IO132160

UNFINISHED REVOLUTION

VIRGINIA HAUSSEGGER AM is an award-winning journalist and gender equity advocate whose extensive media career spans four decades. She has reported around the globe for prime-time Australian news programs on Channel Seven and Channel Nine, and was lead anchor of ABC TV News Canberra for 15 years. Virginia publishes across Australian media, with commentary in *The Sydney Morning Herald*, *The Age* and *The Canberra Times*. She is a Member of the Order of Australia and was 2019 ACT Australian of the Year. Her first book, *Wonder Woman: The Myth of 'Having It All'*, was published in 2005.

'Here is contemporary history at its best. Virginia Haussegger presents Australian feminism as a promise of liberation that gutsy, passionate and brilliant women have pursued not in waves but persistently, across eras and generations. *Unfinished Revolution* should be compulsory reading for anyone serious about understanding, in its historical and global context, Australia's own #MeToo "moment" of 2021 as well as the wider possibilities for a resurgent feminism amid continuing gender discrimination, male violence against women and anti-feminist backlash.'
Frank Bongiorno AM

'Virginia Haussegger is not just a brilliant journalist, but an original and insightful thinker and feminist. I will read anything she writes. And I recommend you do too.'
Jane Caro AM

'In *Unfinished Revolution*, Virginia Haussegger stares down a terrifying global swing to the far-right and yells: Enough. This is the battle cry we desperately need right now, one that refuses to be watered down into niceties that ask politely for equity. This is a book that dares to fight back, and pulls no punches.'
Hannah Ferguson

'At a time of global backlash against women and the women's movement, *Unfinished Revolution* is a spirited piece of feminist scholarship. It practically hums with righteous fury. For those who were at the pointy end of some of the historical changes in the Australian cultural zeitgeist that it charts, it is a timely reminder of what can, and has been, achieved. It acknowledges that there have been some painful moments along the way. That change is not always linear, that setbacks abound, but none of these things are cause for despondency and complacency. There is a relentless, almost bloody-minded optimism in these pages. It feels like a book which urges women to pick themselves up, dust themselves off, and just keep marching.'
Louise Milligan

'A brilliant read. And a reminder that feminist change is possible and it's happening right now. *Unfinished Revolution* honours the Australian feminist movements past and present that have shaped our lives today. A must-read for every young Australian woman ready to build the next chapter of the feminist fight.'
Yasmin Poole

UNFINISHED REVOLUTION
THE FEMINIST FIGHTBACK

Virginia
Haussegger

NEWSOUTH

UNSW Press acknowledges the Bedegal people, the Traditional Owners of the unceded territory on which the Randwick and Kensington campuses of UNSW are situated, and recognises the continuing connection to Country and culture. We pay our respects to Bedegal Elders past and present.

A NewSouth book

Published by
NewSouth Publishing
University of New South Wales Press Ltd
University of New South Wales
Sydney NSW 2052
AUSTRALIA
https://unsw.press/

Our authorised representative in the EU for product safety is
Mare Nostrum Group B.V., Mauritskade 21D, 1091 GC Amsterdam,
The Netherlands (gpsr@mare-nostrum.co.uk).

A catalogue record for this book is available from the National Library of Australia

ISBN: 9781761170102 (paperback)
         9781761179327 (ebook)
         9781761178580 (ePDF)

Cover design Alissa Dinallo
Cover image Long representing women, the Venus symbol was combined with the raised fist, a symbol of solidarity and resistance, during the 1960s and '70s – thus becoming a powerful symbol of women's empowerment and the fight for liberation. shutterstock / durantelallera
Internal design Josephine Pajor-Markus
Printer Griffin Press

All reasonable efforts were taken to obtain permission to use copyright material reproduced in this book, but in some cases copyright could not be traced. The author welcomes information in this regard.

CONTENTS

Dearest Mark SD – busy with revolution – back soonish xx

Why does such a movement seem so anachronistic today? Have we moved away from the radical feminist discourse of 'liberation' and 'revolution' to a more 'acceptable' language of 'diversity' and 'equality'? What happened to this social movement?

Don't women need liberating anymore?[1]

Elizabeth Reid

PREFACE

A fightback: Why now?

The rumble of the huge crowd rolled up the hill, right to the door of Parliament House. As soon as I stepped outside, into Canberra's brilliant morning sunshine, I was hit by the wave of noise.

My phone rang. It was ABC Radio. Could I speak on air right now? Sure.

With the phone pressed to my ear, I struggled to hear the host's question. It didn't matter. A government minister who was also live on the line jumped in. 'The fact is,' she said – words which should be read as political code for 'I deal in alternative facts' – 'the fact is that no one knows what this protest march is all about. There is no clear message.'

I heard that bit.

My response was as crystal clear as the big blue sky above. 'Minister, if you don't know what this is about,' I said, walking towards the mass of people, 'if you can't understand why women are so enraged, well, then you are just not listening!'

On 15 March 2021, the sound of women's anger exploded around Australia. The chant 'Enough is enough!' ricocheted from one end of the continent to the other, as over 100 000 loud, furious and fed-up women rallied in unison. They filled town centres and community halls, spread through city streets and converged on state parliaments.

At midday that day I stepped onto a makeshift stage outside Parliament House in the national capital, the epicentre of feminist rage. The noise was deafening. Brittany Higgins had just addressed the crowd before me.

A team of opposition politicians had come outside to hear us speak, walking together in a sombre band. Like most of us, they were dressed in black. Some wiped away tears as they listened.

What a mess we were in. All of us. Anger, frustration, indignation – women across the nation were awash with it.

How in hell did we get here?

The crowd was bigger than any of us had expected. Bigger than I had ever addressed in my life. Sitting in a TV news studio speaking to perhaps a million viewers is nothing compared to this. This surreal moment in a crowd so big you can't see where it ends, when a massive sea of faces is turned up towards you: expectant, anxious, hungry for words.

The challenge for me right then, along with the dozens of speakers at nearly 40 locations around the country – women spanning generations, colour, race, religion, even political divides who just happened to find themselves at the pointy end of history that day – was to give expression to the hot, caustic, female furore burning across the nation.

Violence and sexual assault had galvanised us, but the roots of this collective fury were enmeshed in the diverse range of women's lives and experiences. It wove an indelible thread through half the population. Men saw it too. Some even joined our march.

This moment marked a nation-wide shift in feminist consciousness. It changed everything. It changed me.

As I looked down from the stage, a woman hoisting a banner high above her head caught my eye. She was wiping tears with her sleeve yet smiling and nodding. Her banner read: 'SAME SHIT – DIFFERENT CENTURY. ENOUGH!'

On stage next to me, feminist legend Biff Ward beamed as she leaned into the microphone, 'I've made it here from the crucible of the '70s Women's Liberation Movement,' she said triumphantly, 'so I have history in my bones.' The crowd went wild with whooping cheers. 'I'm excited to see the seeds we sowed … flowering into this great uprising, here now. I didn't think I would live to see this day.'

The March4Justice is the biggest women's protest rally in Australia's history. It grew from a simple Twitter post to a national movement in a matter of weeks. But this was no accidental 'moment'. It had been brewing for a long, long time.

Not days, weeks, but decades. Five long decades.

*

Australian women are good at revolution. We know how to organise and mobilise. We know how to fight back. We did it in the past, during the revolutionary surge of Women's Liberation and the explosion of consciousness-raising in International Women's Year 1975. And we did it again in 2021 with the March4Justice. We have a strong, proud legacy of rebels, revolutionaries and reformers. Their work is our lifeline to a strong, feminist future. Their mode of operation is a blueprint for the feminist fightback.

In 2022, I was invited to guest-curate an exhibition at the Museum of Australian Democracy titled *Australian Women Changemakers*. I can't tell you how many sleepless nights I had worrying about who to feature in the exhibition's central display. There was only room for seven changemakers. Our list of names began with over 200. As a nation we have no shortage of extraordinarily gutsy, bold, innovative, fabulous feminists – living legends, young and old.

But how do they do it? How do women work together to mount a fightback against pervasive patriarchy? How have they done it in the past – back when second-wave feminists sent radical shockwaves through the nation, declared a war on sexism, picked a fight with the media and shook Australian misogynists by the balls? How does that legacy influence and shape what we do today? How are women pushing back? Is sisterhood alive and flourishing?

Most importantly, how do we regroup collectively in the face of the biggest, ugliest, vilest and most vicious backlash against women sweeping the globe right now?

This book grew from my own desperate need to locate and understand the epicentre of feminist fight in Australia. Where is it? And how 'fight ready' are we? How prepared are the nation's feminist foot soldiers for the battles ahead?

Fuelled by a brewing rage at the global treatment of women as inferior, subjugated servants of men, I wanted to know if we were ready for a new, 21st-century fightback. *Really* ready. Because the stakes are higher now than ever, as toxic male supremacy and new modes of anti-women fascism slam down on women's rights and autonomy. We know this is happening around the world, and you and I both know Australia is not an island – not when it comes to misogynist ideologies.

As a journalist for nearly four decades, with most of my career spent as a reporter and presenter in TV news and current affairs, I find it frankly impossible not to feel outraged at the weak and weakening status of women right now. I have witnessed too much backlash. On a few occasions – in the distant past – I've even been party to the big lie myself. (Monica Lewinsky, if you are reading this (!), I am eternally sorry, and utterly embarrassed, for spending an hour of prime-time commercial television telling Australians you were a seductive temptress and a political slut. In the 1990s, powerful, sex-crazed presidents weren't considered the problem. Women were. We had no language for what happened to you. 'Sorry' doesn't cut it.)

These days I am often appalled by the very industry I have dedicated most of my life to. However, the outlook is not all bleak. The research and interviews for this book have at times shot me high with new hope, even joy. Some of the stories here have reignited my love and admiration for journalism and that small cabal of incredibly smart and deeply thoughtful people who still work at the coalface: the journalists, editors and photographers who still genuinely believe in diversity, integrity and women's rights, and who try to change the world story by story.

I don't think I 'became' a journalist. Like most journos I know, I was born this way – obsessively curious, with an insatiable desire to know 'why'. Why are we the way we are? And how did we get here? I've always had a sharp nose, too, for the power trail. Finding out who has power and how they use it has fascinated me ever since I was a kid. I grew up in a suburban world where not a single woman I knew held a position of public power. Not one. All the women within sight were support acts to men. Even the nuns at school had to answer to a male god. As a newly minted political journalist, I dared ask a male business leader to name five powerful women in Australia. He stumbled. Then he told me women didn't have 'power'. They had 'influence'.

Perhaps it won't surprise you that I start this book with a riff on power.

*

The book is presented in four parts and tells the story of women's revolution and feminist fightback in Australia – in a backward motion. Backwards because I start with now and work back 50 years, to 1975. Whereas books of this type might typically start with the history and take the reader forward through time, the impatient journalist in me couldn't do that. It just didn't feel right. Then I found a hidden gem from British feminist theorist Juliet Mitchell, who happened to visit Australia in 1975 to speak at a women's conference in Canberra. Plied with questions about understanding female oppression and how it connects to the past, Mitchell told her Australian audience: 'Start with the present and work backwards, rather than starting with the past and working forwards.'[1] I took that to heart.

But there is another reason **Part 1** starts in the mid-2020s with '**Our New Now**', rather than with a history of 1970s feminism in Australia. The situation today feels urgent, as the tectonic plates of gender equity are splitting apart, shaking the very ground we walk on. I suspect you picked up this book because you feel that too. The impact of world events on women's lives right now, including women close to home, is always at the forefront of my mind. I sometimes feel like I'm drowning under a daily news feed of stories from an undeclared 'war on women'. I needed to know how we are positioned in Australia today. Are we muscling up, or demurring? Are we well placed to fight back? What is the media doing – hindering or helping? How has the disgraceful period of Julia Gillard bashing, when Australian misogyny went mainstream, impacted the women in parliament who followed her? What have we learned? How well have those lessons armed us for the fightback?

Spoiler alert – the news is good!

In **Part 2**, '**The awakening**', I take a deep dive into the early 2020s and an unprecedented period of national consciousness raising that exploded into the March4Justice. This covers the stories of some of the exceptional young women who took a gutsy, public stand against sexual assault, violence, coercion and rape culture – women such as Grace Tame, Chanel Contos and Brittany Higgins. Their impact on shifting Australian conversations around women's safety worked hand in hand with a substantial upset in mainstream media's centre of gravity. As you may have guessed, the role and behaviour of media is a focus throughout this book. By unpacking the nuts and bolts of how the March4Justice grew into Australia's biggest women's rally, triggering an unprecedented moment of cultural shift, I also explore how women's revolution starts at the kitchen table. Literally! The sisterhood fostered during this time is testament to the enduring power of friendships forged through shared feminist values. Some of the women you'll meet here had me in tears and laughter – often both at once. Part 2 also explores the pressing question of 'What changed?' Once all the noise died down and the protest banners are packed away for posterity, what had shifted in practical terms?

Another spoiler alert – a lot!

Part 3, 'Feminist foundations', takes us right back to a critical point of beginning. Hot on the heels of the 1960s sexual revolution – a fab time for the fellas – women began to unpack what *they* wanted from a social revolution. And here's another spoiler – they weren't interested in equality with men. Far from it. Their quest was liberation. Part 3 is a fabulous journey into the timely birth of Women's Liberation in Australia and the movement that changed women's lives irreversibly. Every piece of current public policy designed to support and empower women has its roots in this time of our feminist history. However, I don't focus on the reformers – as much as I love and thank them. Instead the lens is firmly pointed to the rebels and the radicals: the women who set out to smash the system, disrupt and dismantle the patriarchy and in short transform society. But first they had to take on the foul sexism of Australian media. These are the feminist foremothers who can teach us the most about collective action and feminist fightback. They are the glorious revolutionaries who are still living the revolution.

Part 4, 'International Women's Year, 1975', tells the fascinating story of Australia's Elizabeth Reid – women's adviser to Prime Minister Gough Whitlam. Although few understood it at the time, Reid was the most radical feminist to hold political power in Australia. She wielded that power with formidable force at the first United Nations World Conference on Women, 1975, marking International Women's Year. Whitlam threw funding and the heavy weight of his government's support behind Reid's vision for a world-class program of feminist transformation and consciousness-raising activities. Women loved it. The media trashed it. Thoroughly! None of it ended well. But the legacy of Elizabeth Reid as an international feminist rock star, the first to shine a global spotlight on the scourge of sexism, lives on in historical accounts and UN circles. The story of her impact and Australia's first, year-long, feminist fightback has been largely unknown until now.

I remain thoroughly in awe of the amazing Elizabeth Reid and while 'fangirl' doesn't quite describe it, I suspect you will not only sense the vibe of deep feminist admiration but quite possibly become immersed in it yourself. A good place to be.

Unfinished Revolution: The Feminist Fightback is an incomplete story. The revolution is not over. Clearly. But the story I tell is also incomplete because the observations, commentary and conclusions I draw are those of a subjective journalist. I make no claim to objectivity here. Nor is this a book of history. I am not an historian. My feminist anger and angst, along with my willingness for a fight, are all personal responses. Writing about feminism is always fraught. Every feminist writer I know says so. There are so many variables and imperfections, along with moments of blissful joy in the discovery of sisterhood. There are also doubts, disagreements and isolation. And occasionally I make mistakes. Like revolutions themselves, writing about them can be a messy business.

This book and the stories in it have been gifted and guided by the wonderful women on whose shoulders I stand. Some appear on these pages, while others who are very dear to me hover throughout the project, their words and thoughts tucked between the lines. I am eternally grateful to all the women who have so generously shared their wisdom, wit and encouragement. The story is not finished.

A note on language

When I wrote my first book back in 2005, *Wonder Woman: The Myth of 'Having it All'*, I wrote under the broad assumption that my readers knew and more or less agreed on a shared meaning of the word 'woman'. I acknowledged the limitations of my lived experience, as a result of where I sat in the ecosystem of privilege and power, and my status as a white, cisgender woman born in Australia – a nation located in the global south which, by virtue of wealth and geopolitical influence, culturally positions itself in the global north. But I didn't include a broad view of gender in my research or writing.

Things have significantly changed in the past two decades. Like many people who grew up with strict and ill-fitting binary definitions of 'woman' or 'man', I have found sweet liberation in melting the rigidity of these terms. I've watched the increasing social acceptance of gender fluidity with joy. Although even the word 'acceptance' is highly charged here, in the face of a global backlash against those who identify as queer, trans and gender non-conforming – a backlash that ricochets from the hollow chambers of the Vatican, across Trump's boxed-in binary America, right across the expanding global map of fascist, fundamentalist states and misogynist theocracies. It's a backlash that has pinged loudly in Australian electorates during election campaigns.[2]

While I identify as a cisgender woman, I slide along the spectrum of socially constructed gender traits and behaviours, despite my gender performance as female. Even the mention of 'performance' here conjures the wrath of some feminist scholars and while I choose to duck that discussion for now, I will boldly quote the doyen of gender theory, Judith Butler, who reminds us that these are tough conversations in 'unsettled' times:

> Feminism has always been committed to the proposition that the social meaning of what it is to be a man or a woman are not yet settled. We tell histories about what it meant to be a woman at a certain time and place, and we track the transformations of those categories over time.[3]

As Sarah Casey and Juliet Watson state in their book *Hashtag Feminisms*, the 'category of "woman" is variegated, and … gender binaries are problematic'.[4] Like them, I don't for a moment suggest that 'woman' is a universal identity. But I do use the term with respect to both its individual and universal connotations. So, for the purposes of this book, I use the term 'woman' in reference to anyone who identifies as a woman. It is the experience of living as a woman that is under the microscope here – in both its collective and individual experience.

The 'we' I speak of includes the women who are actively part of feminist discourse, along with those who are not. It includes the millions of women here in Australia and billions around the globe who, like most women I know, are trying to carve out meaning, purpose and a place for themselves in a world that is increasingly hostile and resistant to women's progress. If you identify as she/her/woman, the 'we' includes you.

But this story is not only for those who identify with its cast of characters. It is a very contemporary reflection on all of us. *For* all of us.

INTRODUCTION

The slow boil:
An education in anger

In the late summer of 2025, I sat with Elizabeth Reid at a café table outside the National Library of Australia. Elizabeth had just finished drafting two extensive academic papers to mark the 50th anniversary of International Women's Year 1975 and the printouts were spread out in front of us. My own book manuscript was overdue and I think I sat there mindlessly stroking the crisp, freshly printed pages with envy.

Elizabeth is in her early eighties and her prodigious work ethic, along with her fastidious attention to fact and detail, makes me feel like my brain has shrunk to the size of half a peanut. But I would never tell her that. She would be mortified to think she has that kind of effect on any woman. Elizabeth's life has been wholly and utterly focused on enlarging women, not shrinking them.

While researching this book, I have come to realise that Elizabeth Reid, this unassuming and exceptionally humble woman sitting before me, is the most radical feminist Australia has ever produced. Not radical in a performative sense. Unlike those fabulously brazen suffragettes from the late 19th and early 20th centuries, Elizabeth has never thrown a bomb, smashed a window or plotted to attack an MP. But she was the first woman in the world to be appointed as women's adviser to a head of government, in 1973, at a time of tremendous social change and upheaval in the status and expectations of women. The role gave her an unprecedented political platform in Australia and propelled her onto the international stage with considerable clout. Elizabeth knew she had a brief window to try to do something no one had done before. A philosopher by training and a radical at heart, she threw everything she had at causing a mass explosion – in women's brains. She did it with the mindset of a political anarchist, which she had sifted through a framework developed by the Australian Women's Liberation Movement.

Although I didn't realise it at the outset, my quest to locate the epicentre of contemporary feminist fight in Australia meant winding a path directly back to the women's movement. Once there, I needed to understand how well Elizabeth Reid and the sisterhood succeeded in blowing women's brains. Because, like every new generation to follow, I'd thought that I, and my peers, had invented the wheel. And feminism.

*

I was in my late twenties when my boss threw a pile of women's magazines at me, bellowing, 'Read them and learn something!' It was 1992, and apparently there was plenty of wisdom about 'what women want' to be gleaned from the glossy pages of *New Idea*, *Cleo*, *Cosmopolitan*, *The Australian Women's Weekly*, *Woman's Day* and a bunch of others. Apparently, too, it was the sort of wisdom I lacked but clearly needed to understand our audience and to do my job as a television reporter on *A Current Affair*, at the time Australia's leading nightly prime-time news program.

It had been a rotten day. The lead story had fallen over and tempers were frayed. But that wasn't why my boss, the show's supervising producer, hurled the mags at me. A decent man at heart, he was wedged hard between his own well-disguised feminist sympathies and one of the most overtly sexist media cultures in the Western world. Australian commercial television in the 1980s and '90s was a cesspit of machismo and misogyny. For a long while I thrived in it.

On the morning that *Woman's Day* et al. were frisbeed at me, I had stomped into the office ranting with indignation. I had just walked past my local newsagent where the latest *People* magazine cover, featuring a nude, dark-skinned woman set against a clinically white background, was splashed across the window and footpath advertising. The woman was pictured on her hands and knees, crawling on all fours, with a dog chain around her neck and a leash pulled taut. Her dull gaze looked off into the distance, in the direction of ... perhaps a dog handler.

Some saw sex. I saw red.

The magazine's publisher, Kerry Packer, was my 'big' boss. He owned the television network I worked for, along with a slew of other media titles and assets. An arch rival to Rupert Murdoch, 'King Kerry' was feared and revered in media land. We Packer minions knew where we huddled along the rich food chain. But that particular day, for a long, angry moment, I forgot.

I was incensed by the inhumane and degrading sexism screaming at me from that cover, so I did what any hot-blooded feminist wearing a short skirt, high heels and Farrah Fawcett hair flicks would do. I marched into my boss's dark den of an office, the one with a bar at one end and soft leather couches at the other, and insisted we do a story on how utterly offensive this image was to women. It was dehumanising and reeked of violent subordination, not to mention hypersexualised commodification. On I railed, in my loudest outdoor voice.

At first he laughed. Then he tried humour: 'You're prettier when you smile.' Then, eventually, the poor bloke flipped with exasperation. 'What kind of idiot are you? Who do you think pays your salary? What chance in hell would a story like that have on this network?'

So, that was that. Story pitch over. As I turned on my heel to leave, he reminded me I could always go back to the network from whence I'd come – the ABC.

As a shiny-new and ambitious cadet journalist, I had arrived at ABC TV News in Melbourne in 1986 on the wings of change. It was two years after Australia had introduced the world's first Sex Discrimination Act, and the year that revolutionary new equal employment opportunity laws were causing a seismic shift in workplaces. By the late 1980s, the world for women was explosive with opportunity. We had shoulder pads, big hair, bright brass buttons and push-up bras. The braless brigade – those Women's Liberationists from the second wave – had done the work. 'Thanks Germaine, Gloria, Elizabeth, Anne, Beatrice, Eva, Quentin, Wendy and co,' we huffed. 'We've got this. We're here now!'

We were the new breed of university-educated feminist foot soldiers, charging forward, laying claim to what was rightfully ours: power, leadership, authority, influence, money and respect. I wanted it all. We all did. We just had to work out how to get it.

For years I thought we were on track. Even King Kerry, back in 1992, was forced to remove the dog-collar cover from public display, following women's protests and official censoring. I wore my highest heels to work that day. And a smile. My boss called me 'smug'.

For more than three decades, I have worked across public broadcasting and commercial media with long periods at the ABC, including 15 years as anchor of ABC TV News in Canberra. In my early twenties I became the youngest woman to host the ABC's nightly current affairs program *The 7.30 Report*, back in the days when each capital city had its own show. I felt like I'd won the lottery when I was sent to Darwin as the new host, supposedly to 'cut my teeth' and learn how to drink beer. I later hosted the show in Adelaide, and took on reporting and presenting roles in Melbourne and Sydney. In between, I spent a few years at Channel Nine. In my mid-thirties I was poached for a senior reporting role on Channel Seven's *Witness*, a show set up in spectacular style by media mogul Kerry Stokes to compete with Kerry Packer's *60 Minutes*. They were fast, fabulous and wildly competitive days.

Throughout it all I've had a front-row seat, bearing witness to some of the most significant changes for women. I've lost count of the number of Australian women's 'firsts' I've reported. First female prime minister, governor-general, chief justice, police commissioner, foreign minister, head of Australia's spy agency … and on it went.

Once 'firsts' were no longer a thing, I obsessed over the numbers of women in leadership roles, and founded a small university-based research hub to track the change, ambitiously called the 50/50 by 2030 Foundation. But not long after setting it up, that too seemed like a false positive. Although numbers were improving, workplace cultures were not, and it took time to unpack that. Women were moving into leadership roles in most places I looked – not fast enough, and not high enough, but the shift was gradually happening.

As we rolled into the 2020s, it seemed as if the work of equal opportunity had largely been done. I even had the wife of a cabinet minister lecture me about the need to 'thank the men who have allowed women to do all these things'. We were sitting at the head table of an official lunch to celebrate the Australian of the Year, and she was stabbing a fork of food in my direction. Before I could open my mouth to respond, or vomit, Kamahl leapt up on stage and began to sing. It was surreal.

Despite all the utter nonsense people speak about gender equality, and all the window dressing of change and pretensions of progress, and all the corporate cupcakes in celebration of women's empowerment, most women I know smell a rat. A thick, foul stench, the source of which is difficult to pin down, because the stink is everywhere, meshed into the wall cavity of our social architecture. Women, not just in Australia but around the world, know the truth. Something is wrong. Dangerously wrong. The pendulum of change is swinging the wrong way.

Did we see this coming?

For a long while now I have felt the heat of brewing anger. At first, I managed to keep a lid on it, while distracting myself with obsessive research. I felt an urgent need to document progress. To pin it down. To convince myself of feminism's forward motion. At times I almost did. Then yet another hideous story of sexism and misogyny would come crashing through. And I'd slip back into a feminist funk.

And I wasn't alone. In late 2023 I joined 150 women at the National Press Club for the annual dinner of the National Foundation for Australian Women. That petite but mighty feminist warhorse, Natasha Stott Despoja, was the guest speaker. Once the youngest woman elected to federal parliament, Natasha struts a powerful global stage these days as an elected member of the United Nations' Committee on the Elimination of All Forms of Discrimination Against Women. She'd just returned from the 'rarefied air of Geneva' and despite her valiant efforts to disguise it, Natasha's mood was glum.

The news was bad. The Israel–Hamas war was raging; transnational feminist fretting about conflict-related sexual violence and the weaponisation of women in war was falling on deaf ears; violence against women across the globe was, she said, 'omnipresent'. Natasha sighed, paused, then pushed on. 'We continue to see egregious examples of the rollback of women and girls' rights around the world,' she said. 'Gender apartheid in Afghanistan, the poisoning of schoolgirls in Iran, the rolling back of *Roe v. Wade*, and the valiant efforts of women in Ukraine to help hold the frontline.' Yet despite this, she noted, 'we still don't have a seat at the table when it comes to peace negotiations'.

Natasha stopped short of reeling off the well-known data. Many of the women seated around me were regular voices in the media who quoted the miserable numbers. Some of us barely bother to mention these days that the World Economic Forum says it will take another 123 years to reach gender parity around the globe, and more than 179 years in our own region of Eastern Asia and the Pacific.[1] Or that the federal government's Women's Economic Equality Taskforce reported that eliminating negative gender bias in our workforce could unlock $128 billion dollars annually. We are weary of these figures. They no longer alarm anyone.

Have we stopped talking about these things because people have stopped listening?

It took only a couple of years after the Global Gender Gap Report first came out, in 2006, for the ABC to stop reporting the yearly results. When I asked one of the news producers, back in 2008, why we no longer covered the annual release of the updated Gender Gap index, he told me, 'We did that story last year and nothing has changed. It's the same old same old.' He wasn't being funny. Nor ironic. He simply failed to see any newsworthiness in the lack of progress.

Now, as we race towards 2030 – the target date for the United Nations' Sustainable Development Goals, including goal number 5, 'Achieve gender equality and empower all women and girls' – not even a growing mountain of evidence and sophisticated data on every aspect of the gender gap stirs media interest, nor the public outrage it deserves. Instead, gender inequity continues to be treated with lethargic inevitability.

It is not considered news. It is simply the norm.

*

As a veteran broadcast journalist and presenter, I've always been a committed, dedicated news viewer. Recently, however, I've found I can barely sit through a single TV news bulletin without sliding into despair. In story after story, global headlines scream of war atrocities, inhumane military policies, humanitarian disasters, climate catastrophe, rising populism fuelled by extreme misogyny, neo-Nazi rallies, theocracies preaching gender segregation and women's subordination, authoritarian regimes led by overt sex abusers, far-right anti-woman dictators waving from victory podiums and deadbeat politicians lying about their actions.

The wallpaper behind this cacophony of talking heads is plastered with men. Always men. There they are, in every bit of video footage, clip after clip: political, military, religious and corporate forums of tight-lipped, dead-eyed men. At the time of writing, more than 55 violent conflicts are raging around the globe, the highest number since the end of World War I. Not *one* of these was instigated by a woman. Wherever there is chaos, men are almost always in charge. If ever we need a reminder that men rule the world, TV news bulletins thrust that truism in our faces daily. It has become a game of Spot The Woman and it's a loser's game.

In what feels like a global tsunami of political action intent on closing women out, Australia is not immune. We may be Down Under and downstream, but the grubby water reaches us too: gut-wrenching stories of violence against women, weekly death counts, humiliation of women leaders through AI deepfakes, online trolling and vicious anti-feminist cyber-rhetoric, sexist slap-downs from the tongues of Teflon men wielding media power, and paper-thin pretensions of equity, diversity and inclusion in workplaces weary of women's needs.

On International Women's Day 2025, the Secretary-General of the United Nations, António Guterres, glumly admitted that 'instead of mainstreaming equal rights, we're seeing the mainstreaming of misogyny'.[2]

This is not how it was supposed to be.

The latest manifestation to be felt unnervingly close to us has its epicentre in a surprising place – one of Australia's long-time allies, the United States. President Donald Trump's determination to overturn *Roe v. Wade* and give control of women's bodies and reproductive rights back to the states took effect in mid-2022, reversing a 50-year-old law. It was a shocking reminder that women's rights are never safe, never locked in – even in the West. They are always at the mercy of the man in charge.

In fact, this was just the beginning of a giddying list of executive orders and direct, government-led attacks on women, feminism and gender autonomy in the United States. On his first day back in office in 2025, President Trump set the frightful pattern in motion with his order on 'Defending Women from Gender Ideology Extremism', which restricts sexual identity to two sexes only – male and female. The new vice president, JD Vance, called on men to be more 'manly', prompting a senior editor at *Newsweek* to rejoice that 'manliness is back!' and that the 'war on men is absolutely *over!*'[3] Unspoken but implied in that noisy rejoicing was the corollary: 'the war on women is back on!'

Is it any wonder women are exhausted? But now is not the time for lethargy. We must overcome our exhaustion. There is work to do.

Men have proven themselves a collective failure at building a safe, peaceful, respectful world, much less a fairer or politically representative one. Yet, globally, half of all people think women's rights 'have gone far enough', and – tragically – 45 per cent of Australian men agree. And it gets worse. A whopping 46 per cent of Australians think we have gone so far in promoting women's equality that men are now the victims of gender discrimination.[4]

It would be easy to suggest men just need a little more understanding. A little more hand holding. Or my favourite admonishment: women need to be a little *less threatening*. All this flat-earth thinking thinly disguises an uncomfortable truth: men have failed, and they will continue to fail. They have held the reins of power for millennia and spectacularly failed to build a world in which men and women share power, resources and opportunity.

The future of the planet and the sustainability of humankind now depends on women taking the lead.

Back in 2020, after slamming all nations for 'agonizingly slow' progress on gender equality, António Guterres used a series of speeches to deliver the most powerful global call to arms directed at women I have ever heard. 'Gender inequality is the overwhelming injustice of our age and the biggest human rights challenge we face,' Guterres said. 'Everywhere, women are worse off than men, simply because they are women':

> From the ridiculing of women as hysterical or hormonal, to the routine judgement of women based on their looks; from the myths and taboos that surround women's natural bodily functions, to mansplaining and victim-blaming – misogyny is everywhere.
>
> Gender equality is a question of power; power that has been jealously guarded by men for millennia.[5]

At the time, I was astounded by the sheer audacity of such comments coming from the head of the United Nations. I had never heard a male global leader say anything as direct as this. But it was far from a fleeting emotive moment. The ravages of gender inequality became a subject Guterres returned to repeatedly in speech after speech. With the gauntlet thrown down, he pulled the metaphorical sword from the stone with an open challenge to women all around the world: 'Power is not usually given. Power must be taken.'[6]

If ever there was an official provocation to women to 'do something', this was it. If we strip away the tight-lipped diplomacy, this is a clear, unequivocal invitation to women to rise up and fight. To fight back!

There was a startling sense of urgency when Guterres uttered those words in 2020. Now, as I write, that urgency is paramount. The almighty anti-women backlash gathering pace and coming our way is not only knocking women off balance, but the Trump-led war on what right-wing idealogues call 'gender ideology' is all-encompassing. Any LGBTQI+ people who don't conform to the ancient rigidity of biblical biology are also in the line of attack. Women who embrace the intersectional values of feminism are the frontline foot soldiers here. The task is to build a solid, sustainable feminist future in which women have the controlling stake. A future that is fortified against patriarchy, misogyny and the pernicious repositioning of gender by the manosphere. And the US president.

I understand some readers may be uncomfortable with the idea of staging a fight, much less picking one! I was too, until a cold, realistic review of the status of women around the world, and here in Australia, shook me awake. I am tired of being nice. I am weary of diplomacy. I am over the nonsense of gender-equality training programs that end at morning tea. I am sickened by patronising male leaders who turn up on International Women's Day looking for a cheap shot at virtue-signalling their feminist credentials. I'm done with mansplaining.

While I am deeply grateful for the awards and accolades I've received for being a good citizen, even a model one, it is time to muscle up. To get sharper and tougher, unapologetic in our demands, and uncompromising in placing women and women's interests first. And yes, if that means shoving mediocre and deadbeat men out of the way, so be it. Guterres' words haunt me like a menacing mantra: 'Power must be taken.'

I know he is right. I suspect you do too.

As we roll towards the third decade of this century, the call to scale up a feminist fightback is not as wild as it may sound. Women have been pushing back against male hierarchies and macho bullies since the beginning of time. Even Eve probably gave Adam a piece of her mind when they were kicked out of the Garden of Eden: 'Don't blame me for your woes. I didn't make you eat the damn apple.. You just took it.'

I know many men who are appalled by the treatment of women, some worried sick about their daughter's futures, their safety and their access to opportunity. Men who are good, decent feminists – whether they call themselves that or not doesn't matter. These men are critical allies. They too have a role in the feminist fightback. Give them a job to do. Get them talking to other men. Hand them discussion topics if you like! You're in charge.

Responding to the call to mount a feminist fightback is a non-negotiable for me. Of course I must. I believe we all must.

The good news is that we are well equipped. The exceptional women – and men – I've met and interviewed while researching this book are testament to that. Fortified by a formidable feminist legacy, we are ready!

However, our pathway to this point of preparedness has been excruciatingly tough. In recent years Australia has been a shameful, global embarrassment, as detailed in Part 1. Yet my purpose here is to shine a spotlight on the moments of cultural shift that indicate our changing public consciousness in Australia, and most of all the upsurge of fightback attitude and grit in women themselves. Australian women have always been tough, but in recent years more of us are baring our teeth. And no, it's not a smile.

When it comes to the treatment of women in this country, we know what is wrong and what is no longer acceptable. Workplaces, business leaders, parliamentarians and even High Court justices are now well attuned to what you *cannot do*. In 2022, workplace laws changed, placing 'a positive legal duty on employers to prevent workplace sexual harassment'.[7] But knowing the 'policy' doesn't make it practice. Personal, deeply held attitudes, beliefs and cultural behaviours remain a wicked battleground.

Get reading. We have work to do.

PART 1
OUR NEW NOW

We're back in the fight! We have no choice.[1]

Hillary Clinton

Angry women burn brighter than the sun.[2]

Soraya Chemaly

1

A FEMINISATION OF POWER

The TV newsreader's chair is a privileged place from which to see the world. Night after night, for 15 turbulent years – just after the World Trade Center's Twin Towers collapsed in 2001 and the word 'terrorism' entered our news lexicon – I sat in the ABC TV studio each evening at 7 pm, in the nation's capital, attempting to convey a calm and orderly control amid the chaos.

News thrives on chaos and the mess of uncertainty. It's what keeps the audience fixated, in a mild state of panic: *What now? What next?* TV news feeds that fixation. But where the news media fails us most profoundly is in telling the story of change – social, cultural and political change.

'News cycles tend to suggest that change happens in small, sudden bursts or not at all,' wrote Rebecca Solnit.[1] But it doesn't. It's just framed that way, to fit tired old templates. In the real world, outside newsroom spin, change is neither linear nor predictable, and it's certainly not straightforward. Understanding our stories of change is central to our ability to adapt and make sense of the shift we feel vibrating through our lives. It's critical to laying claim to our future. So why do we attempt to comprehend change only in hindsight – and fail to see and feel it as we live it?

In her essay 'Hope in the Dark', Solnit laments the media's repeated announcements, around the turn of the century, about the death of feminism. In 2002, Australia's prime minister,

John Howard – a media hound from way back – grabbed those 'feminism is dead' and 'post-feminism' headlines and ran with them, saying that for young women 'the feminist battle has been won'.[2]

He was wrong. Very wrong.

We were only just getting started!

An 'end of days' vibe

The Australian media scene back in the 1990s was fuelled by testosterone and stunk of Brut cologne. When I first strutted the corridors of commercial television in my early twenties – ambitious, competitive and perhaps a little over-dabbed in Dior Poison – women were rated and promoted primarily on their decorative value, regardless of their skills and talents. There was a glaring absence of women in senior roles or any position of editorial authority. For young recruits like me, it was a constant battle to be taken seriously. The men in charge were mostly overfed salesmen – anti-intellectual, sexist spivs. Yet, thankfully, despite the unabashed sexism, in my experience the culture was not overtly predatory on women. With new laws about sex discrimination and equal opportunity still fresh in the minds of media bosses, women in the workplace were considered a necessary fixture – as long as they could just work out how to fit in.

My regular complaints at Channel Nine – they called them 'whinges' – about women being routinely assigned 'soft' stories, along with my repeated requests to be sent to the frontlines of the Bosnian War, were met with little more than shoulder shrugs. Girls weren't considered for those assignments; even at the ABC, female foreign correspondents were a rarity in the early 1990s. After one particularly energetic argument with my boss, in which I railed about my value as an experienced reporter and the female lens I could bring to war reporting, I was sent out on a shoot and returned hours later to find a large, fat, black-rubber penis sitting upright on my desk. Attached was a scribbled note: 'Now you've got one!'

The penis proved useless. Days later I was told to pack my passport and head for the airport. I was flown to Hawaii to cover the Ford Supermodel of the World competition and interview glamour model and host of the show, Christie Brinkley. My colleagues thought it was hilarious. I have hated Hawaii ever since.

But what now? What is going on now in those networks I once worked for?

It's August 2024, and I'm with ABC investigative reporter Louise Milligan. We have just listened to the promo of her *Four Corners* program 'Don't Speak', an exposé of the bullying, harassment and misogyny in commercial television news.[3]

I shake my head slowly, flabbergasted: 'It's worse than I thought.' Louise nods in agreement.

The show focused on news programs on Channel Seven and Channel Nine's TV networks, in which both of us have worked over several years. In the promo clip, a well-known lawyer calls television news media 'the industry #MeToo forgot'. The aggressive language used by executives, alarming gender pay disparities, punishing work schedules and outright hostility towards some of the women journalists interviewed was breathtaking. One of those women quit her job the day the story went to air. Another spoke of being so broken by the treatment she received working at Channel Seven that she tried to commit suicide, throwing herself in front of a passing car outside the station headquarters. It was horribly distressing stuff.

A couple of days after the broadcast, Louise and I were deep in conversation on the podcast *Fourth Estate*, discussing TV news culture with host Tina Quinn. Quinn wanted to know if I was shocked at what I'd heard and if the situation for women in television journalism seemed worse than when I'd first moved into commercial TV almost 30 years ago. My answer was, 'No, sadly not shocked.' And, 'Yes, it's worse. Much worse.'[4]

Louise's program, and the legal action taken by women journalists who have quit or fled, are testament to how dramatically and horribly these places have changed. Built up through the lavish excesses of late-1990s media moguls, with a history of fat advertising revenues, bloated pay packets and prime-time dominance, the young men who had mooched about in the shadow of those days appear to have grown old with no sense of workplace self-restraint, and no clue as to what healthy, sustainable, 21st-century leadership looks like. Instead, a dirty, careless, aggressive machismo and masculine vanity had taken hold. By the time of Louise's exposé, it was a toxic culture out of control.

'Where do these blokes get this stuff from?' I ask Louise, referring to the foul language one of the TV executives, someone I once worked with, is reported to have used when speaking to a producer. 'At what point did things get so off the rails that the men in charge thought they could treat people like this?'

Louise smiles, still shaking her head with incredulity: 'Yeah, it has an "end of days" vibe about it. It's like the last days of the empire!'

We both laugh.

Despite the revolting content under discussion, and the toxicity of commercial news media culture – in an industry still owned and controlled by men – this moment in time marks its nadir. Louise and I were laughing because we knew it. We could feel it. The line had been drawn.

Abusive men in positions of power have been put on notice. Women working in broadcast media are now wilfully calling them out. Sexual harassment, bullying, intimidation, sexual predation and objectification – all the filthy stains of a deeply sexist culture – are getting a public airing as employees push back, their stories not just heard but amplified. This is new. The rumble of complaints and accusations that for decades has been largely contained to gossip, tears and anger over drinks at the bar after an exhausting shift has finally burst the privacy bubble.

Two months after Milligan's *Four Corners* story, Nine Entertainment hung out its grubby linen for everyone to see. On 17 October 2024, the media conglomerate publicly released an independent report into its workplace culture, *Out in the Open*.[5] Alarmingly frank and excruciatingly detailed, it is a sickening read. I suspect some of the anonymous employee comments it highlighted were triggering for women who have worked in commercial television. Nine's broadcast division – TV news and current affairs – fared worst, with more than half the employees reporting bullying, discrimination or harassment; nearly two in three experiencing 'abuse of power or authority'; and 30 per cent subjected to sexual harassment. Interviewees told the inquiry that the newsroom 'reeked of a man's locker room', where men 'boisterously joke about sexual assault'. Another said, 'It would not be uncommon to be asked or hear: "Who did you fuck last night?" or "Someone is going to get their dick sucked."' In a culture in which entitled, sexist and demeaning behaviour was so normalised, one employee said she was told by her supervisor to steer clear of a particular manager: 'Don't let him touch your boobs.' Sage advice, no doubt. Another said, 'He made me feel like I was just a piece of meat to be ogled at.' And on it goes.

Nine Entertainment is the largest employer in the Australian media industry.[6] To commission a workplace review such as this, when you know it's going to get very, very ugly and the organisation will be brutally exposed, was a bold step. None of the pus that oozed from this long-festering cultural sore was a great surprise. The report had been commissioned three months before Milligan's *Four Corners* revelations.

In the climate of our New Now, with women increasingly stepping up and speaking out, it would seem Nine knew the 'last days of the empire' were upon them. But as far as masculinised media machines go, Nine is far from alone.

On 12 March 2021, just days before hordes of rowdy women protesters hit the streets for the March4Justice, a somewhat nervous and softly spoken but defiant former News Corp photographer, Anna Rogers, appeared at a Senate committee hearing into media diversity in Australia. Rogers, who had been made redundant in 2020 after more than two decades working across several News Corp newspapers, had made a submission to the Senate media inquiry. She said she wanted to address, 'the portrayal and treatment of women by News Corp and the toxic work culture'.[7] Rogers explained to the wide-eyed senators that editorial instruction about photographing women was overtly and unapologetically sexist. When working on the *Sunday Mail*, Rogers said she was 'told by the acting picture editor that they did not want any photos of "pigs in lipstick" … which meant that women who were overweight or over 35 did not get a run in the paper'. She was also instructed to get photos of 'yummy mummies' and 'pretty backpackers'. Rogers went on to explain how news journalists and photographers felt compelled to scan court lists to look for young, attractive women facing minor charges – some as simple as driving offences – who had hot bikini or lingerie selfies posted on their social media that could be lifted and published in the paper. Effectively, it was a way of creating a ready supply of 'Page 3 girls' – big breasts, semi-naked – for reader titillation, under the guise of 'news'.[8]

Chairing the Senate committee, Senator Sarah Hanson-Young (who knows a great deal about public slut-shaming, as discussed in Chapter 3), asked Rogers numerous questions about her employer's representation of women before attempting to draw her into a broader discussion: 'We are in the midst of a national conversation right now about the treatment of women, the way we speak about issues specific to women, and the way leaders respond to those issues,' she said, before asking the question on all our minds: 'How does a newspaper report on that fairly if they have a toxic culture?'

It's the media riddle of our times, which of course takes more than a Senate inquiry to answer. Rogers took it as a rhetorical question but looked utterly deflated as she almost whispered her answer: 'I don't know.'

Anna Rogers began her career in news media photography in the late 1980s, around the same time I began working as a TV journalist. When I contact her to chat about the Senate committee hearing, two years after her appearance, she is still grappling with a deep and personal frustration over media hostility to women. We share stories about how as younger women we felt we needed to 'man up' to work in news media, and how we now regret that we weren't more vocal about the sexism and simmering misogyny we witnessed over years. 'I was just so conscious of fitting in and providing the product they wanted,' Anna says. Ditto to that.

We both agree: those days of staying silent are over.

As if a tap has been turned on with full force, stories calling out sexual harassment, sexual harm, bullying, intimidation and systemic gender-based discrimination have been pouring out of workplaces and industries since the early 2020s, and not only from commercial television and the media. The hospitality industry and the Australian music industry, both large employers of women, have also been the subject of explosive media revelations of sexual exploitation and assault, prompting government investigations, workplace reviews and industry-wide reports. In early 2025, following a particularly alarming series of stories in *The Sydney Morning Herald* on the hospitality behemoth Swillhouse, a group of former employees who alleged they were sexually assaulted, harassed or discriminated at work set up a fundraising collective to help fight their employer in the courts.[9] Their events to raise money and highlight the issue of sexual assault and abuse in hospitality were so successful that they took their awareness campaign global.

So why the change? What brings about the sort of 'end of days' vibe we're sensing and the bold actions we are witnessing as women choose to stand up and speak out in our New Now? What makes organisations commit to clean up their rotting culture of sexism and abuse? Bad publicity and the threat of legal action are obviously powerful prompts. And the 2022 change to the Sex Discrimination Act that imposes a 'positive duty' on employers to prevent workplace sexual harassment was clearly one such prompt.[10]

But when it comes to dramatic social change, law reform comes last. Personal pushback comes first. It takes courage and bold risks by individuals who are prepared to buck the system and say, 'No, we will not accept this', regardless of the intimidation and dangerous backlash they face.

Our New Now has emerged as a result of countless courageous and pissed-off women speaking out, taking action and fighting back – many of whom you will meet throughout this book. It starts with a trickle, builds to a chorus, and explodes into an army of protesters. There is tremendous power in numbers, as you will see. But first we need to ponder the nature of power itself.

With the words of António Guterres echoing loudly throughout this journey – 'Gender equality is a question of power; power that has been jealously guarded by men for millennia' – it is important to understand how power itself is changing in our New Now.

A gendered shift from 'influence' to power

For most of my working life I have collected news clippings, articles and feature stories about women's progress and power. It began as journalism research and quickly became a lifelong obsession – a method of keeping track of change. Among my bulging boxes of archives is a thick stack of power lists. For a couple of decades, power and leadership lists were my grown-up stamp collection. I pored over every iteration, every new release, looking for evidence that women were cutting through. The holy grail listing – an Oscar nomination for the power hungry – is the annual *Australian Financial Review* Power List. It began in 2001 supposedly to refine Australians' understanding of how power works. Marking the 20th birthday edition in 2020, editor Brook Turner said the newspaper launched the list because 'Australia didn't have a really sophisticated understanding of the currents of power and how they coalesced.'[11]

While we may have been vague on the ebb and flow of power currents, there was little doubt about who owned the currency: overwhelmingly, a bank of men. For years women were rarely included among the top ten most powerful people. Two women made the list in 2001. By 2020, there were three. For several years when former prime minister John Howard topped the 'Overt Power' rankings, his wife Janette was repeatedly listed in the 'Covert Power' list: always the lone woman. For a long while, spotting a woman with power in Australia was a bit like catching a shooting star – rare and fleeting.

Twenty years ago, I asked an auditorium of university under-grads to name the top five most powerful people in Australia. They quickly ran up a list of men: politicians, media moguls and sports stars. When I flipped the question and asked for the top five most powerful women, they seriously struggled. Three women on television were suggested … and the prime minister's wife.

One of the judges of the inaugural Power List was a man of considerable power and political clout himself, former Labor Party pollster Rod Cameron. Cameron headed up one of the nation's leading polling companies, ANOP, and given his talent for reading the mood of the electorate ahead of elections and correctly forecasting voting intentions, for a time he seemed to be the man with the crystal ball. So, when he first predicted a 'feminisation' of Australian leadership, many took note. Me included.

Cameron laid out his thesis in a 1990 speech with the lofty title 'Feminisation: The major emerging trend underlying future mass audience response'.[12] In it he suggested the few (very few) women who had risen to prominent leadership roles in Australia at that time – women such as Carmen Lawrence, the first female premier of Western Australia; Joan Kirner in Victoria; and celebrity journalist Jana Wendt – were collectively evidence of a new community appreciation of values and virtues that he insinuated were innately female. And this is where it gets messy.

In a bout of 'neurosexism', Cameron attributed various 'soft' traits to women.[13] He suggested the appeal of these leading women was because the community was tired of 'the old macho ways' of leadership, and hungry for 'a commonsense, managerial style which is in touch, honest and direct' – characteristics he viewed as female, along with 'creativity'. Cameron argued that when it came to 'credibility and values', women had an 'advantage' over men. Which, when you stop to think about it, is a damning indictment of men. Of course male leaders are capable of demonstrating credibility and a commitment to ethical values just as much as women – if they want to. After all, empathy is a human trait and not exclusive to any gender. Perhaps what Cameron should have been investigating back then was why men in leadership opted for a brute style of machismo instead.

When I interviewed Cameron in 2007 for a magazine feature I was writing on 'Sex and power', he proved a little prickly when I asked if he thought power sat comfortably on women.[14] '"Power" is the wrong word to use,' he said. 'Power is a male thing.' (Yes, he said that!) The word he thought I should use was 'influence'. Women had 'influence', not power, he stated with impressive confidence about the delineation, and women were in fact more 'multifaceted' than men. 'Women are more interested in exploring new [intellectual] horizons than men,' he said, while also insisting that the 'trend towards feminisation' of leadership in politics, business and media was happening at breathtaking speed.

Cameron was wrong about that. It wasn't breathtaking, nor at speed. Data on the representation of women in ASX leadership between 2004 and 2015, for example, shows an increase from a tiny 2.3 per cent to 4.2 per cent – hardly evidence of a fabulous female 'trend'.[15] Nevertheless, the question of the feminisation of leadership continues to dominate public discourse – usually when things go horribly wrong. Early in the global Covid pandemic, between May and June 2020, a rush of international news headlines drew attention to emerging evidence that countries led by women were coping much better in the crisis than nations led by men, particularly bullish 'strongmen'.[16] *The Atlantic* even suggested New Zealand prime minister Jacinda Ardern 'may be the most effective leader on the planet', citing her 'empathy' and her ability to reach her constituents on an 'emotional level', with messages that were 'sobering and soothing' during anxious times.[17] The ability of Germany's Angela Merkel to listen deeply and consult widely on appropriate vaccinations was also pitched as a feminine virtue. European news platform *Social Europe* went even further, with data-driven research titled, 'Women in power: it's a matter of life and death', suggesting women-led countries flattened the epidemic's curve and had fewer Covid deaths than countries led by men.[18]

For a short time in our recent history, the concept of the feminisation of leadership was quite a 'thing'. Fascinated by that global vibe, in 2022 I ran a series of interviews on my podcast *BroadTalk*, specifically asking prominent Australian leaders if they believed we were indeed witnessing a new style of 'feminised' leadership in which women operated differently from men. Julia Gillard was particularly astute on this, gently pushing back on the assumption embedded in my question. A fan of psychologist and philosopher Cordelia Fine, Gillard said, 'I am not a believer that men and women's brains are inherently different,' adding that, like Fine, she believes 'we are not inherently different but we are socialised differently'. However, Gillard pointed out that when other women pave the way, there is greater scope for women to be expansive in their leadership style: 'Jacinda [Ardern] has been very clear that she's got more political space because she is the third woman to lead the country, and has foregrounded kindness in a different way of doing things.'[19]

When I interviewed Dame Annette King, at the time the New Zealand High Commissioner to Australia, in August 2020, she was clearly proud of Ardern's global appeal. But interestingly, when I asked if Ardern had 'shown us a new way' of doing leadership, she replied, 'I think she has, but it's not just her.' A couple of fundamental factors enabled Ardern's natural personality and leadership style to shine through, unfiltered, said King. One was 'a whole generational shift' among new parliamentarians, women and men, who like Ardern were in their thirties and forties. She argued this cohort, unlike the baby boomers before them, 'are led by a feeling of kindness and compassion' and are unafraid to demonstrate it. The other factor, as Gillard has suggested, was precedent. Ardern was New

Zealand's third female prime minister, and King explained that this had created an 'expectation' that women could and would be successful: 'I think it's in the psyche of New Zealanders. It's not a surprise to have a woman.'[20]

The new power paradigm

For too long we have mistakenly assumed that increasing the numbers of women in leadership will naturally lead to a widespread feminisation of power, the assumption being that 'women will act for women'. I plead guilty to this – albeit for a short while. As previously mentioned, when I set up a small gender-equality research and advocacy hub at the University of Canberra in 2017, which I called the '50/50 by 2030 Foundation', our focus was primarily on getting more women into public leadership. We operated under a vague premise that the numbers alone would shift the gendered nature of power. However, it soon became apparent that gender equality is not just a numbers game. Increasing the numbers of women working at, or close to, the centre of power normalises the presence of women, but it doesn't necessarily serve the interests of women in general. It doesn't mean they will throw down the ladder, or work to change the system to support and empower other women. That kind of focus requires concerted effort, energy and a deliberate values-driven commitment to the 'feminisation of power'.

Before I unpack what that means, first let's be clear. There is now ample evidence, around the globe and in Australia, to show that increasing the number of women in key leadership roles in business will improve corporate profitability.[21] But that has little to do with feminism per se. There may be some corporate stars and wealthy celebrities who call themselves feminists, but productivity improvements and better bottom lines do not constitute feminism simply because they involve women.

We do know, however, that increasing the number of women with *political* power does positively impact laws that govern the lives of all women. A 2025 study examined more than 1000 private member's bills in Australian parliament from 1995 to 2022.[22] These are bills a parliamentarian can put forward – independent of their political party – in an attempt to introduce new law, but without the need to necessarily 'toe the party line'. Politicians usually use them to pursue an issue of personal importance, or something directly relevant to their electorate and called for by constituents. The study found that female parliamentarians not only introduce more of these bills, but they are considerably more associated with 'feminized issues' than those proposed by men. The researchers also found the language female legislators use when addressing gender-neutral issues – such as climate change, or migration – is 'more human-centered, welfare-oriented and rights-focused'. This is a form of feminised power in action.

So what *is* feminised power?

Feminised power is purposeful and values driven. It is about rewriting the rules of engagement. It's about bringing a new lens to how we view systems and structures. It consciously centres women's needs and interests. It looks carefully at how an action will impact *all* women: the collective above the individual. Feminised power also aims to dismantle systems that privilege some people above others. It seeks to end all forms of discrimination. It brings an intersectional sensibility to deliberations. Feminised power is not transactional. It is not power for power's sake. Nor is it a zero-sum game – I win, you lose. Feminised power is ambitious, confident and collaborative. It is about 'we' – with women front and centre.

Men may have jealously guarded their power and thwarted gender equality, but in our New Now women are redefining what power is, what it looks like and how it works.

Power as a current, not a currency

One of my journalist heroes, the acclaimed Canadian war correspondent Sally Armstrong, made a remarkable claim in the
opening of her 2019 book *Power Shift: The Longest Revolution*.
While acknowledging that 'the promise of equality has eluded
half the world's population', she insists that 'There's never been
a better time in human history to be a woman.'[23]

Although written before Trump 2025 and the ensuing chaos
he has rained down on women, Armstrong's argument is nevertheless based on her several decades of global roaming and
reporting. She says that in the decade leading up to 2019 she
witnessed a profound change in conversations right around the
world, with a new and sustained focus on the rights of women
and girls, 'whether in the forests of the Democratic Republic of
Congo or the savannah in Kenya, in the deserts of Afghanistan,
or the college campuses in North America'.[24] With women's
futures front of mind, the 'power shift' Armstrong describes
centres on *who* is driving the agenda for change. Whereas once
we had to rely on 'political will' and 'the stroke of a politician's
pen', Armstrong argues that 'personal will' is now the major
driving force of change. Most importantly, it is tech-savvy,
digitally connected and emboldened women who are leading
this fundamental shift around the globe.

Here in Australia, the idea that 'personal will', exercised by
women, is driving public and political change resonates loudly.
We know this to be true!

The 'end of days' vibe seeping through outdated workplaces
right now, which is exciting media veterans like Louise Milligan
and me, reflects a concerted shift in power in this country. It's a
tectonic shift in which a single woman's voice raised in protest
at sexism, harassment and misogyny potentially carries weight
and power that was previously unimaginable, even a few years

ago. The old style of power once celebrated in glossy power lists, traditionally held by people with significant social status or political positioning, is out. New power is in.

An epoch-changing switch has been flicked.

Australian big thinker Jeremy Heimans flagged this shift in his 2018 book *New Power*, co-written with British CEO and philanthropist Henry Timms. Exploring the phenomenal success of people movements such as #MeToo and #BlackLivesMatter, the authors argue that by harnessing personal power, we are reshaping just about everything we do – from politics to business to how we run society. They separate 'old' and 'new' power as a change from 'currency' (which can be hoarded) to 'current' (which flows freely). 'Old power works like a currency,' say Heimans and Timms. 'It is held by few. Once gained, it is jealously guarded, and the powerful have a substantial store of it to spend. It is closed, inaccessible, and leader-driven. It downloads, and it captures.'

Old power is jealously guarded by the patriarchy. It's not for sharing; it's for wielding. But – and here is where this concept gets exciting – new power is not held or traded like a currency. Instead, it is fluid and accessible. 'New power operates differently, like a current. It is made by many. It is open, participatory, and peer-driven. It uploads and it distributes. Like water or electricity, it's most forceful when it surges. The goal of the new power is not to hoard it but to channel it.'[25]

The global juggernaut of the #MeToo movement, started by a single tweet, is one example of an explosion of new power. In October 2017, accomplished Hollywood actor Alyssa Milano was enraged by a story that had just broken in *The New York Times*, which outed film producer and Hollywood kingmaker Harvey Weinstein as a deviant sexual predator who assaulted numerous young women and actresses over several decades. Milano, a friend of Weinstein's ex-wife and some of his victims, encouraged women on Twitter to self-identify as victim-survivors: 'If you've been sexually harassed or assaulted, write "me too" as a reply to this tweet.'

Triggering 55 000 replies in a matter of hours, Milano unwittingly kickstarted a tsunami of #MeToo responses, with global celebrities adding their names to what immediately became a worldwide reckoning on sexual harassment and assault. Later, in Australia we experienced the force of this new power as the March4Justice movement, which was also triggered by a single tweet. At that moment, we didn't just see new power in action, we *felt* it (see Part 2).

'New power doesn't hold to the old traditional leadership style,' writes Sally Armstrong, 'it relies instead on mass participation. It also relies on a frame of mind that says enough is enough.'[26] This, too, Australian women know to be true. The courage of women to speak up is self-generated. It is not a courage born of entitlement or career prestige. Women are using their voices to call out intolerable and unacceptable behaviour that has, until now, simply worn us down.

Now, as we clock past the first quarter of this new century, revelling in our New Now and a major shift in power, the role of men demands scrutiny. Friend or foe – men are an integral part of this story. Finding their footing in the face of the feminist fightback is disorienting for men. Some never will. But others? Let's see.

2

MEN MANNING UP

On the cusp of the 50th anniversary of International Women's Year in 2025, something unheard-of happened in Australia that shifted the conversation about women.

Men got involved.

It was new, it was raw and, like all revolutionary gear shifts, it unfurled in a chaotic mess. Nevertheless, it happened. Men started talking. About men. They started talking about what a violent, dangerous, misogynistic lot they really are. And it wasn't just any men saying this. It was men in power, in politics, in media; men who held court in public; men who happened to be sharing a Zoom meeting with me. Even the elderly gent sitting next to me at the ballet as the curtain came down on *Carmen*: 'Bit violent, eh?' he said. Then, before I could answer: 'Do you know how many AVOs against men there are around the country? More than 30,000.'

He was wide-eyed, appalled, and he was right to be horrified. But he was wrong on the data. That whopping annual figure for apprehended violence orders was for New South Wales alone. The number was fresh in his mind because Australia was rowdy with talk about violence against women. But in a dramatic turn of events, unlike our repeated conversations of the past, this felt different. In a moment of public purging, amid saturation media coverage, suddenly men were talking too.

It had taken a long 50 years, but this had become part of our New Now.

At first it was an arm's-length acknowledgment. It was a Monday evening in mid-April 2024, several hours after the Federal Court's Justice Michael Lee handed down his historic judgment in the *Lehrmann v Network Ten* defamation case. This had been one of the most eagerly anticipated legal events in recent history. Almost 50 000 people tuned in to YouTube that afternoon to watch a live stream from the court as Justice Lee summed up the 'omnishambles' of a case that had become a long, drawn-out, salacious media train wreck and cultural flashpoint across the nation.

It wasn't the defamation that we cared about. It was the allegation of rape. Three years earlier, Brittany Higgins, a young former political staffer, appeared on television and told the nation that she had been on a drunken binge late one night with a work colleague, Bruce Lehrmann, and that he had taken her back to Parliament House and raped her in the office of the defence industry minister. By 2024, Brittany Higgins was a household name, and it seemed that every Australian had a view about the validity of her story. So, finally, there was to be a judgment. Of sorts.

Reminding his audience that this was not a criminal trial but a civil matter, and therefore the finding was 'on the balance of probabilities', Justice Lee slowly read aloud an extensive summary of his 324-page judgment. And there it was, in paragraph 620: 'Mr Lehrmann raped Ms Higgins.'[1]

Unremittingly forensic, the judgment was a stunner. Justice Lee will go down in feminist history as the man who 'got it'. It was not the confirmation of rape that marked this turning point. Rather, it is what Justice Lee said about rape and how the trauma of sexual assault can distort a victim's responses and their post-assault behaviour. His judgment was stunning in both its language and sentiment. While acknowledging Brittany Higgins was a 'complex and unsatisfactory witness', and that her actions had on occasion been erratic and appeared inconsistent, Justice Lee gave unprecedented weight to the disorienting power of sexual trauma. In short, he chose to believe her: the messy young woman who woke up half-naked, sprawled across the couch in her boss's office, drunk and confused, who said she had been raped but had no proof. Faced with a choice, he chose to believe her. Bruce Lehrmann maintained his innocence, denying any sexual contact occurred, and in early 2025 appealed the finding, citing 'inconsistencies' in Justice Lee's judgement.[2] For media, this was the story that just kept giving.

Back on the evening of the judgment, a high-profile corporate heavyweight asked me a fascinating question. As we waited for others to join our scheduled Zoom meeting, we talked about the day's big story. 'Do you think Justice Lee could have made that judgment 20 years ago? Or perhaps even ten years ago?' he asked. Before I could answer, the other men on the Zoom chimed in. 'No way,' said one. 'Not before #MeToo,' said another. 'Not before 2021 and Australia's March4Justice,' I suggested. Everyone nodded, thoughtfully.

Justice Lee had embraced a nuanced, trauma-informed understanding of what it may be like for women living and working in a world made unsafe – and powered – by men. A world in which disempowered, humiliated women, racked with shame, are forced to make unreasonable choices in an attempt to salvage any dignity, while trying to keep their jobs and career ambitions afloat. The language Justice Lee used in his judgment, along with the reasoning and sentiments he expressed, were unprecedented from such a high-profile man of law. This was new. This was progress.

As the business of our Zoom meeting got underway, I couldn't help but muse over the shift we had all felt. It was a fundamental shift in public consciousness. This judgment was an important turning point. It indicated a journey of awakening. And not just for Justice Michael Lee.

As 2024 rolled on, it became clear there were men in positions of public power who were listening to women talk about their lived experiences, and who were thinking more deeply about the damage inflicted on women's lives by social and cultural norms steeped in patriarchy. It was as if a little of the fog had started to lift and a new gender-sensitive lens had been applied. This new thinking had all the hallmarks of a national consciousness-raising experience. We just didn't know it.

The creeping presence of femicide in our news

Australian news media have never been comfortable using the word 'femicide' when speaking about the targeted murder of women. The United Nations defines femicide as 'intentional killing with a gender-related motivation'.[3] It's both complex and alarmingly simple. Femicide is about power: men exercising lethal power over women – because they can, and because such men believe they have some form of rights, ownership and/or entitlement over the women they kill. Even if, ultimately, they're killing for kicks.

Rather than call it what it is – 'femicide' – we collectively blur the brutality of women being hacked, burned, stabbed or pulverised to death, often by men they know, perhaps even once loved, as either 'DFV' – domestic and family violence – or 'VAW', violence against women. We use those abbreviations to box it and explain it. As a young journalist on police and court rounds, I frequently heard the phrase, 'It's *just* a domestic' – to minimise the news value of a female homicide, or infer it was none of our business. But violence against women *is* our business. Everyone's business. It's taken Australia a long time to realise this. Along with that realisation is a sharper focus. In our New Now, our lens isn't on women's safety as much as it is on men's violence.

In early May 2024, after a shocking and sustained period of femicide in Australia, journalist Rick Morton, writing in *The Saturday Paper*, reflected on 'five weeks of wall-to-wall coverage about the hideous nature of male violence'. His story focused on a Queensland domestic violence call centre that was experiencing 'a small but significant surge in men calling about their own use of violence'. Director of the service, Michelle Royes, told Morton, 'As a result of the media coverage and the significant injury and murders that have happened in the last few weeks, we've actually seen more men reaching out saying, "I'm worried about my use of violence."'[4]

Guardian columnist Van Badham blew a bugle announcing the shift in narrative: 'Australia's public conversation about male violence has never been so loud,' she wrote, noting that even the conservative Sky News was reporting that Australians 'want immediate change to combat the domestic violence crisis'.[5] Barrister Geoffrey Watson SC added his voice to palpable community frustration, penning an opinion piece in *The Sydney Morning Herald* suggesting men need to man up:

> We are failing to face up to what must be done. It is now
> obvious that our laws restricting males from stalking
> females (oh, and let's get this straight – this is a male
> problem) are grossly inadequate ... Stronger action
> must be taken against men credibly accused of stalking,
> threatening or abusing women ... We need to do more;
> we need to do things differently.[6]

Around the same time, co-host of Channel Ten's *The Project*, Waleed Aly, engaged in a bit of public problematising over what makes men violent towards women. Musing over former prime minister Malcom Turnbull's now famous mantra that 'disrespecting women doesn't always lead to violence but all violence against women begins with disrespecting women', Aly suggested the claim was wrong.[7] He argued that men's brutality towards women is not rooted in disrespect and gender inequity but in male feelings of 'humiliation, shame and guilt'.[8] Journalist Jess Hill, who had made this link years earlier in her book *See What You Made Me Do*, joined the chorus of commentators writing about this new narrative on women and violence. While expressing support for victim-survivors, families and friends of women recently murdered, she assured readers there were encouraging movements and policy shifts going on 'behind the scenes'. 'It feels like a brave new world,' she wrote.[9]

Even the right-wing shock-jock Ray Hadley, now retired but known back then as the booming bloke from radio 2GB, penned a passionate opinion piece in *The Sydney Morning Herald* about the 'growing number of women' murdered by men: 'We're all sick of the soundbites. They think inquiries and gabfests are going to solve the problem. They won't ... It is time for society to stand united.'[10]

Hadley emphatically called for a toughening up of bail laws for all men charged with rape and sexual assault. It was an interesting foray into the debate, given Hadley's own wife had briefly taken out an AVO against him ten years earlier. When I quizzed *Sydney Morning Herald* editor Bevan Shields about the potential disconnect here, he smiled, agreeing that it was an 'unusual' op ed, as a bloke like Hadley is not who readers expect to see featured in the *Herald*: 'Yes, it's rare that the *Herald* and Ray Hadley would agree on anything. But I have to say, in fairness to Ray, he has been banging on about bail reform and judicial reform in relation to violence against women for a long, long time ... I think he is right.'

Given the saturation media coverage of what we still shied away from calling femicide, one of the greatest male bastions in the nation, the AFL, was moved to take action. On the first weekend of May 2024, before each Round 8 match, opposing clubs formed large rings at the centre of the oval, standing arm in arm, for a minute's silence. The gesture, according to AFL CEO Andrew Dillon, was 'to unite and remember all the women who have been killed as a result of gender-based violence and stand in solidarity in committing to do more to stop this community-wide problem'.[11]

Performative? Yes. But poignant. And new.

Despite my deep dislike of football and its blokey traditions, and my inherent cynicism of corporate virtue-signalling, even I was moved by the AFL minute of silence. I scanned the crowds shown on TV and wondered how many men, among the 400 000 people attending that weekend, might be witnessing a united male rejection of violence against women for the first time in their lives.[12]

Femicide: But is it 'terrorism'?

As always with major shifts in public discourse and media commentary, the groundwork for change is laid well before the apparent trigger moment. In early 2024, Australia had experienced a hideous kaleidoscope of tragic trigger moments.

In February, shock over the murder of two gay men by a Sydney police officer reverberated across the harbour city. But as the 'Counting Dead Women' tally continued to grow around the nation, the sabre rattle of public frustration got louder. Then the unthinkable happened.

On a pleasantly warm Saturday afternoon in April, as shoppers casually strolled through the Bondi Junction shopping centre in east Sydney, a piercing scream ripped through the mall, followed by another, then another. A lone attacker, 40-year-old Joel Cauchi, was on a bloody rampage, armed with a large hunting knife and what appeared to be a mission to kill as many women as he could. In the brief six minutes before he was shot dead by police officer Amy Scott, Cauchi had brutally stabbed 16 people, the majority of them women. One woman, who had crouched down in a shop as Cauchi walked right past her, told the BBC the phones of terrified shoppers hiding with her lit up with frantic messages that one, two, then at least three women had been stabbed. The horror hit home. She said, 'I thought, "He's going after women."'[13] Six people were killed: five women, aged between 25 and 55, and a young male security guard on his first day at work.

Two days later, after reviewing hundreds of phone videos and CCTV footage, police confirmed as 'obvious' what women everywhere feared most – this was a deliberate massacre of women. 'The videos speak for themselves, don't they,' said police commissioner Karen Webb. 'The offender focused on women and avoided the men.' Later, Cauchi's deeply distraught father told the media pack outside his home that his son had been diagnosed with mental health problems. When asked, 'Do you have any reason or understand why he would have targeted women?', Andrew Cauchi was blunt: 'Yes,' he said without hesitation. 'He wanted a girlfriend and he's got no social skills and he was frustrated out of his brain.'[14] In a chilling interview on Nine News, one of the women who survived the stabbing said Cauchi spoke just two words as he plunged a dripping knife into her body: 'Catch you.'[15]

At the time of this attack and in the months following, the sobering reality of a killing spree centred on women forced new conversations in Australia. This was femicide on a scale we had not seen before. But was this the sort of mass-murdering misogyny played out around college campuses in the US?

It was soon obvious that Joel Cauchi was no Elliot Rodger – the Isla Vista killer who in 2014 killed six people near the University of California, before killing himself. Rodger, a sexually frustrated 22-year-old virgin, left a long trail of anti-women hatred in his wake, including a video expressing his desire to 'punish' women and a 141-page manifesto that 'documented his rage against women for rejecting him'.[16] Cauchi left nothing to indicate his motive. Despite the NSW police commissioner's statement that women were clearly the target, the coroner's inquest in May 2025 threw doubt on that. The lead police investigator suggested Cauchi killed 'whoever was in his way'.[17] Cauchi's former psychiatrist told the inquest the rampage was due to his 'sexual frustrations, pornography and hatred towards women' but later withdrew those claims, saying they were 'conjecture'.[18] The inquest also heard that Cauchi had appealed to a health clinic to help him curb his porn addiction by limiting access to pornography on his phone.[19] Without any specific statement from Cauchi, we will never know what enraged him, or why he raised his arm and plunged his killer blade into so many women's bodies. But what we do know is – he did.

The Bondi Junction attack is the worst single case of mass femicide in Australian history. But was it terrorism? An act of terrorism against women? Is such terrorism part of our New Now?

The question of terrorism shot into the media frame following another stabbing attack just two days after the Bondi massacre. On this occasion, no one was killed. On the other side of town, a 16-year-old teenager entered a church during the Monday-evening service, walked straight to the altar and stabbed the priest several times, injuring him badly. Violent clashes involving community members outside the church led to a late-night stand-off with riot police, all of which was live-streamed across social media. In the heat of this high drama, some six hours after the stabbing, police declared the incident 'terrorism', because the stabbing appeared to be 'religiously motivated'.

It's important to note that the official classification of terrorism not only upped the media stakes at the time but, on a purely practical level, enabled the government to throw a lot more resources at investigating the crime. The next morning a very earnest-looking Prime Minister Anthony Albanese held a press conference flanked by national security chiefs. Australia, he said, is a 'peace-loving nation' in which there is 'no place for violent extremism'.[20] They weren't exactly fighting words. In fact, more like being hit with a wet lettuce. But gnawing at women watching on was the burning question: 'If this is terrorism, why has the massacre of women in Bondi Junction not also been declared terrorism?'

When asked about this, the director-general of the Australian Security Intelligence Organisation (ASIO), Mike Burgess, was uncompromising: 'The simple answer is to call it a terrorist attack you need indications of information or evidence that suggests the motivation was religiously motivated or ideologically motivated. In the case of [the Bondi Junction attacks] that was not the case.'[21]

Feminist writer and polemicist Mona Eltahawy, never one to pull her punches or dither over discourse, vehemently disagreed. The Egyptian-American journalist, bellowing from New York, was quick to call the Bondi attack an act of terrorism against women. 'Patriarchy is the ideology,' she wrote in her essay 'Femicide – The approved terrorism':

> Patriarchy socializes men to believe they are entitled to the attention and affection of women and a 'no' – whether it's a refusal to give them a phone number or not consenting to become a girlfriend – becomes a death sentence that men

like the Sydney killer carry out on women, any women, for the temerity of refusing to submit body and cunt.[22]

While not quite so blunt, back in Australia, it wasn't just women asking aloud why Joel Cauchi's killing rampage wasn't labelled terrorism. Men also asked the same question. One of the nation's most respected political broadcasters, David Speers, wrote a provocative editorial comparing the incidents. 'Both involved extreme violence. Both caused fear in the community. So why was one labelled terrorism while the other was not?' he wrote. 'Is targeting someone for being a woman somehow less serious than targeting someone for their religious views?'[23]

At the same time, Greg Barton, a professor of global Islamic politics, wrote: 'So, if someone is targeting a specific group of people, isn't that terrorism? Why does it matter if they were killing based on gender or religion? Is misogyny not terrorism?'[24]

This was the first time Australia had engaged in media discussion about the potentially lethal impact of misogyny and the necessity of calling it what it is – terrorism against women. While some legal experts continue to argue that to describe a massacre as an act of terror it needs to be driven by an ideology that includes belief in a 'higher cause', I cannot separate the hostility towards women from fundamental feelings of terror. Internalising those feelings of fear – as women do – is to be terrorised. When men believe that women should be subservient, malleable and available to them, they are identifying with – and perhaps fantasising over – a patriarchal world order in which men are the natural commanders who enforce the rules. A world in which men have an indisputable, gendered right to take control.

This belief is born of ideology. When women don't conform to patriarchal demands and expectations, their rejection, or even their very existence, triggers raw fury. This is when misogyny is weaponised and wielded as a tool of the patriarchy. At its extreme, misogyny gives rise to violence and ultimately murder: femicide. These acts are attempts to reverse the wrong. To take back masculine control and power. To restore patriarchal order. *This* is the 'higher cause'. *This* is the political ideology.

Tragically, what followed shortly after the horror of these incidents was further confirmation that terrorism against women is an indelible part of our lives.

By the time the hideous murder of 28-year-old Molly Ticehurst hit media headlines in late April 2024, a woman had been killed every four days in Australia since the beginning of the year. *The Sydney Morning Herald* led with a front-page headline screaming 'THIS HAS TO STOP'. The booming editorial cut straight to the chase with a national shaming: 'How many more women have to be beaten to a pulp, strangled, stabbed, shot, drowned or set on fire before Australia gets serious about confronting the many causes behind our epidemic of gendered violence?'[25]

Molly Ticehurst lived alone with her one-year-old child in a regional town in the Central West of New South Wales. In early April she reported her ex-partner, Daniel Billings, to police. He was charged with rape, stalking, harassment and property damage. Yet, despite the obvious threat he posed, Billings was issued with an interim AVO, granted bail and allowed to walk free. A local housing support service called Molly and promised to install security measures in her house, including outdoor lighting and cameras. But before any of that happened, Billings was back. And Molly was dead. One of the region's detective inspectors told reporters that he had been in the police force for 34 years, including time as a homicide detective, but the discovery of Molly's body had rattled him. 'It was terribly violent ... quite brutal,' he said.[26]

It is too reductive to say that Molly's death in 2024 was a tipping point. Australian women had already been well and truly tipped over: lied to, yelled at, ridiculed, humiliated, gaslit, bullied, demeaned. By the time young Molly Ticehurst's senseless and shocking death was in the media spotlight, women – and men – around the nation were livid. Michael Salter, a leading academic expert in gendered violence, wrote that 'National anger at men's violence against women is at boiling point. After multiple killings, Australians are marching on the streets demanding change. Governments are nervous ... searching for new solutions.'[27]

Media in the spotlight

On the weekend after Molly's story broke, 'No More' protest rallies were held across five cities, gathering crowds of several thousand women and men. The snap rallies were organised by a little-known activist group called What Were You Wearing (WWYW). I joined the crowd in Sydney's Hyde Park, at which activist Hannah Ferguson delivered an impassioned and furious invective at mainstream media. She skewered news media for exploiting women's trauma for commercial gain, and for using language that ameliorates the violence and responsibility of perpetrators. We all know the predictable words and rhythms: we've been reading them for decades.

Journalist Jane Gilmore drew national attention to the ubiquity of our exonerating language in her book *Fixed It*.[28] Headlines such as 'Football star charged with glassing girlfriend' rather than 'Violent man disfigures and maims woman', or 'Loving father attacks cheating wife' instead of 'Violent man kills woman trying to escape him'. You get the drift. As I watched Ferguson – a powerful young woman, and a formidable voice of our New Now – expertly lasso the crowd and berate the media, I wondered what male editors of legacy news organisations might think about this attack on media integrity.

But first, political leaders were also in the firing line.

Ferguson castigated the NSW premier, Chris Minns, for leaving the Sydney rally 'halfway through the first speech! I watched him walk!' she bellowed to the crowd. Then she ripped into the hypocrisy of all political leaders: 'what they're doing is leaving as soon as the fucking photo is taken'.[29] It's a fair cop. But not always. In Minns' case, he was leaving to see his dangerously sick father, who had been rushed to hospital and died three days later. While Ferguson is perfectly justified to be angry at failed political leadership – as we all are – I nevertheless include mention of this misplaced attack as a sobering example of how, at times, we are all capable of misreading motivations and actions.

However, at this time of intense anger and frustration, no one got it as badly wrong as Prime Minister Anthony Albanese. The day after the Sydney rally, Albo – as he likes to be called – turned up at the Canberra 'No More' rally, flanked by his loyal women comrades: Katy Gallagher, Minister for Women, and Amanda Rishworth, at the time Minister for Social Services. In front of a crowd of close to 5000, the PM was heckled and challenged, which was to be expected under the circumstances. However, after 23-year-old rally organiser Sarah Williams delivered a harrowing speech about her personal experience of rape and living with violence and homelessness, the microphone was waved at the PM. He was not scheduled to be a speaker on the day but, given the heat of the moment, he took the bait.

What followed was classic political tin-ear awfulness. In a spectacular failure to acknowledge the personal trauma Williams had just shared with the crowd, Albanese instead quibbled over not being officially invited to speak. Offended, Williams told the crowd that was 'a straight-out lie' and burst into tears. The PM looked baffled and turned away. Her friends rushed to comfort her. And Albanese, demonstrating all the empathy of a bollard, blustered onward and made the moment all about him, lecturing the crowd and defending his government's record on combating gendered violence. It was awful. Gobsmackingly awful. For a moment, an ABC camera lingered on Minister Gallagher, who looked like she was about to be sick.

Later, Annabel Crabb, the sharpest wit to walk political corridors, summed up the spectacle with a heave of exhausted humour:

> The world is full of imponderables at the moment. And for Australian women, you can add a new one to the list: How long is it going to take for us to get a prime minister whose response to reasonable female anger isn't to trip spectacularly over his own tackle?[30]

Turning up the media heat or flaming trauma porn?

Over at *The Sydney Morning Herald*, Bevan Shields was keeping a sharp eye on the 'No More' rallies. Shields, who was in his mid-thirties when he took the reins of the *Herald* in 2021, does not defend past wrongs of the news media; instead, he's intent on forging a new discourse. His front-page editorial on the day before the Sydney rally called for two royal commissions into violence against women: a federal commission to look at cultural and social issues, and one in his own state of New South Wales to examine judicial issues and law reform. Like most women I know, I groaned reading that. *Really? How many more talkfests are needed? How many more reviews, reports, summits?* Australia has a National Action Plan to End Violence Against Women and Children – the result of thousands of hours of talk and expert research. How much more talk is needed?

When I sit down to talk to Shields, before I can launch in

and make this point he starts his own groaning. 'How many more repeated cycles of violence do we have to have before something changes?' he asks. 'This thing is so big and so complex, and there is such a cycle to these things, which I just found after 15 years in the media completely depressing.'

He runs through what we both know is the typical media cycle for a horror story like Molly Ticehurst's: shock headlines, a young woman's pretty face flashed across screens, details of her brutal murder, thoughts and prayers to her family; then the political outrage, a call for more funds from women's services, more political thumping from the opposition, talk of 'what we need to do'. At this point, Shields isn't trying to hide his contempt for a repeated media-led process that delivers nothing and fails everyone.

'Everything just moves on,' he says. 'Then, six months later … 12 months later, here we are again at the start of that cycle!' For a moment we both sit there, looking glum. These are depressingly well-known media cycles. And yes, there will be more Molly Ticehursts. Which is why Shields insists there should be a royal commission now, rather than wait another decade, during which there will be numerous repeats of this same cycle. He's even done the sums, to prove what a tiny portion of government spending it would take.[31] There is solid precedent for state-based royal commissions. Victoria was first, completing its Royal Commission into Family Violence in 2016. Seven years later, by January 2023, all 227 recommendations had been implemented. The southern state is often referred to as the standard bearer when it comes to policy settings and a nuanced political understanding of the issues: proof that change takes time but can happen. In 2024, South Australia launched its Royal Commission into Domestic, Family and Sexual Violence, chaired by Natasha Stott Despoja.

Not surprisingly, the Sydney paper's call for a royal commission was met with political deafness at both state and federal levels. Undeterred, Shields and a small team of journalists at the *Herald* pushed on.

In April–May 2024, *The Sydney Morning Herald* ran daily stories about violence against women in a concerted campaign to drive public discourse beyond the usual femicide 'shock horror'. The aim was to unpack the cultural and social drivers enabling it. Some were hard-to-miss front-page screamers, like 'Misogyny driving violence'.[32] Others were deeply personal accounts in which a woman's family, friends and community members were interviewed, providing a fully rounded picture of a woman's life before she was hacked to death. Day after day, it was tough reading. At times, I found myself turning away. But Shields says that was the point. He wanted to 'force' the public to see the faces of women whose lives were being taken, 'to see what is being lost'. The relentless repetition of similar stories was to emphasise that these are not fleeting or unusual incidents but part of an epidemic of violence against women.

While I understood the *Herald*'s well-meaning intentions behind the dogged campaign, I was also unnerved by it. Unsure. At what point does all this female horror simply become clickbait to drive up audience numbers and sell papers (to those who still read them)? After all, attacks on women and violating their bodies is prime entertainment. Our movies are full of it. TV series thrive on it. So where is the divide between journalism and horror-porn?

It's the sort of question that would normally get any news editor squirming, but to my surprise, Shields relishes this discussion. He says the small team assigned to work on this campaign were worried that the opposite of clickbait would occur. They feared readers would avoid these stories, turned off by the horror and the relentlessness of gender-based violence. It was a tricky call for Shields, who makes a strong ethical case for 'public good' publishing, while also acknowledging a journalist's need to be relevant: 'If you are going to ask your reporters and photographers and others to put their heart and soul into this kind of thing, you want to make sure it is read as widely as possible.'

Explaining that an advocacy 'campaign' in the *Herald* – such as calling for a ban on gambling advertising – might take between two and four months to 'take off' and filter through to public debate, Shields says the *Herald*'s Violence Against Women campaign had immediate impact. 'The truth is, in the past, it has been hard to get readers to engage with stories about violence against women,' he says. 'But what really surprised us here is that there was a massive audience, from the moment we started doing this. It didn't take any time to build. There was a real hunger for depth and for substance.'

One of the critical points of interest for the readers, as demonstrated by the *Herald*'s analytics, was the data. Lots of it. Until recently, we have had very little national data on violence against women, leaving media free to peddle old assumptions and myths. Most importantly, the lack of data meant stories about family and sexual violence were invariably treated as ghoulish, horrific and singular events that only happened to unlucky individual women. The systemic patterns and epidemic rates of violence went unreported. Now, thankfully, access to solid, longitudinal data tells a deeper, truer story, and it's a story audiences want to understand.

When researching the birth of the Women's Liberation Movement and its battles with appallingly sexist media, it didn't surprise me to learn that some feminists in the US, as far back as 1968, refused to talk to male reporters at all. They told media outlets to send a 'woman reporter' or go to hell – although usually in more colourful words. But given the increasing number of male journalists and commentators writing about violence against women, I asked Shields how much this shift was a concerted effort or a conscious decision by *The Sydney Morning Herald* to get men writing about women and violence.

His response was emphatic.

> I think people in media have felt conflicted about this in the past, because there's been an absolutely misplaced perception that this is a women's issue, and so you can only have women write about it, or report on it. I just think that is complete bullshit. It's everyone's issue. This is not for women to solve. This is on everyone to solve. Men, in particular, have an obligation to be part of this.

They were impassioned words. I just wish Kerry Packer was still around to hear this. Perhaps such enlightened male activism has him turning in his grave!

The sort of enlightened thinking demonstrated by a small cohort of millennial men who wield media power is still a work in progress. A slow and lumbering yet demonstrable shift is underway, but only in narrow sections of the media. Not fast enough, and not around the power corridors and old mahogany rows where media moguls and CEOs amble, nor in those media executive suites where money decisions take priority over editorial. But there is a new male scent wafting up from the lower floors, less cheap cologne and perhaps more green tea. These are men who are comfortable sharing space with women who challenge them – women who are often smarter than them, perhaps even more ambitious. It's a slight shift, but an encouraging thread in the story of our New Now.

However, to reach this point has taken much more than a handful of male feminists who can apply a gender lens to reportage and the complexity of entrenched discrimination. It has taken a painful, prolonged period of darkness and denial. We have had to work through a shameful period in which

Australian women supposedly in positions of privilege and power have been openly bullied, brutalised, humiliated and demeaned – in public. This of course follows an unspeakably long history in which generations of woman have endured these blows in private.

The mythology around Australian mateship and the larrikin bloke has given cover to a culture grounded in sexism and inequality – a culture in which women have had to fight for the most basic human rights, including the right to vote, study, work, love freely, and have full control over our bodies and sex lives. For Australia's Indigenous women, every battle for equal rights and recognition has been overlaid with racism. For migrant, disabled and impoverished women, layer upon layer of disadvantage have long rendered their rights and needs invisible. Arriving at our New Now does not for a moment suggest these burning disadvantages have been dissolved. They clearly have not.

But here's the key message: no woman's voice will again be silenced. No act of gender-based brutality will be shoved back in the shadows.

We are out now.

3

MISOGYNY, PARLIAMENT, WITCHES, LIARS AND LEERS

After I was struck down with Covid in 2020, I seemed to develop olfactory superpowers. My sense of smell was off the charts. Which is fine around jasmine and daphne but it proved overbearing when I walked into Parliament House. The place stunk. An awful stench of wasted women infused the air. Women's frustration, anger and a general sense of being pissed off was overwhelming – if you had a nose for it. Women who were passionate about politics and worked like warhorses to try to muscle in change were being ignored, belittled and at times outright abused.

But that was just the surface stuff. Beneath the performance of politics was the undercurrent of a dirty, toxic culture steeped in misogyny. It was an ocean of dangerous rips, pulling women under, using them as expendable political cannon fodder for pot shots and playthings. Yet no one seemed to be noticing. Most of all, the press gallery.

Occasionally, the most obvious story is right under our nose, but we just can't smell it, much less see it. Sometimes, we might get a whiff of it but we choose to ignore it, or we just don't care.

Missing a story was always my biggest fear as a young journalist. As a junior press gallery journalist in Victoria, I was unspeakably grateful to be included in the 'bloke's caucus' after each premier's press conference. So raw and green was I that I often left those regular 'pressers' not sure what the story was or who I should be chasing for interviews. Thankfully, the older blokes, my ABC colleagues and some of the commercial TV reporters would gather like a male cabal for a 'So, what do we think, gang?' session. I took copious notes!

Journalists hate to hear this, but the toxic culture of the Australian parliament and its inherent misogyny is one of the biggest missed stories in Australian political history. Bevan Shields, once a prominent member of the press gallery, was not the first bloke I berated about the media's failure to report on the overt sexism and toxic work culture brewing within Parliament House. But he is perhaps one of the most honest in response: 'I've definitely spent a lot of time soul searching,' he says. 'Why did we not look at this earlier? Why did we not see this as clearly as we, as media, should have? Why didn't we see this when it was clearly happening in plain sight?'

Groupthink is an indisputable characteristic of political reporting. To be in the group is to exist in a bubble. In the nation's capital, at the seat of power, it is called the Canberra Bubble. But what happens when the bubble is so enveloping, so self-referential, that everyone in it misses the same story – collectively? What about when the whole press pack has its eyes wide shut?

Julia Gillard lets rip

Misogyny in politics doesn't start or end with Australia's first female prime minister, Julia Gillard, but she sure became its poster girl.

When I first interviewed Gillard back in 2003, in the days when she was a junior minister and rising star in the opposition, she skirted my questions about feminism. Asked what she thought was 'the biggest problem confronting women right now', she responded in abstract terms about work and family-life balance, admitting it was not something she herself had to contend with.[1]

From the outset, Gillard presented herself as the 'model post-feminist woman'. Unlike leaders like Hillary Clinton, Gillard refused to acknowledge gender as an important and defining issue, instead insisting she preferred just 'getting on with it'.[2] Which, mostly, she did.

Until she famously, spectacularly, didn't.

Once described by another woman MP as 'one of the most controlled human beings on the planet', Gillard's resilience and calm demeanour were legendary.[3] But on 9 October 2012, Julia Gillard blew a gasket. I was at my desk in the ABC Canberra newsroom watching the live feed from parliament when a ferociously cool Gillard walked to the dispatch box during question time, paused a beat, and then began a searing evisceration of the opposition leader, Tony Abbott, as she ripped open the wound of misogyny:

> I was offended ... by the sexism, by the misogyny of the Leader of the Opposition catcalling across this table at me as I sit here as Prime Minister ...
>
> I was offended when the Leader of the Opposition ... stood next to a sign that said, 'Ditch the witch' ... and stood next to a sign that described me as a man's 'bitch'.
>
> I was offended by those things. Misogyny, sexism, every day from this Leader of the Opposition. Every day in every way.[4]

Shot with adrenalin and exhilarated by what I was hearing, I clipped an edit of the 15-minute speech while Gillard was still talking and posted it on Twitter, as fast as my fingers could work. Others were doing the same. Within minutes #Gillard was trending. My favourite tweet, from an unknown bloke, simply read, 'Tony Abbot [*sic*] raised 3 daughters, I think Julia Gillard just raised a generation of them.'[5] And so she did.

Years later, I was speaking with Amaani Siddeek, at the time a journalism student at the University of Technology Sydney. A Sri Lankan–born Muslim, Siddeek was making a documentary on the Misogyny Speech, which intrigued me, and I asked, 'Why?' She said the speech exposed her to a whole new world of feminism, and although she was too young to have heard it at the time, Siddeek, like the students around her, discovered the speech in 2019 via a global TikTok lip-sync craze. Many of the hip young women mouthing Gillard's words didn't know a jot about Australia's former prime minister or her parliamentary record. But they clearly related to the underlying message of sexism and misogyny 'every day in every way':

I will not be lectured about sexism and misogyny by this man.

I will not.

And the government will not be lectured about sexism and misogyny by this man.

Not now, not ever.

The Leader of the Opposition says that people who hold sexist views and who are misogynists are not appropriate for high office.

Well I hope the Leader of the Opposition has got a piece of paper and he is writing out his resignation.

Because if he wants to know what misogyny looks like in modern Australia, he doesn't need a motion in the House of Representatives, he needs a mirror.

That's what he needs.

There is profound irony in the fact that the single most quoted and talked-about speech in Australian political history is a speech about misogyny and sexism. More academic articles, PhDs, essays, songs, musicals, theatre, video reel, media space and discussion forums have been devoted to Julia Gillard's Misogyny Speech than any other parliamentary speech in Australian history. Not one of the 30 men who have sat in the prime minister's seat since Federation in 1901 has ever made a speech that has been discussed around the world like this one. All because Gillard called out and railed against a fundamental sexism and misogyny that just about every woman in Australia, and beyond, felt and understood. Even if the parliament and the press gallery didn't.

The speech was pure poetry, belted out with the rhythmic thwack of a steel bar across the opposition leader's head. But was it politics?

For women, it was personal. For the press gallery, it was political.

Over the days and weeks that followed, most commentators sifted Gillard's words through the functional funnel of the Canberra Bubble. They reviewed the speech as a strategic ploy by the prime minister to distract from the turbulent politics of the day, in which the speaker – a member of parliament Gillard relied on to maintain her minority government – had been caught out sending lewd and sexually inappropriate text messages to his former boyfriend.

Some weeks later, on the ABC's prime political talk show *Insiders*, host Barrie Cassidy took a swipe at his media colleagues for failing to understand the cultural importance of the speech, and its powerful and obvious resonance with the public, pointing out that it already had three million views on YouTube. With an eye towards the next election, Mark Kenny, then chief political correspondent of *The Sydney Morning Herald* and *The Age*, responded: 'A lot of these three million people aren't voting in Australia.' Cassidy bristled and snapped back, 'I'm not talking about it in terms of shifting polls, I'm talking about it in terms of the significance of the speech and the fact that it was virtually ignored by the Canberra press gallery.'

It was an 'ouch' moment. In fact, a double ouch for Kenny and me. Mark Kenny is my husband – yes, still is – and this was an issue we had discussed at length. (The personal is always political, and vice versa, in our household.) Mark had previously written about the attacks on Gillard's legitimacy as being inherently sexist, but such commentary got little traction at the time. No one seemed interested in connecting the dots between deep-seated gender discrimination and the fundamental rejection of a woman's equal right to claim political power in whatever way the politics of the day required.

Witch, liar, bitch: Australia's 'inner misogynist' let loose

The appalling disrespect levelled at Julia Gillard during her tenure as prime minister was unprecedented. So too was the ferocious language used to describe her, which was often highly sexualised and violent. Not only was social media an open cesspit of hatred and bigotry, but the unabashed, foul-mouthed taunts spilled into radio talk shows, public rallies and even dinner speeches. Gillard was frequently referred to as a bitch, a witch, a lying cunt, a moll and a slut, and her image was plastered on banners screaming 'Sack the crack' and describing her as 'a lying scrag'. We had never seen or heard anything like this directed at a public person, much less a prime minister. Veteran journalist Anne Summers suggested Australians had 'discovered their inner misogynist' when Gillard became our first female PM.[6]

A Liberal–National Party fundraising dinner, awash with champagne and rancid testosterone, boasted a menu offering 'Julia Gillard Kentucky Fried Quail – Small Breasts, Huge Thighs & A Big Red Box'.[7] Even the ABC viewed a female PM as fair game for ridicule. The public broadcaster's dreadful production, *At Home With Julia*, used slap-stick cliché to mock Gillard's position, her efforts to exert authority and even the way she spoke. One tacky episode showed Gillard having sex on the floor of the PM's office under the Australian flag. When I complained to my employer, I was told it was 'funny'. It wasn't. It was abusively sexist. The national broadcaster has never produced a television series openly mocking any of Australia's long line of male prime ministers, or their wives.

For some women in the media, cringing on the sidelines, it was just too much. On the ABC's *Q+A* program in October 2012, Catherine Fox, a business journalist and expert commentator on women in leadership, almost choked up as she lamented: 'I do think our standards have declined. I think we have become desensitised since we have had a female PM and that saddens me more than I can say.'

Perhaps the worst example of media desensitisation was the press gallery's collective blindness, or wilful disregard, of the unprecedented political attack unleashed by cartoonist Larry Pickering. Obsessed with the prime minister's body, breasts and genitals, Pickering sent daily 'hate-filled commentary', along with pornographic material, to members of parliament. Some of the smut included fake nude photos of Gillard and cartoons of her wearing an enormous dildo. These mail-outs went on for an extended period. Amazingly, not one member of the press gallery chose to expose or report Pickering. Not one. The material was not a secret and was easily available to anyone who asked for it. It took Anne Summers, an outsider, to break the story and most importantly ask 'Why?' Why had hordes of people privy to this 'undeniably sexist' and vile persecution of the prime minister watch the material circulate Parliament House and not do anything about it?

Summers is a forensic and formidable journalist. Her examination of the Pickering campaign led to a broader investigation of the material floating freely online, particularly on Facebook, that sexually abused, attacked, vilified and threatened violence towards the prime minister. In late August 2012, Summers presented her findings in a public lecture at the University of Newcastle titled 'Her rights at work'. In it, Summers methodically mapped the depth and breadth of sexist and misogynistic abuse of Julia Gillard and asked what no one else had thought to ask – why weren't employment and anti-discrimination laws being used to stop it? Or at least stem it? If Australia was a corporation and Gillard the CEO, there would have been legal prosecutions aplenty.

Summers' presentation was R-rated. Literally. Some of the material she found was so foul that she zipped the worst of it into a locked appendix. The 'milder' stuff that Summers shared included a series of Facebook pages by a bloke called Alf. Here's a snippet (brace yourself):

> In particular, one shows Alf saying: 'Julz you fucking slut' on top of a photo of Gillard which has superimposed over it the words: 'Smash my box Alf'. Under that is another photo of Alf, and the words: 'If I wanted a greasy red box I'd go to KFC ya slut'.[8]

Caught up in the hurricane of misogyny that spun around Julia Gillard, the media failed to connect the dots. It was a failure to look more deeply, beyond each day's crass slur, to the environment within parliament and more broadly across the media landscape. It was a failure to see that the cultural norms driving acceptance of the unacceptable and providing cover for a mass desensitisation were in fact toxic cultural norms that urgently needed to be exposed, unpacked and addressed. It was a failure by media to collectively ask, 'What is really going on here? How are we enabling this?', and a failure to explore the muscular misogyny on display and peel away its corrosive power on women – any women – who dare step up. It was a failure to look more broadly at Australia's deeply entrenched culture of disrespecting women, particularly in politics, a confounding disrespect that years later saw global headlines about our national sexism that asked why politics is 'toxic' for Australian women.[9]

Why were none of Gillard's own colleagues yelling loudly about this, pushing back at media complicity and public indecency? Years later, former senior women parliamentarians such as Kate Ellis, Tanya Plibersek and Penny Wong pondered that question publicly. In her 2021 book *Sex, Lies and Question Time*, Ellis says she still holds a grudge about the treatment of Gillard, and still asks, 'How could we have prevented it? What should we have done differently?'[10]

But why was it up to the women to call out abusive sexism anyway? Media enablers are not the only blinkered sloths or misogyny deniers here. Where were the male members of the Labor Party at the time? I could name and shame each of them right now but the list is too long. Of course some journalists, including members of the press gallery, viewed the attacks as awful and inappropriate. But there was little more than a collective, uncomfortable shoulder shrug in response, fed by a crusty cynicism and sense of inevitability. After all, Gillard was tough; she provoked them, didn't she?

This is not a singular story about Julia Gillard. What happened to her would have happened to any similarly ambitious and politically sharp woman who fought her way to the top and boldly attempted to assert authority and exercise power. By now, we all know the roots of patriarchy run deep in Australia. According to that global anthropological authority, the BBC, Australia favours 'larrikin' and 'aggressor' MPs.[11] While I suspect that privately some male politicians might be proud of those descriptors, they should be seen for what they are: an indictment of Australian political behaviour, not a compliment.

This is not the story of one woman. It's a story about a system – about a system's failures to support and protect women from abuse that goes well beyond political differences or political anger. It's a story about how deeply misogyny resides in the Australian psyche, and how rampant it runs when threatened by serious female progress. Pink cupcakes on International Women's Day don't incite this fear. But formidable women focused on seizing leadership and 'running the joint' do. Media were clearly primed to frame the narrative around Gillard as a story about the danger of female ascendance.

If this can happen to a woman with privilege, clout and democratic endorsement as the leader of the nation, what hope is there for women without that kind of power – for women thought to be powerless? And what hope has Australia of ever living up to its claim of representative democracy if women are shunned from politics? What then?

That was the story the media missed.

Sadly, tragically, many more women would be sacrificed on the public stage before we finally woke up, connected the dots and saw the well-stitched pattern of patriarchy at play.

Creeps in parliament ... and the phone booth

Since Julia Gillard's 2012 speech shot through the stratosphere, even the dictionary meaning of misogyny has officially expanded. Previously defined as a 'cultural hatred of women', misogyny has broadened to encompass what Australian philosopher

Kate Manne refers to as 'the hostility and hatred faced by girls and women that serves to police and enforce patriarchal norms and expectations'. As such, misogyny is something we 'face', rather than something men 'feel'. Media often confuse sexism and misogyny, using the words interchangeably, when in fact sexism should be seen as the belief system – the scaffolding, if you like – that props up patriarchy. Understood this way, misogyny then is the behaviour that kicks in when the assumptions of sexism prove incorrect: when a woman proves she is neither inferior nor willing to be subservient.

Increasingly, misogyny has become a tag word attached to feminism. That too is best explained by Manne, who says the two are 'in lockstep as cultural forces': hand in hand, for all the wrong reasons. 'Misogyny,' says Manne, 'is frequently a response to the anxiety that comes in the wake of feminist social progress.'[12]

According to the great British classicist Mary Beard, misogyny 'has been hardwired into culture from ancient times onwards, which is one of the reasons it has proved so hard to get rid of'.[13] It's also one of the reasons it is so hard to identify and call out. In *Not Now, Not Ever*, a collection of essays edited by Julia Gillard, Beard repeatedly comments on her shock at how much misogyny she missed throughout her long research career. 'Over years of close reading,' she writes, 'I am ashamed to say I had simply not noticed.'[14]

She is far from alone. Australians have been remarkably tolerant of excessive levels of shameless harassment, sexism and misogyny in our politics and public leadership, and elsewhere. It's tempting to say this bullish, hypermasculine behaviour is so ubiquitous we don't even notice it. But that is a lie. Of course women notice it. And feel it. Many of us grew up conditioned to believe there was nothing we could do about it.

As a 23-year-old junior reporter for ABC TV working in the Victorian press gallery, it didn't occur to me to complain.

About anything. I didn't dare complain when a senior member of parliament followed me into a phone booth in the corner of a parliamentary meeting room, ran his hands over my body, heaved alcoholic breath down my neck and pressed his penis against my thigh. All of this while the opposition leader was conducting a press conference. The commotion caused by my demure and embarrassed rejections made enough noise to annoy the man out front addressing the TV cameras. Jeff Kennett raised his voice above the seated crowd and told me to 'Keep it down.' Me! A kid in stockings and court shoes, with bright-red lipstick and what looked like her mum's bauble earrings! The slimy politician laughed as he rubbed me roughly on the back and pushed me out the door. Of course I didn't complain. What would I say? To whom? And who would care? Besides, I had a career to build and a reputation to protect. Shame can be shattering for a girl with ambition.

It takes guts – big-girl guts – to refuse to be shamed. Fortunately, Australian Greens senator Sarah Hanson-Young is one such gutsy role model. During a Senate debate on women's safety in 2018, in what is now an infamous moment of misogyny in Australia's parliament, Liberal Democrat David Leyonhjelm yelled out to Senator Hanson-Young, 'You should stop shagging men, Sarah.' She remembers that moment as if the words 'flew across the chamber like bullets'.[15] When she later confronted him about it, the Senator smirked. She said, 'You're a creep.' He shot back, 'Fuck off.'[16]

Leyonhjelm had just 'slut-shamed' Hanson-Young in a rather spectacular and crude fashion. Reputation is everything in politics, so inferring a woman is somehow sexually and morally lax and of dubious character can be a career killer. Often based on something as benign as how a woman looks and what she wears, slut-shaming is an insidious way of using sexual connotations to humiliate, undermine and shut women out.

It was a popular practice in the early 2000s, wrote US journalist Jia Tolentino, then went through a cultural metamorphosis and became a 'what not to do buzzword in the late 2000s'. By 2018, Tolentino argued, slut-shaming had become 'a hard cultural taboo'.[17] Sadly, as with many cultural advances, Australia proved slow to catch on.

Leyonhjelm's outburst might have been the end of it, but Leyonhjelm later expanded his slut-shaming outside parliament, talking up the story on radio and TV, even incorrectly naming who Hanson-Young had slept with. Senator Hanson-Young then did something women in politics studiously avoid: she went on the offensive and publicly demanded an apology. As she later wrote in her book *En Garde*:

> Leyonhjelm supporters were in overdrive on online forums and social media, writing foul and vulgar comments: 'Sarah's always been a slut', 'Why would anyone fuck that fat arsed slut anyway?' … 'Face it, you are a slut. No one is trying to shame you because sluts like you have no shame.'[18]

One caller to her office said if Hanson-Young didn't stop demanding an apology from Leyonhjelm, he and his mates would find her and rape her. Another caller threatened to rape her nine-year-old daughter if Hanson-Young didn't shut up.

Hanson-Young sued Leyonhjelm for defamation and, eventually, she won. Outside court she said it was an important win 'for all women'.[19] While that comment was broadly true, once again the vile attacks and brutal harassment experienced by Hanson-Young were reported as a disturbing but singular occurrence. Media didn't start looking for the patterns: the pattern of foul behaviour towards women parliamentarians, or the systemic, gender-based attacks experienced by women in any other industry or workplace – especially women without Hanson-Young's privilege and public profile. Yet there was plenty of it going on. In plain sight.

The following year, while conducting a round of research interviews, I found myself sitting in the office of Labor MP Emma Husar. I'd run out of tissues and her flood of tears meant this distraught and lonely woman needed a box of them. For a short moment in 2016, Husar had been the Labor Party's 'It Girl'. She had managed to unseat a popular Liberal MP, Fiona Scott, who Tony Abbott had famously praised for her 'sex appeal'.[20] But parliamentary life had not gone well for Husar and by the time I met with her she had fallen victim to a disgusting sex scandal: a so-called 'Sharon Stone' moment. It was alleged Husar had sat knicker-less in the office of her colleague, Jason Clare, and crossed and uncrossed her legs several times, while Clare sat on the floor playing with his kids. Both Husar and Clare vigorously denied this ever happened. But someone within Husar's orbit told journalists it did. The salacious details were repeatedly reported across mainstream media. Eventually a tearful Husar did a TV interview with the ABC's Leigh Sales, in which she said slut-shaming was a 'common tactic' used against women in politics: 'It's almost used as a method of torture,' she said. A later inquiry – while upholding other complaints about Husar's managerial behaviour – rejected the allegations of lewd conduct.[21] But it was too late. Husar was a goner.

Slut-shaming is one of the most devastating political strategies weaponised against women, and it was happening openly in parliament. Yet when her story made headlines there was no further effort to dig beyond Husar's singular experience. There was no investigation into the arsenal of gender-based and sexualised tactics used to berate and brutalise women in politics – or women in positions of power outside politics.

Turning up the gaslight

Not long after Scott Morrison usurped Malcolm Turnbull as prime minister in 2018 – following a party-room coup that blithely ignored the most qualified leadership candidate in the room, Julie Bishop – grumblings about the Liberal–National government's 'women problem' began to hit the headlines. Soon it was a daily story. Since #MeToo had exploded into public consciousness the previous year and media men had begun to realise that women were 'a thing', the indefensibly low number of women in the Morrison government also became 'a thing'. A big thing, because the number was so small: just 19 seats out of a total of 227 were held by women in the Liberal Party.

Around this time, I interviewed a number of female members of parliament for a research project exploring the potential for a multi-party parliamentary women's caucus. Similar groups had been established in the UK, New Zealand and other Commonwealth parliaments, providing support networks and the sort of collegiality that was clearly missing in Australian politics at the time. The overwhelming message I heard from women MPs and senators, across all political parties, was that they felt isolated and lonely in parliament. Despite it messing with their heads and attacking their confidence, no one seemed to know what to do about this female-specific isolation and loneliness – other than just suck it up. Many spoke of bullying and intimidation. Some even detailed awful examples of being physically stood over, eyeballed and yelled at by male opponents, with spit landing on their faces. Yet despite these disgraceful behaviours, I was repeatedly told that most women will 'never admit to being bullied'. Instead they choose to hide it.

But, like most things in life we try to hide, the cracks eventually surface. Some of us attempt to cover them up. Others take a hammer to them.

Julia Banks knows how to wield a hammer. Working under Scott Morrison meant she got to exercise her grip and eventually take a swing! She had been a star recruit to government. A smart corporate lawyer from the Victorian conservative heartland, Banks should have been given a seat at the cabinet table. Instead, she found herself fending off overt physical harassment from within her own party, along with the sort of sexism and misogyny that corporate workplaces outlawed decades ago. By the time she stood up in parliament and announced she was quitting the Liberal Party, slamming what she called a 'scourge of cultural and gender bias, bullying and intimidation' of women in parliament, the boys in charge had already set out to seize the narrative and spin a new story. Julia was sort of unwell, we were told – kind of nuts. The prime minister pulled his 'sad dad' face and went on TV saying, 'What is important right now is Julia's welfare … My first concern is for Julia's welfare and wellbeing … I'm supporting Julia and reaching out to Julia and giving her every comfort and support.'[22]

Banks was not sick at all. She was enraged. She later wrote: 'He kept using my first name like we were somehow close friends or colleagues, which we weren't … It was infuriating, condescending and misleading.'[23]

Julia Banks had been gaslit – in spectacular fashion. A day or so later I phoned her to ask if she was alright and, naturally, to ask her for an interview. After sitting for over an hour in my cold car, in a darkening car park, listening to a rattled woman who was clearly distressed, frustrated and shocked at how quickly a false narrative had taken hold, I found myself doing a very anti-journalist thing. I suggested to Julia that she not speak to any media for a little while – me included. She needed to pull back and rethink her next move.

Two years later, she returned to the public spotlight to launch her book *Power Play: Breaking Through Bias, Barriers and*

Boys' Clubs, a devastating attack on Liberal Party hypocrisy, and the misogyny that propels men forward and flattens women who get in their way. She did countless media interviews detailing how the men in her party treated her like a dispensable fool when they discovered they couldn't dictate what she said, nor control what she did. Her now-famous description of prime minister Scott Morrison as 'menacing, controlling wallpaper' made headlines, as women squirmed with recognition. For Julia Banks, and the numerous women cheering her on, it was a stunning exercise in fightback.

Playing it like a woman

There is a classic line from the legendary Liberal Party icon and former prime minister, Sir Robert Menzies. After listening to the campaign speech of Nancy Buttfield, a Liberal Party candidate back in 1954, Menzies gave her the sort of advice women like Julia Banks – and women the world over – are done with hearing. 'Nancy,' he said with great earnestness, 'I suggest you don't play it as a woman. That won't win you support.'

In our New Now, women and nonbinary people moving into positions of power that are fiercely coveted by men know full well that 'playing it like a man' is simply not an option. It's not just a matter of authenticity; it is about reality. Apart from overwhelming evidence that men are lousy at leadership and don't deserve to be considered the standard-bearers, the reality is that our democracy will never strengthen and flourish while it remains stuck in the age-old assumptions that leadership is naturally a male trait – and it must be done in a 'male way'. Yet most of us find our unchecked subconsciouses darting to the image of a man when we think of key leadership roles.

In Australia, it's not hard to see why. Our history books boast 30 male prime ministers and only one female; 28 governor-generals, and only two women; 20 men appointed chief of the defence force, and no woman. And the same goes for our top 20 ASX-listed companies – as of late 2024, none were chaired by women.[24] Across 300 ASX companies in the same year, only 25 CEOs were women; 20 companies had no women on their executive leadership team at all.[25] Is it any wonder we trip up and forget to assume a woman might happen to sit in the big boss chair! It takes personal vigilance, but we actively need to self-correct every single time we slip to the male as default.

As an infuriating reminder that women are odd outsiders when it comes to leading Australia and shaping the laws under which we all live, one only needs to visit the headquarters of the Department of the Prime Minister and Cabinet (PM&C) in Canberra. When you enter through the staff car park, even before you're through the lobby turnstile, you are confronted with a glass wall showcasing every Australian prime minister since 1901. Other than Julia Gillard, stuck stiffly between Kevin Rudd and Tony Abbott, it's a large grey sea of 30 all-white, all-middle-aged men. For those who work in that building, it's a daily reminder before you clock on as to what power looks like in this country – and what it doesn't look like. Then when you head upstairs and stroll down the executive corridor to the office of the head of PM&C, the most powerful bureaucrat in the country, there it is again: a gallery of former heads of department, all white men in a row.

These sorts of visual symbols have untold impact, seeping into our subconscious, calcifying old gender and cultural stereotypes for both men and women. Which is why I was delighted when Frances Adamson was appointed the first female head of the Department of Foreign Affairs and Trade back in 2016, well before she became governor of South Australia. Not long after Adamson moved into the foreign affairs headquarters, just down the road from Parliament House, women working in the building took it upon themselves to fix the problem of the long 'gallery walk of men' by simply reversing the order in which the portraits hung. So when you arrived on the executive floor, the first power portrait you saw was a smiling Adamson. It didn't quite provoke 'a last days of the empire' vibe, but it was a signal of change.

Every revolution needs symbolic moments of defiance – big and small. Sometimes those unexpected acts of individual fightback can surprise and delight. Particularly when they come from a woman perhaps expected to be compliant, to placate her masters and protect her privilege. When such a woman turns snarly and grits her teeth, I've got to admit – I get a bit of a feminist thrill.

When corporate boss of Australia Post, Christine Holgate, was blasted by the prime minister for gifting expensive Cartier watches to four executives – who had secured lucrative deals for Australia Post – he bellowed that she 'must go!' Ten days later, shattered with humiliation, Holgate did resign. But a year later, in 2021, she too made a spectacular return to the public spotlight and mounted her own form of fightback. Called to appear at Senate Estimates and explain herself, Holgate fronted up to the inquisition flanked by two women executives. As they took their seats in front of the cameras, opposite the panel of senators, a few tight smiles swept around the committee room. All three women were wearing white suits. Amid the traditional sea of men in dark suit and tie, the blindingly bright blazer suits sent an unmistakable message of unity: female unity. Sisterhood.

Reminiscent of the crisp white dress worn by Julie Bishop on the day she quit parliament (after being done over by her male colleagues), Holgate's white team shone with its reference to female protest and bold suffragette pushback. With the TV cameras trained on her, Christine Holgate proceeded to rip into the dubious ethics of the men who had bullied her out of her job.

'I was humiliated and driven to despair,' she told the committee. 'I was thrown under the bus [so] the chairman of Australia Post could curry favour with his political masters. But I'm still here. And I'm stronger for surviving it.'[26]

As far as fightbacks go, it was a ripper.

A 'sex pest' in the High Court: Female fightback in unison

Isolated pocket grenades of female fightback in the early 2020s weren't just happening within Parliament House and the political sphere. They were popping up even in the most self-protecting and reverential of all-male bastions – the legal industry.

In June 2020, journalists Jacqueline Maley and Kate McClymont, from *The Age* and *The Sydney Morning Herald*, broke a story that shook Australia's legal industry to its core. Former justice of the High Court, Dyson Heydon, was found to have sexually harassed six young female associates. Revered and feted as 'one of the nation's pre-eminent legal minds', Heydon was also one of the most powerful: he belonged to a class of men once considered untouchable.[27] Yet it turns out this 'sex pest' – known to some as 'Dirty Dyson' and 'Handsy Heydon' – had been at it for years. For well over a decade, Heydon's proclivity for groping and harassing attractive young women, luring them into his private chambers behind closed doors and trying to kiss and caress them was an open secret that had long circulated in legal circles.[28] Once again, this was abuse happening in plain sight, yet not one of Dyson's peers who observed his well-known pattern of behaviour tried to stop it. After all, what do you do? Old men rule, don't they? As for the girls … well, as always in such situations, they are considered invisible, expendable and replaceable. After all, smart young women desperate for a job as a judge's associate are pouring out of universities in droves.

Some might slink away after a nasty round with Dirty Dyson, but there will be others. Won't there?

Poring over these stories, I was struck by the inaction of Heydon's colleagues. What were the men who observed this 'sex pest' in action thinking? I wonder how many thought of their own daughters?

The consequences for the women cornered by Heydon were life changing. Despite being earmarked for elite legal careers, some of the women quit their jobs and others left the law altogether. One of them, Chelsea Tabart, told McClymont and Maley, 'the culture was broken from the top down'. She said she felt she could never be safe 'from powerful men like Heydon, even if I reported them'.[29]

It was heartbreaking stuff, with the detritus of women's lives and careers scattered wide. But what was remarkable about this story was that despite years of living with the insidious episodes buried away in the past, the women chose this moment in time to come forward, formalise a complaint and collectively initiate action. In a tremendously gutsy move, the women took their allegations to the chief justice of the High Court, fully understanding the intense and invasive scrutiny to which they would be subjected. Given these were historic complaints, some of which dated back over a decade and a half, the obvious question was – why now?

Also in plain sight was one of the obvious answers. After 113 years, the High Court finally had a woman in charge.

Susan Kiefel was appointed the High Court's chief justice in 2017. When the women took their very private complaints of sexual harassment to her in 2019, she took action immediately. Kiefel set up an independent investigation and, once handed the findings, she took the unprecedented step of issuing a public statement. It was an extraordinary public apology in which she said the High Court of Australia was 'ashamed that this could have happened' and she personally apologised to the women, saying that 'their accounts of their experiences at the time have been believed'. There was almost a coded message in that statement to other young women: a message to say the ground has shifted, the rules have changed, and women coming forward will be heard. It was a powerful, transformative moment.

For his part, Heydon, 'categorically' denied the allegations against him. Through his lawyers he questioned the validity of the High Court's investigation as 'an internal administrative inquiry ... without statutory powers'.[30]

The independent consultant who conducted the internal investigation, Vivienne Thom, later told me she thought Kiefel 'really changed the world'. When I asked Thom if any of this would have happened if there was a man in the chief justice's chair, Thom just smiled. I think we both knew the answer to that.

Connecting the dots

A few months after the High Court bombshell, there was another female-fuelled detonation back in Parliament House. In November 2020, ABC reporter Louise Milligan's *Four Corners* story, 'Inside the Canberra Bubble', took a hammer to what she outed as a 'culture of silence' within parliament that 'allows sexist behaviour to thrive'. The story was explosive because it focused on the then federal Attorney-General, Christian Porter, and his 'deeply sexist' behaviour towards women. A former legal colleague, barrister Kathleen Foley, who had known Porter since their student days, didn't hold back, saying Porter was 'misogynist in his treatment of women'.[31]

Milligan's story included descriptions of Porter sexually cavorting with a young staffer in a Canberra bar in 2017, in front of journalists. The Attorney-General was married with a toddler at the time, and frequently used his credentials as a father and family man to promote his conservative, 'wholesome' values. The incident was fascinating because several press gallery journalists were present and, according to Milligan, one even snapped a photo of the Attorney-General 'kissing and cuddling' the staff member. The photo never surfaced. Even more astonishing was that none of the journalists ever reported the story. For three years, the 'culture of silence' that protects powerful men within political ranks held firm. Until it didn't.

Rachelle Miller held the complicated dual role of media adviser and mistress to the Attorney-General's close mate, cabinet minister Alan Tudge. Miller had been in the bar with Tudge the night the Attorney-General was spotted with the staffer. She told Tudge to tell the journalists to delete the photo and back off. He did. Word of Porter's night out reached the then prime minister, Malcolm Turnbull, who was interviewed in Milligan's story. He said he spoke to Porter and warned him that his behaviour was 'unacceptable' and exposed him to 'the risk of compromise'. There was no mention of risks or career damage to the young woman involved. A year later, after another political staffer became pregnant to her boss, Turnbull declared an astonishing new rule – a 'bonk ban' on sex between ministers and staff. We all laughed. Given the heat of the times, it was absurdly funny.

The ban, of course, was ignored.

Miller says her affair with Alan Tudge was consensual but abysmally unbalanced. After it ended, she no longer worked for Tudge and gradually grew disillusioned by the overt gender inequity around her and the constant turnover of female staff. Miller says watching other young women fall prey to the predatory and sexist behaviour of entitled men in parliament eventually became too much. Emboldened by the growing number of women speaking up and fighting back – inside and outside politics – she too decided to shelve her shame and call it out. Interviewed by

Milligan for the *Four Corners* story, Miller detailed how her affair with Minister Tudge, at the time a married father of three, was wracked by emotional and verbal abuse and based on a 'significant power imbalance'. Her awkward and painful claims that he kicked, demeaned and yelled at her, and that she felt 'completely under his control', were excruciating to watch.[32] Tudge responded saying he 'completely and utterly rejected Ms Miller's version of events.'[33]

Dramatic as the allegations about both Porter and Tudge were, what was most powerful and enduring about the *Four Corners* story was the pattern of behaviour Milligan began to identify. Sex scandals in politics make great headlines, although they are nothing new. But this was the first time a substantive media spotlight focused on the 'culture of silence' within Parliament House and how that 'heady, permissive culture ... can be toxic for women'. It was a serious attempt to look beyond the singular story and connect the dots to tell the cultural story.

Nudging our New Now, women across the country began to see how these stories – of abuse, humiliation, shaming, sexual harassment, predation, bullying, brutalisation and violence – were all connected, whether in politics, the law, the media, corporate Australia or any woman's workplace. It didn't take long before women everywhere were also connecting the dots. A mood was brewing. We could feel it. There was a grubbiness, a stench wafting around men in positions of power. The rumble of a public pushback from women began gathering pace. Soon that mood would breathe fire into a national movement. Women were ready to line up.

We won't go quietly ...

In mid-2021, I interviewed the former-politician-turned-misogyny-whistleblower Julia Banks in front of a packed house of several hundred women – and a few men – at the Australian National University, to celebrate the launch of her book. Compared to those dark hours in which we had spoken at the height of her distress, she was now in a very different place. After spending a few years to process what had happened and unpack how calculated her political gaslighting had been, Banks was now sharp, cool and focused. She had shaken off any mantle of shame. Now she was back in the spotlight to talk about blame. She was in full fightback mode.

At the conclusion of our interview, one of Australia's most revered and respected political commentators, Niki Savva, gave the vote of thanks. Both tiny and almighty, Savva is a wonderful conundrum. One of the oldest women on the political beat, Savva's smiling demeanour and impeccable presentation belie a fierce, formidable female power. She can slice through political nonsense with a single glance. Few politicians dare ignore her calls. On this occasion, Savva's comments were profound, verging on the prophetic. While noting that Banks had 'experienced firsthand the bullying, the belittling, the thuggery' meted out to women who speak up against sexism and gender bias, Savva flagged a growing sense of sisterhood around the nation: an intergenerational sisterhood that was standing up and fighting back.

'It was said that older women become invisible. That is no longer true,' said Savva, taking a moment to scan the crowd. I noted a number of women nodding with tight but knowing smiles.

> Together with the younger women who have stepped
> out of the shadows, they have combined their formidable
> power. They have challenged the most powerful
> people and institutions in the country. Everywhere you
> look, women are leading or dominating the national

conversations – in politics, in media, in health and in social reform.

Referring to then prime minister Scott Morrison, she added: 'And if he or anybody else thinks they – we – are going to go quietly into the night, they are kidding themselves.'[34]

There was a long, loud and energetic applause, before the evening came to an end.

We certainly didn't go quietly into the night.

For years we had watched, feeling powerless, as our federal parliament descended into a bull pit of testosterone-led power battles, where sexist slander was so ubiquitous it barely raised a headline, and women were routinely discarded as collateral damage. With the tone set at the top, corporate untouchables publicly slapped down women with ambition while promoting the very men accused or even fined for sexual misconduct.[35] Women who dared push back were demonised and, like modern-day witches, chased out of court by hungry cameras capturing frazzled portraits of them for news clicks.

For a long while, a malaise of hopelessness crept through women's networks. The comprehensive trashing of Julia Gillard, as many of us stood back, aghast and feeling utterly powerless against the onslaught, had worked like an anti-feminist venom. It anaesthetised us – for a while. As former Labor minister Kate Ellis acknowledged, she still holds a grudge, wishing she and others had acted in retaliation. She didn't. We didn't. No one did. Gillard did that on her own. The Misogyny Speech didn't save her career, but its legacy has infused and empowered new generations of feminists and countless careers.

As I noted earlier, understanding our stories of change is central to our ability to adapt and shape our future, rather than allow it to shape us. The daily flood in our news feeds of rapid movement and global-sized mess makes it impossibly difficult to discern the undercurrents, the systemic patterns of misogyny that filter through our everyday lives. Particularly when media headlines hoot over the appointment of a woman to a position of power as if all claims of sexism are now null and void. *Women are on top!* Instead, it takes concerted weaving together, piece by piece, the stories and memories, to see clearly how and where women's progress is failing.

When I watched the video of former News Corp photographer Anna Rogers shrug her shoulders apologetically, and say 'I don't know', when asked by the chair of the Senate committee how a news organisation can report fairly if it has 'a toxic culture', I didn't just hear her response; I *felt* it. Women's sense of powerlessness in the face of patriarchy is deeply buried in us all. We internalise what the world tells us about women's innate inferiority. We believe it. It infects our thinking and polices our actions. The humiliation and foolishness I experienced when being felt up in a phone booth by a senior politician still inhabits me. When Dyson Heydon's associate Chelsea Tabart said that she could never be safe 'from powerful men like Heydon, even if I reported them', the long brew of anger in me flared.[36] I know and hate that personal sense of disempowerment. When Christine Holgate said so boldly, so publicly, 'I was humiliated and driven to despair', I felt that too. When Julia Banks described her boss, Scott Morrison, as 'menacing, controlling wallpaper', I squirmed. I've been wrapped in that wallpaper by men too. The terror felt by the woman crouched in hiding as Joel Cauchi strode past with blood dripping from his knife, when she thought, 'He's going after women' sickened me, as it no doubt sickened you too.

Women know too well what all these comments mean, how they make us feel. Piece them together and the big picture comes into focus. Australia has misogyny flowing through its cultural veins. Recent years have proven that – for those who needed proof. But when collated, these stories are also evidence that a strong feminist spirit stirs within women – and increasingly men – across this country. Feminised power, which centres women and seeks to end all forms of discrimination, has taken a strong and deliberate foothold. Our New Now is a place in which we are alert to the flagrant abuse of power and collectively ready to fight it.

To get to this point, to reach our New Now, first there had to be an awakening. This came in the form of a big, loud public reckoning. It thundered so loud that it surprised even those at the centre of the noise. The groundwork had been laid. The feminist foundations had been building over years. But, in the end, the fuel that flamed the 'moment' came from a chorus of young women who were all new to centre stage. They are the rightful caretakers of our New Now.

PART 2
THE AWAKENING

Australian women … are stirring in a way
that I have never seen in my lifetime.[1]

Tanja Kovac

Power is never shared without a struggle,
and the stakes have never been higher.[2]

Sara Dowse

4

THE MOOD THAT TRIGGERED
A MOVEMENT

It was March 2021, and I was being interviewed by a journalist from France 24. The torrent of questions she fired made Australia sound so shocking, so crazy, so filthy that I was momentarily stunned.

Yes, it was true a young staffer had alleged she was raped in a federal minister's office by her colleague. Yes, young men had videoed themselves masturbating over a female member of parliament's desk. Yes, female ex-ministers were 'blowing the lid' on vicious bullying by their party colleagues, who proudly called themselves the 'big swinging dicks'. Yes, historic sexual assault allegations had been levelled at the Attorney-General, Christian Porter; no, he has not resigned; yes, he remained in cabinet. Yes, a former High Court justice had sexually harassed six young female associates. And yes, woman were afraid for their safety.

'So,' the journalist asked, in summary, 'is there something particularly "toxic" about Australia's political elite, or does it reflect the broader Australian culture, indicating something is fundamentally flawed in how men and women relate in your country?'

It was such a good question that I laughed ... before the weight of it hit me like a blow to the head.

Misogyny was bleeding from the elite corridors of powerful law makers into the wider community. Slut-shamed, ridiculed, trampled, dismissed, smudged out of view: yes, Australia *did* feel toxic for women. Sam Mostyn, who would later be appointed Australia's governor-general, wrote in early March that year about the 'distressing whirlpool of shocking allegations' and 'toxicity', which she said extended 'right to the top, right into the halls of political power'.[1] The fact that the most powerful person in the country at the time, Prime Minister Scott Morrison, seemed to regard women as some kind of irritant provided the backdrop to a hypermasculine culture ripe with entitlement and sexism. On International Women's Day 2019, he had reminded men that his government did not 'want to see women rise on the basis of others doing worse'.[2] Myriad examples of sexism and misogyny had been on open display in our national parliament and for a long time reported by the media as if they were business as usual.

It took an explosion of women's anger to wake Australia from its stupor, and for the media to pay attention to what was happening in plain sight. Was it rage that we felt? Or was it something more? What could be stronger than our collective rage? What else had the power to shift a nation?

On 15 March 2021, we would find out.

The March4Justice, initiated by Janine Hendry – a woman with no public profile or political credentials – saw more than 100 000 women take to the streets in a nation-wide movement. It became the biggest women's protest rally in our history.

To understand the transformative power of that day, and how it changed our national conversation and revived a long-dormant focus on women's collective anger and activism, it is important to understand not only why the march happened but how it unfolded. There are valuable lessons: what we learned, what cut through and what has since been taken forward.

Most importantly, the March4Justice is a fascinating story about contemporary consciousness raising, with powerful echoes and a direct line of connection to the Australian Women's Liberation Movement that sprang to life in the 1970s, and kickstarted a seismic shift in women's lives.

A chorus of young women's voices rise

Four years after #MeToo had first exploded in the US, Australia was finally ready for its own #MeToo moment. We had witnessed a small but steady upswell of women speaking out: some accusing high-profile men of sexual harassment, indecent assault and bullying; others boldly challenging gender inequities in our justice system. By 2021 a new power was shooting through Australia like an electrical current. It was not fired by those with political currency, but rather by the voices of 'nobodies' – female nobodies. Young women's voices had begun to crack through, telling their own private and painful stories of sexual abuse and vile coercive control. Some of it was almost too shocking to hear.

Feeling the pulse of that switch, journalist Annabel Crabb observed how the voices of young women in particular were rising to national prominence and taking charge. 'It's a new head of power,' she wrote. 'And what's extraordinary is that it's been generated nationally by the voices of people conventionally thought powerless, or near enough to powerless for the difference not to mean much.'[3]

In their late teens and early twenties, smart, gutsy and truthful, one after the other, these young women found a platform, stood up and braved the onslaught of public ridicule. But here's the amazing thing. They weren't ridiculed. Instead, an unprecedented shift in media gravity, led by a small handful of senior women journalists, gave space to these deeply personal stories of abuse and the festering culture of misogyny that had kept them hidden. The impact of this shifting media lens was critical to moving the national dial on community awareness, and the shock that followed.

All these young women acted alone. They hadn't come through traditional feminist networks or advocacy organisations. In fact, feminism perhaps wasn't even on their radar, nor was 'feminist' a descriptor they would necessarily have used about themselves. Yet being digital natives in the age of 'fourth-wave feminism', these young women were excellent collaborators when they needed to be. Typical of their generation, they were also well grounded in the politics of intersectionality and could sniff out structural inequity.

Women arrive at feminism in myriad ways. For some it is simply in the breastmilk, a natural way of being. For others it's a gradual awakening. For me it was as British journalist Helen Lewis experienced it, 'through a pervasive feeling of wrongness with aspects of my life that I couldn't quite articulate'.[4] Feminism provided the language and the framework. These young women are adding the fire.

Grace Tame: Turning up the 'noise' on a nation

For many Australians, it began with Grace Tame.

On a hot, dry summer's evening in Canberra, on the eve of Australia Day in January 2021, I sat sipping champagne in the audience of the ABC live telecast of the Australian of the Year Awards at the National Arboretum. I was delighted that for once, with no formal role, I didn't have to do anything but kick back and enjoy the show. Two years earlier I had sat, sweating profusely, in the same venue as one of the eight nominees for Australian of the Year. So, for me, this night was pure enjoyment. And a special kind of thrill. For only the second time since these awards began in 1960, each of the four award categories were won by women. Isobel Marshall, a 22-year-old social entrepreneur and medical student, was named Young Australian of the Year; Dr Miriam-Rose Ungunmerr Baumann AM, an Aboriginal elder, activist and legendary teacher, was named Senior Australian of the Year; and Rosemary Kariuki OAM, a former Kenyan refugee and tireless advocate for migrant and refugee women, was named Local Hero.

I was feeling jubilant about the stunning female power and talent on display … and then the final announcement was made. Taking us from a trifecta of women to a superfecta, 26-year-old Grace Tame was named 2021 Australian of the Year. Looking calm and poised, Tame walked to the lectern and stared out at the audience with her piercingly clear blue eyes. Little did we know what was coming.

As she began to speak, my muscles tensed and my jaw clenched. I dug my fingernails into my palms. Soon I could barely restrain myself from shooting to my feet and yelling out, 'No, stop! Don't do it. Don't say it. Stop now!'

I've often thought about the intensity of my reaction at that moment. Decades of working in news media had primed me to fear for any woman, particularly a young woman, who unwittingly and naively exposed her vulnerability in public. Although I didn't know it then, I soon learned that there is nothing naive about Grace Tame! But my visceral response at that moment was a primal urge to stop her talking. To protect her.

'I lost my virginity to a paedophile,' Tame said, sweeping a challenging gaze across the audience.

'I was 15, anorexic; he was 58. He was my teacher. For months he groomed me and then abused me almost every day. Before school, after school, in my uniform, on the floor. I didn't know who I was.'

As she spoke with raw, unfiltered honesty about the shocking sexual abuse she had endured, I thought of the million or so Australians who were watching this broadcast on television, and the news media machine that was capturing and filtering her every word, her every inflection. My media head was in overdrive.

'I remember him towering over me, blocking the door,' Tame told us. 'I remember him saying, "Don't tell anybody." I remember him saying, "Don't make a sound."'

By this stage I was rigid in my seat, holding my breath, terrified by what might come next. And Tame didn't hold back: 'Well hear me now. Using my voice, amongst a growing chorus of voices that *will not be silenced.*'

She breathed in, then roared, 'Let's make some NOISE, Australia!'[5]

It was gobsmacking. Mesmerising. A thunderous applause exploded. Everyone was on their feet. I wasn't the only woman in the audience with tears in her eyes. Like most of those tears, mine were ones of admiration and awe. But I also had a deep sense of foreboding. I didn't believe mainstream media could digest this young woman's story without skewering her in the process, distorting her message and ripping her apart.

Until this time, reporting of sexual violence, abuse and harassment of women in Australia had been uncritically formulaic, underpinned by abject sexism, driven by hackneyed gender tropes and perversely sympathetic to perpetrators. However, in January 2021, mainstream news media picked up a shift in public sentiment and many began to work with it, rather than against it. Grace Tame's courage and consistency of message was pivotal in pushing the pendulum towards that change. Tame quickly proved a formidable talent at both judging and dealing with media. Yes, there were rounds of thinly disguised perverted questions about rape, but her exceptional communication skills, sharp intellect, piercing gaze and unrelenting call for victim-survivors to be heard and believed helped prise open a new national conversation.

Six weeks later, Tame delivered the International Women's Day address at the National Press Club, in which she warned journalists to 'tread carefully' when reporting sexual violence and dealing with survivors of abuse. She railed against the 'commodification' of victim-survivors' pain: 'Listening to survivors is one thing,' she said, as she swept a steely expression around the packed room. 'Repeatedly expecting people to relive their trauma on your terms, without our consent, without prior warning, is another.'[6] Despite her youth and inexperience in such forums, Tame spoke with considerable authority. I looked over at colleagues on the press table, normally a site of cynical mutterings and side remarks, yet every set of eyes was fixed on this remarkable young woman and her uncompromising message. This was new. The winds of change picked up apace.

The following year, as guest curator of an exhibition at the Museum of Australian Democracy, I chose Grace Tame as one of our featured Australian women changemakers, writing in the exhibition notes that Tame's 'intelligence, integrity and deep conviction have fast-tracked her rightful role as an emerging feminist icon'. Each of the chosen changemakers was asked to lend the museum a personal item that represented a pivotal moment in their changemaking journey. We were delighted when Grace Tame gave us the original, huge and very heavy petition book containing more than 5000 signatures that she, along with 16 other survivors, collected as part of journalist Nina Funnell's #LetHerSpeak campaign.

That unprecedented petition and Tame's vigorous advocacy led to her home state of Tasmania legislating to change its gag laws for victims of sexual assault, which had prevented victim-survivors from speaking about their experiences publicly – despite perpetrators and media being free to do so. Although the law was originally intended to protect victims' identities, it had in fact worked to silence them and render them effectively invisible. Tame's relentless campaigning across borders led to similar victim gag laws being reformed in most Australian states and territories.

Chanel Contos: The meaning of consent

In the same year, 22-year-old Chanel Contos was also showered with government praise and public accolades. Singlehandedly, Contos focused national attention on to a subject we had studiously avoided – sexual consent. Her brilliantly uncomplicated call to action, 'Teach Us Consent', prised opened new conversations and forced dramatic changes to the Australian curriculum and sex education in schools. The organisation she founded in 2021 had global reach within a few years, providing education and advocacy that has helped build a global consent movement.

Contos shot to media fame in February 2021 after a now-famous social media post in which she simply asked: 'Have you or has anyone close to you ever been sexually assaulted by someone who went to an all-boys school in Sydney?'[7]

Since leaving an elite all-girls school and moving to London to study a master's degree, Contos had been nursing a slow, angry realisation about the extent of rape culture and the normalisation of sexual abuse that she and her schoolfriends had endured, and enabled through naivety and inaction. In a late-night, stingingly honest discussion with close girlfriends – echoing the classic consciousness-raising circles held by Women's Liberationists of the past – the proverbial penny dropped. Each of the young women revealed they had experienced forced sex in their teens, mostly with schoolboys they had known and trusted. On one occasion, when Contos and several others had dragged a drunken teen friend away from a party – at which the friend had just been subjected to non-consensual sex, then rolled off a bed half-naked – other partygoers, including girls, laughed, calling Contos and her friends 'cockblocks'.[8]

Within hours of posting her Instagram message, it went viral. Contos quickly set up a website and an online petition, 'Teach Us Consent', which attracted tens of thousands of online signatures, along with thousands of written testimonials from young women:

It was at a ballroom dancing class …

Her brother's friend made me have oral sex …

I started crying with the pain … then he said 'I'm done'

His friends watched and laughed cheering him on …

He asked to see my room … he anally raped me. I didn't know what anal sex was.

Shortly after turning 16 … he 'won' me in a poker game …

I … [was] raped by my completely sober best friends … my friends laughed it off. I laughed it off too …

I was drunk … giving oral to a guy from my school … he asked to take a photo … I didn't know how to say no … the photo [was] sent to many students in my year level.[9]

The testimonials reeked of pain, humiliation, confusion and an overwhelming sense of female degradation. Young women and girls, some as young as 14, who assumed they had the world at their feet and lived in a gender-equal society – one in which the sexism and machismo of their mothers' generation were just quaint quirks of the past – were in fact themselves mired in a world of aggressively brutal misogyny. Sexual debasement was so normalised that no one was calling it out.

Days after Contos's post went viral, I interviewed the 2021 Young Australian of the Year, Isobel Marshall, and her friend and business partner Eloise Hall, for my podcast *BroadTalk*. I wanted to talk about their fabulously successful social enterprise, Taboo, but when our talk turned to the news headlines about Contos and the online testimonials, I was gobsmacked to hear Marshall say that none of the revelations shocked her 'in the slightest'. But even worse was her depressingly sad admission that she felt she had been 'one of the few lucky ones' who had not been sexually abused or assaulted during her school years. 'I know that a lot of my friends have,' she said, 'and it speaks to a culture, a very hypersexualised culture, that isn't questioned by many students when they're in that situation.'[10]

Lucky? Yes, she did say 'lucky'. What kind of society have we created when teenage girls and young women think they are 'lucky' to be one of the few who escape sexual abuse?

When I heard Contos on morning radio, I was astonished by her calm, articulate and detailed account of just how pervasive sexual assault was among teens and young Australians. But most impressive was her uncomplicated solution, shaped by her own lived experience. At that moment it was obvious to me, and just about every other female journalist I knew, that a powerful new voice had emerged.

Until that moment, rape culture discourse had been largely hidden from the general public, reserved instead for academic and specialised forums. Chanel Contos hurdled all that by gathering irrefutable evidence in a matter of days and laying it all out on the breakfast table. Armed with a simple tool – a petition – and an unequivocal, clear message of 'teach schoolkids about sexual consent', she quickly garnered the skills and networking talents of friends and family to establish a crack support team that included pro bono lawyers. Later, when interviewing Chanel for my podcast series on changemakers, she said the pivotal moment that gave her campaign lift-off was when Senator Sarah Hanson-Young – who had herself been subjected to abhorrent slut-shaming in parliament – took an interest in what Contos was doing and set up an online federal parliamentary briefing.[11] Logging on at around 3 am London time, Chanel was staggered to see 50 or so Australian members of parliament join the call. Later, the prime minister also agreed to a meeting.

Education ministers around the country met with Contos in late 2021, and by February 2022, just one year after that first Instagram post, she'd done it. Contos had brought all parties to the table and won an unprecedented agreement: all the state and territory ministers for education unanimously agreed to include mandatory education about consent in their schools. As a result, all Australian students are now taught about respectful relationships, sexual coercion and consent, from their foundation schooling year right through to Year 10. In my interview at the time, Contos somewhat modestly attributed part of the stunning success of her campaign to 'kind of just ideal timing'.

It is true, as Contos told me, that by 'absolute heavenly luck' the Australian curriculum, which is reviewed every five years, just happened to be up for review at the time she hit the airwaves with her 'Teach Us Consent' petition. Yes, timing was on her side. But it was so much more than that. Beyond her own outstanding talents and skills as a communicator, Contos has been a powerful figure in a unique moment in Australia's feminist history and women's progress, when individual young women's voices coalesced into a collective power that clamoured for change.

Saxon Mullins: 'That girl' who changed the law

Before Chanel Contos raised her voice for every teen who has endured unwanted sexual contact, another gutsy young woman, barely out of her teens, took on the seemingly impossible task of fighting to change consent laws. By 2021, Saxon Mullins found herself joining other speakers on stage, outside Parliament House in Canberra, listening to an almighty roar of applause and appreciation.

In 2013, Saxon Mullins had been the victim of a gut-wrenching sexual encounter in which she didn't give consent; she endured it in a state of frozen fright. She had only recently turned 18 years old and was a virgin when she found herself on her hands and knees, in a dark alleyway behind a nightclub in Sydney's Kings Cross, being penetrated anally by a man she had just met. Mullins endured a protracted and brutal five years of legal battles, with two trials and two appeals; then she watched as the man who she alleged had raped her walked free. In fact, not only did Luke Lazarus walk free, but on the day he was acquitted he threw a party at his father's nightclub, the very place where the alleged assault had occurred.

Unlike Grace Tame, Saxon Mullins remained a voiceless victim throughout the legal ordeal. However, in 2018 she decided to go public. *Very* public. She chose to work with *Four Corners* reporter Louise Milligan and tell her very personal story of degrading sexual humiliation and despair for one single reason: she knew the law around consent was wrong. It fundamentally discriminated against women by providing men with a seemingly irrefutable excuse.

Despite District Court judge Robyn Tupman finding that Lazarus 'did have sexual intercourse' with Mullins, the judge viewed the issue of consent had not been established in the negative.[12] In other words, this teenager – who was terrified when Lazarus ripped her stockings off and told her to 'put your fucking hands on the wall, get on the floor and arch your back' – never actually said the word 'no', or 'I don't want to have sex with you', or some other version of formally denying consent. Like hundreds of millions of women and girls before her, Saxon Mullins froze. But she knew her inaction did not mean she consented to the hideous debasement she endured.

With gag laws in place, similar to the gag laws Grace Tame would go on to fight in her home state of Tasmania, Saxon Mullins could not speak freely, so the *Four Corners* producers had to apply to the court for victim suppression orders to be lifted. Once unshackled, her words were utterly chilling. In the program titled 'I Am That Girl', Mullins' quiet and gentle voice belied her exceptional strength, providing the narrative with a steely spine.

Her story set off an unstoppable domino effect as a slew of law reforms were introduced or amended around the vexed issue of consent. Numerous academic studies have chronicled the impact of Mullins' decision to go public, and her one-woman challenge to sexual consent laws that invariably favoured and forgave male perpetrators. A University of Melbourne study found the *Four Corners* episode 'caused an immediate sensation when it was broadcast'.[13] The next day the NSW government announced an inquiry into consent laws. Rolling reviews and reforms of sexual consent legislation around the nation quickly followed.

In late November 2021, Saxon Mullins, the unassuming young woman who found herself at the centre of a pivotal moment in history, smiled softly for the cameras at a press conference as the NSW Attorney General, Mark Speakman, announced new consent laws had passed the NSW Parliament. He then turned and thanked Saxon Mullins for her 'extraordinary bravery' and 'tireless advocacy'.[14]

Brittany Higgins: The fuel that flamed the fire

Among those young women whose names dominated media headlines and airwaves in 2021, Brittany Higgins was most prominent, unfortunately for all the wrong reasons. Her story was explosive. It was February of that year when the former Liberal government staffer Higgins alleged she had been raped by her colleague Bruce Lehrmann in a minister's office. For news media, the story was a riveting combination of booze, sex and politics. It featured highly visible and public characters: a frazzled cabinet minister forced to take mental health leave; a slippery prime minister who notoriously offended and gaslit women; and an articulate yet traumatised young woman intent on exposing political expediency and reclaim her own agency, along with her integrity. For political journalists, the salacious chaos was media gold.

Back in 2019, when Brittany Higgins was 24 years old and only months into what she described as her 'dream job' – working as a junior communications adviser for a minister – she was out on a Friday night doing what many young, single Australian women do after a solid week's work – kicking back and drinking with friends and colleagues. On this occasion she drank way too much, a mistake that resonates with many of us. But what makes Higgins' story of sexual assault after a drunken binge differ from every other woman's horror story is where it occurred: Parliament House, in the office of Senator Linda Reynolds, the defence industry minister.

In the dark hours of Saturday morning, 23 March 2019, Higgins, sick with booze and in some kind of shock, opened her eyes and stared blankly at a female parliamentary security guard who came to do a 'welfare check' on her at 4.20 am.[15] Higgins was naked and lying prone on the lounge in the minister's office. The man she'd accompanied to the office around 2 am, Bruce

Lehrmann, a 'rising star' among Liberal Party operatives, was long gone. So, what happened?

Higgins said she passed out on the couch and woke to find Lehrmann on top of her, sweaty and 'mid rape'.[16] She said she cried and told him to stop, and he didn't.[17] Later, during a defamation trial that Lehrmann himself brought against media, Federal Court judge Michael Lee found Lehrmann had been 'hell-bent on having sex' with Higgins. He noted that she was excessively drunk and that Lehrmann not only encouraged the drinking but did 'not care one way or another whether Ms Higgins understood or agreed to what was going on'.[18] Although this was a civil defamation case and not a trial about the allegation of rape per se, Justice Lee found that on the balance of probabilities, 'Mr Lehrmann raped Ms Higgins'.

Shortly after Justice Lee handed down his judgment in the defamation matter, Brittany Higgins made her own public statement, saying, 'I was raped. No judgment was ever going to change this truth. I lived with the shame, humiliation and fear of what telling my story would mean for my life and career, like so many other survivors.'[19]

The long saga of several legal battles that centred on Higgins, the truth of her allegations, the damage done by association and even her social media posts continued to fill media space for several years after her story first broke on 15 February 2021. In the 12 months after going public, Brittany Higgins was the subject of around 12 000 media mentions. With the sordid details and suggestions of a possible cover-up – along with political efforts to contain and control the narrative – the media quickly and understandably became obsessed with 'Brittany'. The ramifications for the government of the day, already bleeding badly over its dreadful treatment of women and culture of bullying and undermining its own women MPs – were political dynamite.[20]

The Brittany Higgins story was broken by journalist Samantha Maiden, national political editor of news.com, and was followed on the same day by an awkwardly intimate, prime-time television interview with veteran broadcaster Lisa Wilkinson, on Network Ten's *The Project*. Both women went on to win awards for their stories: Wilkinson a TV Logie, and Maiden the highest journalism honour in Australia, the prestigious Gold Walkley for her sustained and prodigious coverage. The story shone a blinding spotlight on the Australian parliament as a workplace, and how badly it failed women. What got less scrutiny, but deserved much more, was how Brittany Higgins was treated by the media.

There is little doubt that Higgins first approached Samantha Maiden and Lisa Wilkinson with a strategic determination to expose what she believed was a hypocritical and humiliating culture within the government she served. Years later, during a defamation trial brought by Linda Reynolds, Maiden told the Western Australian Supreme Court that she believed Higgins' motives in going to the media were 'altruistic'. 'She wanted to achieve reform of the parliamentary workplace,' Maiden said, adding that Higgins was anxious her story might end up being little more than 'a one-day wonder'.[21]

The overwhelming power imbalance in the parliamentary workplace had Brittany Higgins sitting at the bottom of the food chain. And for a couple of years after her revelations she stayed there, wounded and immobile. In what Maiden called a 'Don't Ask, Don't Tell' culture at Parliament House, Higgins had found herself wedged between wanting to keep her job and career within the Liberal Party, which she repeatedly said she 'loved', and the overwhelming trauma of feeling herself sidelined the moment she reported the rape. Although various workplace protocols were followed, and Higgins was told she should consider reporting the 'alleged rape' to police, she said didn't feel believed or understood. Instead, she began to see the fabulous career she'd mapped out for herself being flushed down the toilet as she became 'a political problem' for the government in general, and the prime minister in particular.

Scott Morrison had already been roundly thrashed in the media for admitting it was his wife who explained and 'clarified' the severity of Higgins' rape allegation for him by saying, 'What would you want to happen if it were our girls?' Days later, Grace Tame publicly lashed the prime minister for his insensitive ignorance, saying, 'It shouldn't take having children to have a conscience.'[22]

Higgins was no media novice. Indeed, she and her partner David Sharaz, were both smart communications strategists. That was their job. Initially, Sharaz did much of the reaching out to individual journalists. Although I'd never met him, Sharaz sent a message to me via my journalist husband (yes, I know – the irony!) to say Brittany wanted to thank me for my 'support'. It struck me as an odd thing to do. I had not sought to interview her. I had written a column, published in *The Canberra Times* two days after her story broke, that reflected the mood at the time. Something was brewing. We could all feel it.

'Occasionally a story breaks that, although the circumstances are not terribly new and on the surface not that surprising, it nevertheless triggers a deeply buried rage within women. A furious, frustrated rage,' I wrote. Watching Higgins tell her story on television had triggered a visceral response in me. Those short breaths, the pant of exhalation delivered with an embarrassed smile, were all classic signs of an interviewee desperate to talk yet finding it excruciating to do so. It was raw. Painfully real. The humiliation, gaslighting and disempowerment Higgins had endured cut through my layers of feminist armament like a gutting. I was furious. This was all about power and women's lack of it.

The words of American writer Soraya Chemaly, who had recently visited Australia, came to mind as I watched Higgins speak: 'If men only knew how angry women around them often are – and understood the structures enforcing women's silence – they would be staggered.'[23] An interstate colleague texted me, saying she was 'floored' and 'utterly sickened'. She wanted to know if there was 'some kind of disease thing going on' in Parliament House.

The immediate pushback Higgins had copped from a government that instinctively dived for cover and control had stirred a rumble. I returned to pounding my keyboard. 'Women's rage over this story is not only due to our lack of surprise over the apparent high-level institutional abandonment of a distressed young woman – although that is petrol to the fire. The full depth of women's rage is fuelled by impotency. Our own. Here we are. Again.'[24]

Although Higgins set out with what appeared to be her own media strategy to control the telling of her story, it quickly escalated well beyond what any one woman could have navigated. Driven by the need for a new angle, media rivals to Samantha Maiden and Lisa Wilkinson turned their spotlight to building sympathy for Bruce Lehrmann. Channel Seven infamously gave him a prime-time interview platform in exchange for $100 000 in rental payments. Along the way there was also payment for cocaine and an evening with sex workers. Although the 'entertainment' costs were covered by a Channel Seven producer, the producer later apologised to his boss for using a company credit card and it was never established as to whether the network authorised those payments.[25]

Despite being hounded by daily headlines, Brittany Higgins managed to maintain an exceptional public dignity. What went on privately is her story. But in public she was astonishing. At every opportunity she did her best to turn the spotlight of media attention towards the bigger picture: the epidemic of sexual assault and rape in Australia, the forced silence experienced by many victim-survivors, and the institutional power structures that attempt to bury stories and women like her.

In late 2021, Higgins was awarded the Edna Ryan Grand Stirrer Award, a fun and riotous annual award established by some of Australia's hardcore second-wave feminist shit-stirrers. They're a raucous and rebellious bunch of older feminists who have done a brilliant job supporting 'the battlers and unsung heroines' whose activity 'advances the status of women'. Recent years have seen Ednas go to a number of young women, including Chanel Contos. In awarding Higgins the accolade, the judges said:

> Brittany Higgins has become the figurehead and
> inspiration for a new force, an influence in reminding
> previously silenced women that they indeed have a voice.
> After telling her story and becoming a political football
> across the media and parliament, the pressures on
> Brittany have been more than most of us could bear.[26]

While the circumstances of Higgins' rape, within the office of a federal minister, were explosive by virtue of the location and political implications, Higgins fully appreciated the Everywoman nature of her story. In responding to the Edna prize, she said, 'The truth is, most women either have a story like mine, or know somebody who has a story like mine.'[27] We know that sexual assault, rape, harassment and gender-based domination is ubiquitous in Australian life: at home, in the community and at work. But what resonates most about the story of Brittany Higgins goes even deeper – to a place we rarely acknowledge.

Women the world over carry private stories of being openly humiliated and intimidated, and made to feel inferior, insubstantial or disempowered because of our gender. It may be a wildly aggressive act, or a series of subtle everyday slights – microaggressions. However they find a way into your memory muscle, once those gender slapdowns are internalised, they become part of life's playbook. We know the story too well: what it looks like; how it feels, sounds and smells; and how it plays out.

All women, at some stage in our lives, will come to realise that the unspoken, unspecified pressure we feel, which works like an invisible but omnipresent resistance, is in fact the press of patriarchy. It presses down on our ambitions, our careers, our confidence, our efforts to politically engage, our desire to take control of our own lives and destinies. Most of all, it presses down hard when we say 'no'.

Brittany Higgins' story is not only one of rape but a classic tale of female subordination and subjugation. As a subordinate, in a fiercely hierarchical system, it appeared as if she was rendered less entitled to dignity and institutional support, or even being believed, when she reported an assault. After Higgins' allegations went public, her boss, Senator Linda Reynolds, privately told staff Higgins was a 'lying cow', a statement she later withdrew, apologising to Higgins for the 'hurt and distress' that comment may have caused. Reynolds also insisted she had 'never questioned Ms Higgins account of her alleged sexual assault'.[28] It must be noted that the suggestion of a political cover-up by Reynolds or her chief of staff, Fiona Brown, was thoroughly rejected by Justice Michael Lee in the Bruce Lehrmann defamation case, who noted that both women urged Higgins to take her complaint to the police.

Nevertheless, countless thousands of women across Australia who witnessed the Higgins saga related to the feeling of being at the mercy of those who have power over you: power to move you sideways, gaslight you, rattle your confidence and kill off your career. The prime minister's irritated dismissal of

Higgins, then his faux concern for her mental health followed by a highly politicised, public apology, gnawed at most women's guts. More patronising from patriarchal chieftains.

We all know it. Every woman around me felt it.

Coming in the wake of a growing chorus of young women's voices speaking out, demanding reforms and commanding respect, Higgins hit the high note of mass attention. The impact was a long, reverberating crescendo.

5

IT BEGAN WITH A TWEET

I suspect there were very few women in Australia in early 2021 who didn't share, read or listen to a deeply personal story about some form of sexual assault or misogynistic abuse. The floodgates had opened on personal disclosures. Many of us began reflecting on our own lives, poking and prodding at previously unacknowledged experiences of coercive control and sexual manipulation. The emotion of it all was overwhelming.

For me, the shared stories came in a flood of emails, texts, whispered corridor discussions and revelations during my podcast interviews; even a staff memo from the dean of my faculty, a professor of law, outlined the psychological trauma she experienced as the result of a teenage rape. Another highly credentialled colleague spoke publicly of the family incest she had endured as a child. I recall her nodding rhythmically as she talked, as if her sentences were being unlocked, one by one, and physically released. It was the gentle bow of a woman finally unburdened.

Now, in addition to lumping around our angry sacks, we were also hoisting sacks of sad and painful personal stories, strapping them across our breasts, near our hearts. Our heavy hearts. 'This howl of pain is the soundtrack to millions of women's lives,' wrote Sam Mostyn in *The Sydney Morning Herald*.[1] It seemed inevitable that sooner or later all those heaving sacks would start to sag and split open. We had had enough.

Like Alyssa Milano's famous tweet on 15 October 2017 that kicked off the global #MeToo movement, Australia's

March4Justice movement also began with a tweet. But unlike the Hollywood fame of Milano, Janine Hendry had no public profile. Unknown in feminist or women's groups, Hendry had no discernible following at all.

A product of Melbourne's high-end laneway culture, Hendry was a 57-year-old woman who exuded arty creativity and had multiple descriptors: designer, interior architect, academic, marketing expert, charity founder and business mentor. 'Social activist' was a new one for her, 'public feminist' even newer. So, the furious and fast Australia-wide response to her tweet calling on women to rise up and take action took everyone by surprise – Hendry most of all.

A single mother of a teenage son, Hendry had heard Chanel Contos speaking on social media about the prevalence of rape culture among teens. She began reading through the thousands of testimonials uploaded on the 'Teach Us Consent' website and, like many women, felt sick. 'Within an hour I was in tears,' she told me when I first interviewed her. 'I just couldn't believe this was happening to young women right now.' Looking at the sixteen-year-old son she would soon be launching into the adult world, Janine says she became alarmed: 'His role models are the men in power in our government, in our law courts, in our major institutions, and they're not actually setting a great example right now,' she told me, with a dry understatement that belied a festering anger.[2]

Eventually, fed up with the litany of misogyny emanating from Parliament House and heartbreaking stories of gendered violence, sexual abuse and harassment, Hendry had had enough. After watching her news feed groan under the weight of daily stories about a prime minister who clearly did not understand, or seem to care, what women wanted him to do in response to sexual assault and violence, Hendry decided to act.

Late on the evening of 25 February 2021, Hendry posted

an idea on Twitter that would unexpectedly trigger a social and cultural shift in gender relations. It was a simple, somewhat wacky tweet that kickstarted a new conversation:

> Ok here's my thought – is it possible to form a ring of people around the perimeter of Parl Hse? Then all of us extremely disgruntled women could travel to Canberra on March 8 and form a ring linking arms with our backs turned toward the parliament and stand in silent protest.

She followed up to press the point:

> I need someone to tell me if this is possible. I then also need someone to estimate the distance and how many women we would need? I'm absolutely serious if this is possible we need to protest at a time and place that tells not only this Govt but the world that we've had enough.[3]

With few followers and not anticipating much traction, Hendry called it a night and went to bed. By morning the tweet had gone viral, with thousands of comments urging action. 'I thought, "Oh wow! This is bigger than what I thought,"' she says. 'I could almost feel the anger, a visceral anger, emerging out of my phone. And I knew then that it wasn't just me.' A Facebook group was set up and within days a movement was born. Some clever soul even measured the perimeter of Parliament House and ascertained that almost 4000 bodies were needed to form a protest ring, if we all spread out and held hands.

Within days, more than 20 000 people had committed to join the action. And that was just for starters.

Our angry sacks split open

As we listened and watched and spoke, a consciousness raising was taking hold across the nation. Women everywhere were connecting the dots, seeing the patterns in patriarchy and its abuses of power. It was a rare moment in Australian feminist history, when the shame, grief, humiliation and embarrassment we had buried, along with the anger – the red-raw anger – would come crashing through like a tsunami.

In those heady days, as feminist fury got louder and the demand for action boomed across airwaves and in cyberspace, I wrote an impassioned commentary for *The Canberra Times*, in which I called this 'a crystallising moment for Australian women':

> There is extraordinary power in the emotions surfacing in women around Australia right now.
>
> The power of this moment is unprecedented. But, as a nation, we must get this right. We must hear the myriad and complex reasons as to why women are so deeply aggrieved and angry.
>
> If those in power, who currently hold the political policy levers, fail to act. Well, god help Australia.[4]

Women around the country were online, talking, sharing and doing what we do exceptionally well – organising! Late one evening in early March, during a hastily called Zoom meeting among colleagues and friends working in the feminist advocacy space, a woman of national profile says, 'You know, I can really feel it – a significant mass movement is developing.' There is a pause, then another exhales loudly: 'Finally, *finally*, we are collectively saying that the treatment of women in this country is unacceptable.'

Australia's sex discrimination commissioner at the time, Kate Jenkins, pointed to the huge cultural change we were all feeling as an historic shift: 'In my time working in this area and particularly looking in workplaces over the 30 years, I've never seen any moment like this.'[5] Sarah Maddison, Professor of Politics at the University of Melbourne, told *Time* magazine: 'I don't think I've ever experienced a period in Australian politics where women, and I include myself in this, have been so personally distressed.'[6]

Just a week after Janine Hendry's tweet, Grace Tame was concluding her televised address at the National Press Club when she was asked by a journalist if would she consider going into politics, following her term as Australian of the Year. After all, there was a federal election due the next year, and the horror of the previous several years had not only blown the lid on the toxic masculinity of Australian politics, but the recent stories out of Parliament House demonstrated how desperately we needed more women in politics. At the time, the federal Coalition government had a grand total of just 30 women out of its 112 members in the parliament. Only 37.9 per cent of parliamentarians were women, which ranked Australia at an embarrassing 54th in the world for women's political empowerment.[7]

Tame didn't miss a beat as she replied to the cheeky but genuine question. She raised her eyebrows, hunched her shoulders and slowly shook her head from side to side, whistling a firm, 'Nooooooo!'[8] Everyone in the audience laughed. Except me. Call me a humourless feminist, but at that moment her answer struck me as a bloody tragedy. Tragic that such capable, clever and savvy young women like Grace Tame were so disgusted by how politics played out in our country that they wanted no part of it. Tame and women like her are precisely who we need in the house on the hill.

At the conclusion of the event, Tame received a thunderous standing ovation. Then she did something I had not seen a young women do in Australia for many years. With her lips pressed tight and an almost imperceptible nod of appreciation, she held up her clenched fist in a salute to sisterhood. I was awestruck by this female boldness, this defiance.

That action carried power; it triggered a visceral reaction in one of Australia's legends from the Women's Liberation Movement, Biff Ward. For Biff, that symbol of sisterhood, popularised by radical feminists during the 1970s, has always been a powerful display of women's solidarity and commitment to fighting the patriarchy. Later, she told me: 'That symbol really matters to me. And to see women do it just makes me burst into tears.' We didn't know it then, but two weeks after Tame's speech, Biff would be seen in news broadcasts around the nation also raising a salute to sisterhood, with me standing by her side. Our clenched fists held high.

As I left the National Press Club that day, a somewhat frazzled woman on a mission stopped me at the door and thrust a scribbled note into my hand. She introduced herself as Kerry Burton, a volunteer with 'the women's rally'. The note was a request for me to speak at the 'upcoming rally', with date TBA, details TBA and a contact number. It was such an odd approach that I wasn't sure if this was legit. I was aware of the social media activity generated by Janine Hendry's tweet, but I was also mindful of the huge amount of time and organisation that goes into planning a women's protest march – often with unspectacular results to show for it. I'd never seen more than a few hundred women turn out in Canberra for the annual Reclaim the Night marches. Even the 'pink pussy hat' women's marches held in Australia in January 2017, in solidarity with women in the US protesting against the inauguration of President Donald Trump, only mustered several hundred women – not thousands.

I thanked Kerry and stuffed her note in my bag, thinking that would be that. *Who are these women anyway?* I thought. *Does anyone know them?* I'd have to ask around later.

I cringe now at how dismissive I must have seemed back then, and my lack of faith in the speed and organisational power of women who are seriously pissed off. Australian women right around the country were buzzing with energy and the need to be heard, en masse.

So who were these women?

'It just happened to be me'

How did women no one had ever heard of build a movement and create an action that shifted the dial? And what made this moment in time so ripe, so ready, to reawaken a dormant feminism?

'This is my very first revolution,' Janine Hendry told *Time* magazine. 'I know that someone had to take a stand and it just happened to be me.'[9]

Within days of her social media call-out, the movement had mushroomed, with women in towns and cities across Australia making contact with Janine to say they too would gather local women and stage a march. 'It was organic,' says Janine. 'That was the beauty. It was totally organic. The women I was working with to put this together I had never met before.'

Right from the outset, there was an uncompromising focus on coordination and collective action. Women who set up their own organising committees around the country – including those who personally didn't like Janine's business-like approach, nor her vertical organisational structure that positioned her at the top – nevertheless intuitively understood that this had to be done in unison, as there would be unparalleled power in the collective voice of Australian women.

'It had to be Janine. Or someone like her,' says a reflective Renee Jones, a few years later. One of the core Canberra committee organisers, Renee, and indeed numerous women I've spoken to, agree that Janine Hendry, despite her lack of activist experience, just happened to be the right woman at the right time. 'For the scale we needed,' says Renee, 'she was able to mobilise groups that had not been engaged outside online spheres before, or perhaps not engaged in a long time.'

Not one for what she calls 'kumbaya' moments, Janine didn't waste a minute trying to meet everyone's needs. 'There were joys and frustrations,' she reflects on the whirlwind that changed lives, including her own. 'You're learning as you go along and you're learning about people's skill sets. And because we had to move really, really quickly, I had to put in a very hierarchical structure just to get things done.'

She set up several teams and delegated specific tasks. She worked most closely with the small but expert media and communications team, perhaps the most powerful cog in the multi-pronged women's wheel. Drafts of key messages were shared among some of the larger organising committees, agreed upon and finalised. A slogan was designed and adopted. And then Janine laid down two important ground rules for the 42 organising committees that had spawned around Australia, with an additional two in the UK.

First, and somewhat surprisingly, she insisted this was to be an 'apolitical movement' – that is, a diversity of politics and political affiliations were to be welcomed. While I appreciated Janine's ecumenical approach, this rule struck me as a little naive, given that politics was at the heart of women's anger. The appalling behaviour of Australia's federal parliamentarians and the chilling lack of empathy shown by the prime minister, along with the repeated failure of public policy to make any dent on the epidemic of violence and sexual harassment in Australia, meant a protest march such as the one building could not avoid the reality: this was political. Deeply political.

The other ground rule Janine stated in the guidelines and governance frameworks she sent to organising committees was that the March4Justice must embrace diversity and intersectionality. While not well-versed in feminist theory, Janine was nevertheless emphatic about this. Diversity and intersectionality had been guiding principles throughout her life and were at the forefront of her charity work building schools in South Asia, which she'd begun after the suicide of one of her children. As far as Janine was concerned, everyone and anyone who wanted to be part of this movement must be made to feel welcome and included.

While this was a seemingly obvious and unremarkable position to take, Janine was knocked sideways when a small but formidable delegation of TERFs (trans-exclusionary radical feminists) infiltrated one of the early online meetings, demanding that transwomen be banned from inclusion in the march. Given Janine had accepted a theory of consensus, this was a sudden and unexpected wedge. 'Remember, my background is not in feminism,' she tells me. 'It's in strategy. I'm a strategist. Yes, I'm a feminist, but I had very little understanding and certainly zero experience in the kind of feminist collectivist model [on] which most feminist organisations had been established, which is about collaboration and consensus thinking.'

For a wobbly moment, Janine felt ambushed. She had worked hard, in the spirit of feminism, to try to accommodate a broad array of demands and suggestions coming thick and fast. But a compromise on the issue of excluding transwomen was simply not up for negotiation. She stood her ground and the TERFs were quickly out-manoeuvred, not to be mentioned again.

We're all here, and we're all real!

Kate Walton's parents were worried she may have fallen in with some kind of cult. Suddenly their 30-year-old daughter, who had recently returned from living in Indonesia, was spending inordinate hours glued to a screen on endless Zoom calls. They heard names like 'Renee', 'Kuljeeta', 'Bethany', 'Peta' ... who were these new friends Kate was staying up late into the night, emailing and talking with? Their daughter seemed anxious but highly energised.

Days after the 'cult activity' took hold, Kate arrived at a suburban house in Canberra. Not sure if she was in the right place, she hesitated at the front gate. A young boy greeted her and asked who she was looking for. 'A group of quite angry women,' she said. The kid didn't flinch. 'Yeah, they're in the backyard.'

Around ten days out from the March4Justice, this was the first meeting of the Canberra organising committee. Ten women turned up. They all came alone. A week earlier, each woman had answered a Facebook call-out from Fiona Scott, a media and communications expert and political strategist who had volunteered to help build the Canberra organising team. Fiona, who worked as the liaison with Janine in Melbourne, was looking for women with skills and time to volunteer. She didn't need to ask about anger and rage: that was a given. While they'd met online and already begun the enormous logistical task of organising a rally for thousands of people – as well as negotiating the fraught politics, permits and publicity – none of these women had met face to face before.

For Kathryn Allan, in her twenties and the youngest of the group, that meeting was a powerful, life-affirming moment, in the heat of the stress. 'There were tears and hugging, and I was like, "Oh my gosh! We're all here and we're all real, right?"' A little overwhelmed at first by the diverse and strong personalities around the table, Kathryn's initial shyness was coaxed out of her. 'Everyone just cared a lot. And they cared for each other,' she later remembered. 'I didn't know these women at all, but they were sharing with me their own trauma stories and their stories of survival of various forms of abuse and harassment, and it became like a healing circle. It was the first time I also spoke about something that happened to me the year before.'

Collectively, these women could see the patterns in their stories of abuse and oppression. What quickly emerged, in the spirit of feminist consciousness raising, was a powerful solidarity and sense of sisterhood. 'I really felt that solidarity, and even though we didn't agree on everything, we could agree on that,' Kathryn says. That afternoon meeting stretched late into the night as the women did what their feminist foremothers had also done: they gave space and time to listen to one another.

Kuljeeta Singh was the only woman of colour around that table. A tough and talented corporate executive in her early fifties, Kuljeeta worked across South Asia and the Middle East. Originally from Sri Lanka, she'd settled in Australia two decades ago. For Kuljeeta, the strength of sisterhood she experienced at these meetings was profound and transformative. 'To be really honest, it was the first time in my life that I actually belonged to this country,' she later told me. 'I felt I belonged. I was part of these women's lives and they were part of my life. It was the first time that I was actually heard without being questioned.'

Like many in this hastily formed collective, Kuljeeta shared a story of sexual assault that she'd long buried. Others discussed private issues around their shifting gender identity, partnership breakdown, divorce, workplace harassment and abuse, or gender-based intimidation. During that first meeting, real estate agent Peta Swarbrick, a middle-aged mother of two, felt she had finally found her tribe: women like her who were going crazy at the blinding level of misogyny all around them, yet felt they were shouting alone into a black hole. Peta was turbocharged into action after her 13-year-old daughter, 'a daggy little introvert', was verbally accosted while walking home from the local shops by a couple of men stalking her and threatening to rape her. Peta couldn't contain her rage. 'She came home really, really frightened. And I just thought, "You're fucking kidding me! This is still happening? I thought we had sorted this. I've been asleep at the wheel."'

When Peta asked her daughter if she had 'told them to fuck off', she says 'her little eyes filled with tears, and she looked at me and said, "What, and make it worse?"' Peta's own eyes filled as she explained to me that until that day, she had never discussed sexual assault with her daughter. 'Now I had to explain rape culture. To my child! And I had this horrendous feeling of how I'd failed her and failed to do anything about it.'

Peta's innate sense of gender justice led her on a journey online to discover feminism and feminist activism. On Twitter (now X), she found a like-minded feminist foot soldier, Bethany Williams, who just happened to live in the next suburb. Sponges to the cause, the two of them spent every spare moment sharing links, articles, webinars and memes. Before long they were reaching out to international feminist giants, like Egyptian-American journalist Mona Eltahawy, to discuss the radical feminists' theory of the 'octopus of patriarchy'.

For the Canberra women, the concept of patriarchy was clear enough: 'a system of oppressions', as Eltahawy puts it, 'that privileges male dominance'. But they thought that definition needed more cut-through. So Bethany was ecstatic when she first heard Eltahawy explaining her more visually powerful definition: patriarchy is the head of an octopus, and each of its tentacles is a form of oppression – sexism, capitalism, racism, ageism, homophobia and so on – and 'those tentacles are working in unison to keep that head of the octopus, which is patriarchy, alive'.[10] For Peta and Bethany, this slimy and vindictive octopus, with tentacles flailing about simultaneously to keep it in control, was the perfect embodiment of the multipronged approach of patriarchy.

Similarly, they also devoured everything Eltahawy wrote about intersectionality to understand how the various layers of identity beyond gender – such as race, ethnicity, age, disability and religious affiliation – can collide and compound the discrimination someone might experience. For the two women, a grasp of intersectionality dramatically changed the way they saw all forms of discrimination around them. It was a matter of 'once you see it, you can't unsee it', they said.

Sadly, the Australian government proved less willing to learn. It had to be dragged into the light when it came to integrating intersectionality into public policy. In early 2017, while undertaking an executive leadership course at Harvard Kennedy School in the US, I received a phone call from the federal government's Office for Women, inviting me to pitch a project for a 'women's leadership grant'. Over $100 000 was up for grabs, so my small team at the University of Canberra, led by Professor Mark Evans, got straight to work and prepared what we thought was a rather fabulous exploration of intersectionality – with a detailed research project on how to unpack this concept for the public service and apply it to government leadership programs.[11] We thought it was bang on the money, so to speak, in regard to what was needed to help advance gender equity, diversity and inclusion. But we were wrong. A somewhat sheepish apologist called to say we didn't get the grant. When I pressed her for feedback, the response was almost comical, it was so honest. In short, the then Minister for Women didn't 'get' intersectionality, or this concept of the layers of disadvantage. 'She just wants an announceable,' I was told – in other words, a headline for a press release. 'Intersectionality', it seemed, had no media sex appeal.

When I shared this story with Bethany and Peta, they roared with laughter. Not because it was funny, but because we all understood how depressingly unsurprising it was. Together, the two Canberra women came up with their own feminist theory about women in Australian politics who kowtow to men who hold the power levers and dominate public space. 'They are the crumb maidens,' they tell me. 'They take the crumbs that patriarchy throw them, and they betray their own gender just to have those crumbs of power.' Peta and Bethany initially coined the phrase as a descriptor for former deputy leader of the parliamentary Liberal Party, Julie Bishop, who famously clicked her sparkling red heels and finally quit parliament after her male colleagues – the 'big swinging dicks' – failed to support her leadership bid. When I mentioned that *Guardian* journalist Amy Remeikis is credited with coining the 'crumb maiden' term, they fall about laughing, telling me they came up with it first, using it across social media well before Remeikis. 'But then, who are we?' they ask. They're a couple of suburban mums. And proudly so.

They are also funny, fiercely feminist and utterly committed warriors for change.

They are Everywoman.

Revolutions are not the miracles of history, written with a Spielberg script, starring glamorous celebrities. They start around kitchen tables, with suburban foot soldiers just like these women. A sustainable feminist fightback needs the clear-eyed, earthy pragmatism and instinct of the Everywoman. The real heroes in the extraordinary story of the March4Justice movement, and the reason it grew the way it did, rests with the countless individual women who came forward and simply said, 'I've had enough! How can I help?'

But 'rests' is the wrong word here. There was nothing restful about the explosive force of power that rolled out on the day we rose up.

6

THE MARCH4JUSTICE HITS THE STREETS

In the pre-dawn hours of Monday 15 March, I sat in the dark at my desk with a dull light bleeding from my laptop and an annoying cursor blinking on a blank page. I typed the words 'March4Justice Speech', then sat staring at that damn screen.

I was exhausted. Not just from lack of sleep, but from months of dragging that sack of anger around with me. We all were. Every woman I knew. Exhausted and frustrated.

Yet the March4Justice had been conceived and pulled together at breakneck speed in less than three weeks. Monday 15 March 2021 would be the day. The day we would collectively gather, right around the country, in the biggest show of feminist force Australia had ever seen.

My cursor became apoplectic with impatience. But how to express all this anger, this tightly bottled rage, in a matter of three minutes? There would be 11 speakers – or 12 if we counted the secret wildcard. *Keep it tight to give it fight* is my mantra for such occasions. Short sentences. Weave in space for breath; scan the crowd; go lyrical; give it rhythm; feel the cadence; write with a beat. For a moment I felt like I was channelling Julia Gillard – 'I will not ... I will not'. 'This is OUR parliament', I wrote. 'OUR House. OUR democracy.' I wrote the rest in a blur of passion and keyboard pounding.

My biggest worry in those dark hours was ... will they come?

For days I had tried to dampen expectations about crowd sizes, particularly for Canberra. I knew women around the nation were dialled in to the swell of activity and felt the powerful vibe of a movement. Women everywhere were energised. But I'm a realist. It was a Monday. Parliament was sitting. The Canberra organising team had originally applied for a protest permit for 3000 people. Days before the event it was increased to 4000, 'just in case'.

Oh, how we laughed about that later!

Mist and mood ... but will there be arrests?

On 14 March, the morning before the march, Dr Tjanara Goreng Goreng walked out of Parliament House in Canberra and onto the forecourt. It was Sunday, just after daybreak; the air was still and a ghostly early morning mist was rising from Lake Burley Griffin. Draped in a cream linen shawl and white tunic, Tjanara – a Wakka Wakka and Wulli Wulli traditional custodian, academic and healer – moved like a luminous apparition. She slipped off her shoes and walked in bare feet over the cold paving stones, towards the centre of the *Possum and Wallaby Dreaming* mosaic that lies in front of Parliament House. Bending forward in a nod towards the mountain in the distance, Tjanara narrowed her gaze, tracing the ancient songline axis that runs through Old Parliament House, up Anzac Parade, through the grounds of the War Memorial and reaches right up to the tip of Mount Ainslie, a sacred place for women where young Indigenous girls were once taken for ceremonies. She closed her eyes, inhaled deeply and began to sing. It was a hauntingly beautiful sound, a call to ancestors to support and protect the women who would soon gather there.

Standing behind her, well back from the mosaic, Janine Hendry watched in awe, deeply moved by the serenity and sheer beauty of the moment. Next to her, also stilled and silent, was Fiona Scott, who had helped steer Janine through the mindboggling maze of national and international media interviews as the original idea for a Canberra rally snowballed into a nation-wide movement. More than 40 concurrent marches and rallies were planned for the next day. Organising committees had sprung up in every capital city and in towns across regional and rural Australia. There were even two events scheduled for Aussie expats living in the UK.

Neither Janine nor Fiona had slept much in the week leading up to this moment. It had been hellishly stressful and unbelievably exhilarating.

On this still morning, Fiona had just ushered Janine and Tjanara through the parliamentary press gallery for an interview on ABC *Weekend Breakfast*. All three women had met for the first time, in person, only a day earlier. Janine had never been inside Parliament House before, and yet here she was, leading what would become the biggest feminist protest rally parliament has seen. It's perhaps an understatement to say that she was feeling stressed. As Tjanara sang, the sound of a deep, ancient echo rippled through the open space around them. Janine and Fiona stood motionless. Tears streamed down their faces.

After the song, Tjanara told both women to take off their shoes. She asked them to inhale oils she had rubbed on her hands, and then held their feet as she quietly conducted a grounding ceremony. Later, when recalling this moment, Fiona's blue eyes brim with emotion. 'There was something so powerful in it,' she says, blinking away tears. 'It was magical, like an enormous weight was lifted.'

Later that day, I met Janine for the first time at a speakers' briefing at the Q Hotel on the edge of Canberra's CBD. With her were some of her handpicked crew of volunteers from Melbourne, including publicist and marketing director Rosemary Hamilton, who was working in tandem with Fiona Scott. It was quickly obvious to me that although these two women were new to the feminist advocacy space, they were highly skilled media and campaign managers. Sharp and fast, they didn't falter when giving Janine sound advice. That said, this accidental protest leader was no slouch when it came to political manoeuvres. Janine Hendry struck me almost immediately as one of those ballsy women gifted with an instinct for political power plays.

By the time we met, the whole country was engaged in the March4Justice action. The speed at which women organised was breathtaking, but so too was the uniformity of message and purpose. Petitions were signed and a list of demands drafted, but the overwhelming focus was a singular scream to the men who ran the country: 'Enough is enough!' The patriarchy was put on notice. 'We see you. Now you see and hear us!'

With parliament sitting on the day we were to rally, and the prime minister and his Attorney-General, Christian Porter, a primary focus of women's rage, it was inevitable the national and international media attention would turn to Canberra. Jacqui True, Professor of Politics and International Relations at Monash University, captured the feeling: 'Many women and men are angry at the ignorance, neglect and failure of the federal government to address a growing reality of egregious sexual abuse and violence against women perpetrated by powerful men.'[1]

I arrived at the speakers' briefing expecting an excited chaos, or possibly even brewing panic, the sort that normally accompanies bold activism shrouded in uncertainty. *How will the police respond? Will there be arrests? How far am I prepared to go?* But that wasn't the vibe I walked into. Instead, a calm and efficient bunch of women ushered me into a boardroom, coffee and tea was laid out, sandwiches were served and, as in any well-oiled board meeting, we quickly got down to business. Introductions were necessary all round because, amazingly, none of us knew each other. Even some of the national organising committee had never met in person before.

This alone is one of the most remarkable aspects of the March4Justice. There was no single group or feminist organisation, no NGO, union, institution, business or university behind what would become a coordinated, collective scream of female anger across the country. Numerous public and private-sector organisations lent support, including local and national NGOs, women's legal and domestic violence support services, unions, student networks, even bus companies, along with some state and territory government departments, local governments and shire councils. But this movement was fastidiously grassroots. It belonged to everyone. Every woman was invested in its success. We had to get this right.

A meeting with the PM?
The movement says 'NO!'

At some point during the briefing, I found myself in a tense discussion in the car park with the woman at the helm, Janine Hendry, along with well-known feminist advocate and seasoned campaigner Helen Dalley-Fisher. A burning issue had erupted about Prime Minister Morrison's possible presence at the rally. Like all members of federal parliament, the PM had been personally invited to attend but not to speak. Liberal MP Bridget Archer was the only member of the Morrison government who had written back and said she would come.

One. Single. Woman.

Unlike the decades of media ridicule to which feminists and women activists are accustomed, in the lead-up to the March4Justice, national media were not only running stories about the march but many were doing so with enthusiasm. 'A time of reckoning for Australia,' bellowed *The Guardian*.[2]

Even the broadsheet favoured by old, conservative white men, Murdoch's *The Australian*, was on board, with columnist Caroline Overington firing a backhander at the prime minister: 'Why all fathers should join the March4Justice.'[3]

While there had been no commitment from the PM's office about his attendance, by late Sunday afternoon media hype and social media traffic about the expected size and passion of the march had escalated dramatically. Western Australia and a few regional towns held their marches on the Sunday, a day before the rest of the nation. Everywhere the turnout was proving bigger than expected. Perth was a big and boisterous success with around 5000 women marching. Suddenly the PM's office smelled a media backlash if he didn't appear to make some kind of effort towards these damn women.

Scott Morrison's office reached out to Janine Hendry, offering her a private meeting with the prime minister on Monday morning, before the rally. Surprised by the phone call, Janine had simply said 'Well, I'll get back to you.' Later she would laugh at the audacity of that casual response, admitting that 'I didn't know what to do.'

Back on the ground, the organising committee posted the PM's offer across social media platforms: should she, or shouldn't she go? Although the self-appointed leader and figure-head of this rapidly rolling movement, Janine instinctively knew the decision wasn't up to her. It was for the 'movement' to decide: the tens of thousands of women whose voices were turbocharging this unique moment.

Nevertheless, at the time, there was something about Janine's hesitation that worried me. I sensed her uncertainty around the politics of the offer, and was concerned that her hesitation in responding could quickly develop into a vulnerability open to exploitation. Given my two decades immersed in the Canberra Bubble of politics, power and media manoeuvres,

I view any slight crack in a political door as an opportunity to push right on in. In the car park that day, I urged Janine to accept the prime minister's offer – conditionally. I was not sure if the ever-diplomatic Helen Dalley-Fisher agreed with me, but nevertheless she began to run through the possible delegates Janine should insist accompany her to meet with the prime minister.

Among the diverse group of speakers and women on the organising committee were numerous sharp and savvy political strategists; young, super articulate activists; well-seasoned unionists; persuasive older Women's Liberationists; compelling women of colour; and highly respected Indigenous women. My thinking was that it was a golden opportunity for some of these incredible women to get in front of the widely despised prime minister and give him a piece of their minds!

Turns out, I was wrong. Very wrong. Women across the nation quickly made it very clear who was in charge of this collective action and what they wanted. A furious and unanimous 'No, don't go!' ricocheted around cyberspace. Scrolling through the noise, I was reminded of Audre Lorde's line: 'Anger is loaded with information and energy.' Right then, women's energy was in overdrive. Unfortunately, a loud chorus online vented its anger directly at Janine, attacking her personally for even considering a closed-door meeting with the chief of the patriarchs. I later learned that the ferocity of backlash winded her badly at the time. But, as an experienced business professional, she parked that pain and got on with the show.

At 5.32 am the next morning, I received a text from Fiona Scott confirming that Janine would not meet with the prime minister, or the Minister for Women, Senator Marise Payne, who had suddenly also found 15 minutes of availability in her busy schedule. In my exhausted dawn haze, Fiona's prosaic message made me smile: 'They can come out to all of us on the lawn.'

The day dawns: 'Mate, it's going to be big!'

By the time I had finished writing my speech and drained a pot of coffee, I had to get to Parliament House. Chris Wallace, my colleague from the University of Canberra, texted to suggest I park outside her house near The Lodge and we walk to the march together. I declined. I needed silence. I don't get nervous but I do become unsociably focused ahead of a big event or speech. That morning I was struggling to get into the zone. I felt a complicated anxiety about the day.

The preceding 48 hours had seen strong and positive media commentary. According to Fiona Scott, organisers had been overwhelmed with a late rush of offers of support; buses, donations and 'anything you need' messages were coming in thick and fast. But the journalist in me knows how quickly these things can turn ugly. All it takes is a flare-up of some kind – a rowdy disturbance during speeches, some anti-feminist nutters – and presto! The substantive story is lost to a media bunfight over a punch-up. Or some such thing. It can happen in a blink.

By the time I arrived at Parliament House mid-morning to do a couple of media interviews, I was cocooned in my own anxious bubble. My friend Kieran Gilbert, Sky News journalist and presenter, met me in the marble foyer to sign me in. Kieran was pumped, excited about the day, striding towards me with a massive smile. 'Mate, it's going to be big!' he said. Famed for his optimism, Kieran also has exceptional media intuition and a gift for forecasting how a political scenario is going to play out. At that moment I could have hugged him.

With a quick pace through the parliamentary press gallery, we arrived at the Sky studio where I met up with Fiona and two students from the Australian National University. Both were in the ANU Students' Association: Avan Daruwalla was the women's officer and Maddie Chia the education officer.

Maddie had just celebrated her 20th birthday a few days before, and both were also listed to speak at the rally.

Sky is perhaps one of the most distrusted media outlets among gender activists and feminists, but on this occasion, with host Laura Jayes asking the questions – like Kieran, also a reputable and admired journalist – we were in safe hands. Watching Maddie and Avan sail through their interviews as they explained the pervasive nature of rape culture on university campuses, and young women's anger at the political failure to address Australia's epidemic rates of sexual violence against women, I was struck by a most unexpected emotion: joy. The language, the arguments, the anger, the demands for change, the political nous – it was all there, solid, informed and passionate. The intergenerational and intersectional strength of a new, emerging movement couldn't have been more evident at that moment. Neither Avan nor Maddie had been into a television studio before. Yet, despite their bellies full of nerves, admitting later that they were 'terrified' when they realised it was Sky News, they blitzed it.

When we finished our media commitments, after taking a bunch of selfies together, we left the press gallery and headed to the lawn area outside where a small stage was erected.

I heard it before I saw it. A band was playing and the noise of a large, jubilant crowd blasted up the hill towards the doors of Parliament House. As we walked over the rise, each of us suddenly stopped, our jaws dropped. We stood staring at what lay ahead. A thick, moving mass of women, clad in black, stretched all the way down acres of lawn, as far back as the eye could see, towards Old Parliament House in the distance.

This was not the crowd of 4000 the permit allowed. This was three, possibly four times that. It was huge! Just huge. We were stunned.

'It was very overwhelming,' Maddie later recalled. 'It's not until you see the crowd that you realise how momentous this occasion is going to be, and the sheer scale of the history that you're about to make.'

As I walked towards the loud, festive hum, I thought of my days at Melbourne University when I was the age Maddie and Avan are now, and how I would nervously meander around the perimeter of women's protest rallies on campus, wanting to join in but always feeling ignorant, an outsider. I'd read the foundational feminist texts, but did I really understand the theory? No, probably not. But sexism, misogyny and gender inequity – these were things I felt in my gut. I always have.

As I looked out at this crowd of women in 2021, I could see quite plainly they were the women I would see any other day at work, in the supermarket, at the gym, walking their dogs. In this collection of women I saw Everywoman: women who, regardless of their connection to feminist theory or activism, collectively felt the power and importance of this moment deep in their hearts and bodies.

As I headed for the stage, with my heart hurting it was pounding so hard, I wondered what the legendary historian Marilyn Lake might have to say about this. In concluding her epic history of Australian feminism, *Getting Equal*, back in 1999, Lake wrote of being 'struck again and again by the creativity and energy of feminists of all generations, their gusto and stamina and ebullience and courage'. After detailing the remarkable linkages among more than a century of women's activism in Australia, Professor Lake signed off with what now feels like a provocative dare: 'It must be hoped that Australian women will be so passionately moved again.'[4]

As a young journalist reading Lake's closing line back then, on the cusp of the 21st century, I had internalised that call to arms, repeating it like a mantra.

So, did they come?

They came alright. In numbers too big to ignore!

Sisterhood, solidarity and listening

By the time the speeches began, the Canberra crowd had swelled to around 12 000. Some reports later put it at 15 000. Across the nation, total numbers were estimated at 110 000, making this, collectively, the largest women's protest rally Australia has ever seen.

By the time I made my way to the staging area, the band had struck up that beloved anthem, 'I Am Woman' by Helen Reddy. Those opening chords lit a fuse in me, a full-body joy! And I wasn't the only one. A bunch of women, including older feminist icons and octogenarians from my mother's generation, were sitting on their picnic chairs near the front of the stage, and they were not going to let such a magnificent moment pass. In a flash many of them were up dancing too. I saw Wendy McCarthy – Aussie trailblazer, feminist icon and mentor to many – among them. We hugged and laughed and jived like mad.

It was 'a wonderful, wonderful moment', Wendy later told me. 'There were all these people in my life I hadn't seen for ages,' she said, but most remarkable to Wendy and her cohort of second-wave feminists was the massive throng of people they didn't know, including the rally organisers. 'That was what was so extraordinarily exhilarating: "So, it's *not* just us!"' she said. 'And it wasn't a march divided on party political grounds. Women came for whom the women's narrative was more important than either [left or right] political narratives.'

In her opening speech at the Canberra rally, Dr Tjanara Goreng Goreng spoke movingly about dadirri, the practice of deep listening. I had heard Dr Miriam-Rose Ungunmerr Baumann, the 2021 Senior Australian of the Year, explain this concept months earlier. Right now, it felt like a timely and precious message. 'The contemplative way of dadirri spreads over our whole life,' Tjanara explained. 'In our Aboriginal way, we learnt to listen from our earliest times. We could not live good and useful lives unless we listened.'

What had been a party mood just moments before now gently shifted into what Helen Dalley-Fisher described as a 'quasi-religious mood'. The massive crowd rippled with seriousness, standing quiet and still as Tjanara spoke. Later she told me she felt her ancestors present in that stillness. When she looked out at the 'sea of faces', she saw 'women who were wanting transformation and change'.

Around the country that day, in nearly 40 locations, women chanted 'Enough is enough' as speaker after speaker echoed the anger, passion and power women were ready to express within the safety of a collective show of force. In Tasmania, Grace Tame stood outside the island state's parliament basking in this fierce, new solidarity. 'My heart is going to beat right out of my chest for all the love I feel here today,' she said, as thousands of voices erupted in a cheer. Urged on, she continued:

This surge, this cultural shift, this paradigm shift of normalising the conversation of sexual abuse – you know where that started? It started here! … We are leading the nation. That is a testament to the power of solidarity. It's a testament to the power of hope, resilience and a refusal to let fear stop us from doing anything!

In Melbourne, Julia Banks addressed the thousands who had marched up city streets and streamed into Treasury Gardens. She too was clearly moved by an overwhelming sense of solidarity and sisterhood, telling the crowd:

When I was asked to speak here today, I said no. I was frightened. I've seen what those in our centre of power will do if you speak up.

They try to silence you. They create fear. They use
their power over you. They threaten legal proceedings.
They paint a picture, create a narrative about you in the
media of someone you're not.

But ... what changed my mind to speak up today –
was because of you. All of you.

Up north, in Queensland's city of Townsville, Ashleigh Met-
calfe from the North Queensland Women's Legal Service
told a crowd of several hundred that 'Change does not happen
overnight ... Take that fire burning within you and nurture that
flame, keep it burning ... You are not alone.'

In Nowra, on the NSW south coast, the late Bonnie
Cassen, activist and march organiser, told a cheering crowd that
'Patriarchal power rules society in this country and inequality
breeds across all divides: in hospitals, preschools, sporting clubs
and communities. Structures exist that undermine the legitimacy
of women, their efforts, achievements, their intelligence and
their value. That needs to end!'

Back in Canberra, I found myself standing at the foot of
the stage as a mob of cameramen – yes, they were all men –
converged like swarming locusts right where I was planted,
knocking me and Biff Ward out of the way. Brittany Higgins
had appeared. Trailed by a team of people, including journalist
Lisa Wilkinson, Higgins looked ethereal in a soft white dress,
in stark contrast to the uniform black the other speakers and
thousands in the crowd were wearing. Biff and I were due to
speak next, but Higgins' appearance suddenly tossed out the
running order. Her participation that day had been kept top
secret, even from some of the organisers. I was glad she was
there. Higgins is a solid, thoughtful speaker and her well-
chosen words have impact.

At the moment of the media scrum I was worried about Biff, who was in her late seventies and had experienced a mild stroke eight weeks earlier. She was pumped with happy adrenalin on this day and seemed fine, but she'd asked me to place my hand on her back to steady her as she spoke on stage – if, and only if, she seemed to be having trouble. So, with a watchful eye on my friend, I glanced over at Higgins, who was now standing under the tiny marquee to the side of the stage. The media crush was pushing in around her, with raucous men shouldering each other out of the way, moving in on her. For what? She was simply standing there alone, waiting. Not saying a word.

Higgins caught my eye and I saw a flash of panic. Her eyes were welling up. I realised she was about to cry. Suddenly I lost it and rushed forward, doing something that for a television journalist is almost unforgivable: I messed up the shot, getting in the way, pushing and pulling the cameramen by their shirts, their shoulders, even yanking one by his cap, interrupting their filming and yelling at them to 'Get back! Shove off!' I was wildly angry at what had rapidly become a feeding frenzy. 'For godsakes, give her some room!' I pushed one of them sideways, off balance. He swung around to face me … and laughed! It was a colleague, an old workmate I really liked. He smirked, backing off, saying, 'Yeah, yeah, okay boss!' I laughed too. Frankly, I was a little surprised at how easy it was to move the mob back. But of course, cameramen will always try it on – until someone blocks them. At that moment, I just happened to be that someone.

Once Higgins was up on stage, the media mob tried again to swarm. This time it was the job of the MC, Julia Zemiro, to spray them down. And she did. Masterfully.

When she finally began speaking, Higgins had the crowd hanging on her every word. 'We are all here today not because we want to be here, but because we *have* to be here,' she began:

I am cognisant of all the women who continue to live in silence. The women who are faceless. The women who don't have the mobility, the confidence or the financial means to share their truth. Those who don't see their images and stories reflected in the media. Those who are sadly no longer with us. Those who have lost their sense of self-worth and are unable to break their silence, all of which is rooted in the shame and stigma of sexual assault.

Acutely aware there would be many women listening to her words who felt overwhelmed by their private grief and humiliation, Higgins encouraged women to know others would support them, just as they had her. 'Take ownership of your story and free yourself from the stigma of shame,' she urged. 'Together, we can bring about real, meaningful reform to the workplace culture inside Parliament House and, hopefully, every workplace, to ensure the next generation of women can benefit from a safer and more equitable Australia.'[5]

At one point, Higgins paused mid-speech. Perhaps thinking the audio was suddenly not working, a man standing near Helen Dalley-Fisher called out, 'We can't hear you.' A woman in front spun around and glared at him. 'She's *crying*,' she said. 'Oh. I'm sorry,' he replied, chastened.

Around that time, freelance journalist Jane Goodall was traversing the crowd when she came across veteran reporter Chris Uhlmann recording a piece to camera. There were a few women watching on, so she joined them, sensing a wariness about how men in the press gallery might report this rally. The observers were listening carefully. Entirely unphased, Uhlmann looked meaningfully down the barrel of the camera and said sternly, 'Rage outside parliament is washing over politics.'

Jane stifled a laugh. He sounded absurd. It seems even

the cameraman thought so. He stopped filming and said to Uhlmann, pointing to the crowd, 'There's no rage.' The crowd had gone quiet. Another speaker had stepped up to the microphone, following Brittany Higgins, and the crowd was doing what it did for much of the rally – listening intently and respectfully. 'Got to wait for the rage,' said the cameraman, with a shrug.

It is worth noting that despite more than 100 000 women – and a guesstimate of several hundred men – taking to the streets in protest that day, not a single person was apprehended or arrested for bad behaviour. Not one. Can you imagine that many men marching in the streets without any arrests? No. Nor can I.

Goodall went on to write a moving piece for *Inside Story* the next day in which she captured the unusual solemnity she witnessed. 'The quietness itself was perhaps the most important message of the day,' she wrote. 'Sometimes you just have to listen. The three generations brought together in this crowd harboured reserves not just of rage, but also of generosity, social maturity and moral intelligence.'[6]

The 'spirit of women's energy' out loud

Speakers at the Canberra rally were asked not to include personal details of their own experience of violence and trauma in their speeches, and none did. Yet when Aminata Conteh-Biger walked onto the stage and stood, still and tall, back from the microphone, I put my hand over my heart. I may have even held my breath. A refugee to Australia, Conteh-Biger escaped brutal sexual slavery in Sierra Leone and her personal story is one of the most horrific I have ever heard.

Watching her at that moment, I was in complete awe. The strength in her shoulders, her pride and her poise spoke volumes about this woman's inner steel. When she stepped forward to speak, slowly, precisely, there was an intense moral power in her words as she addressed the crowd, asking the question no one had yet posed: 'If the politicians don't believe a white woman, what is the hope for black women?'

The crowd roared and rippled with a collective 'Yeahhhh.' I looked around me and saw every face turned towards Aminata.

The day before the march, Aminata and I had sat together at the speakers' briefing and fell into deep conversation. Her shocking story of capture and enslavement as a child was almost too much to bear. I found it hard to fathom how any girl could survive what she did and grow into the woman who sat before me: wise, calm, compassionate and super quick to flash a fabulous smile. Aminata told me she didn't know anyone on the organising committee, or indeed any of the women around us that weekend. I laughed, telling her I didn't either.

Later, she said was surprised and delighted to see women dancing before the rally began. A display of joy and laughter within rage and anger? Now that was unusual! When she stood on the stage, looking out at the thousands and thousands of open, expectant faces smiling back at her, she felt a powerful surge. 'What I felt was a refusal to be silent anymore,' she said. 'I felt a spirit of women's energy coming together … and I was so proud to be part of that contribution.'[7]

By the time ANU students Maddie and Avan stepped up onto the stage, they were pumped with adrenaline and pride. They had written their speech together and delivered it in a lyrical rhythm, each speaking a line at a time.

'We are too young to be standing here alongside these incredible women, knowing that our fight for safety and bodily autonomy will continue for the rest of our lives,' they said. 'We are too young to be so unsurprised by these reports of gendered violence. And yet we are. We aren't shocked, we are pessimistic. We have been taught to accept toxic masculinity as the norm.'

As I listened, I caught myself heaving deep breaths. Their clarity of conviction was stunning, but my god, they seemed so very young: too young to be so profoundly despairing about sexual violence and misogyny. Yet their words were wise and ancient, born of lived experience. Yes, I wept. 'We are too young to be called "angry feminists" for calling out blatantly violent behaviour and standing up for our basic rights … We are too young to have lost faith in the justice system and the reporting process. The deep-rooted patriarchal values of our society mean that survivors must suffer.'

At this point in their powerful duet, I was standing at the side of the stage and noticed Maddie grip Avan's hand and squeeze it tight. I could see they both were blinking back tears. They finished triumphantly: 'Look to your left. Look to your right. These are your allies. We love you, we believe you and we are here for you. We stand with survivors.'

Later, Avan told me she became overwhelmed as she looked out at the huge crowd and realised that many of the thousands of women in front of her were there because they too had a story of abuse or belittlement buried somewhere in their lives. This expansive blanket of empathy and compassion became a rolling theme in each interview I did about the March4Justice. Every person who attended any of the rallies around the country took a little piece of that collective empathy home with them, for safekeeping.

If I had been worried about Biff Ward before we went on stage, I quickly realised there was no need for concern. This revolutionary from way back was in her element. She beamed with joy. 'This is a huge crowd and you look fabulous!' she laughed into the microphone. The crowd roared. 'This is an historical moment,' she said in a more serious tone.

More roaring. Biff was on a roll. 'I've made it here from the crucible of the '70s Women's Liberation Movement, so I have some history in my bones,' she told the crowd. 'I didn't think I would live to see this day. This great uprising here, right now … It feels like a tidal wave of rage is sweeping the land.'

Unsurprisingly, those last two lines gave headline writers their cue as they dubbed the March4Justice 'the Great Uprising'. My phone soon pinged with Biff's words, summed up by Jewel Topsfield at *The Age*, who called the rallies 'a tidal wave' that had swept the nation.[8] Seizing her moment, Biff used the platform to speak of the thing dearest to her heart: sisterhood. 'What is it?' she asked, then answered, as the crowd cheered her every sentence: 'Sisterhood is understanding that the personal is political. It is supporting each other, battling together for change. It's what has created and driven today!'

Jubilant at the noisy response and electrifying energy shooting through the crowd, Biff concluded with her fist clenched tight by her side, at the ready. 'We have reached critical mass. The days of the patriarchy are numbered. We are counting down. Sisterhood is powerful!'

We both raised our arms and clenched fists in a salute to sisterhood. It was a moment I will never forget – a pinnacle in my feminist life.

I paused before stepping up to the microphone. Many of the speakers had addressed violence. I wanted to zoom in on Australia's shameful political failure and backsliding. 'Once we were a proud leader when it came to women's rights. What the *hell* happened?' I roared. The crowd roared back. I was in the zone now. 'Women's anger has deep and ancient roots,' I said, bringing the tempo down. 'But there is positive power in our anger. This is a crystallising moment for Australian women. But as a nation we must get this right!' Letting the staccato rhythm do its work, I could feel the energy building to a crescendo.

Then I let rip: 'If those in power ... fail to act, well, *god help Australia!*' The rally chant rang out: 'Enough is enough!'

Unsurprisingly neither the prime minister, nor his firmly silent and absent Minister for Women, showed up to the march. They remained hidden inside parliament throughout the day. In fact, Minister Payne made invisibility into an art form in the women's portfolio. Her occasional scripted utterances were mind-numbingly dull and bureaucratic. Like the good girl who handed in her homework, Payne proved proficient at ticking boxes yet incapable of engaging with the very women she was supposed to represent and support.

Later that day, Scott Morrison told the parliament it was a 'triumph of democracy' that we weren't shot. 'Not far from here, Mr Speaker, such marches, even now, are being met with bullets,' he announced.[9] It was a shocking but perhaps not surprising statement from the prime minister. Under intense pressure, his natural reflex was to evoke images of retribution, of violence and even military massacre: a warning to those mouthy women that if it wasn't for men like him, their protest banners would be no barrier to bullets. It was also a coded reminder of who was in charge. Him. Anne Summers nailed the prevailing view days later when she rather politely said that 'Scott Morrison and his government is not just unresponsive but is actively hostile to women.'[10]

While the women around me were horrified, I was glad the prime minister had revealed his hand. His statement solidified our success. The words of Rebecca Solnit came to mind: 'Those who doubt that these moments matter should note how terrified the authorities and elites are when they erupt.'[11]

When I look back now at the footage of Biff Ward and me on stage at the March4Justice – at the conclusion of our speeches, as we stand with fists raised – I have a visceral reaction. Biff is beaming with joy, but I look worried. Heavy hearted. My mouth is tight. I am not smiling.

As I stood, arm around Biff, the answer to that burning question I have been lugging around most of my working life began to crystallise. *What has changed irrevocably for women?* The answer was right here. Amassed right there in front of us. *This is what has changed*, I thought. *Us*. Women. Our collective consciousness. The March4Justice and all that led to this explosion of frustration and collective anger shifted us. Fundamentally. Powerfully. The huge turnout at the rallies around the country validated our anger.

Now we would be emboldened to push forward. There could be no going back.

Watching it now, I slow the footage down, squinting to see what I was feeling at that moment, and there – I can see it! It's as if the penny suddenly dropped. I can see it in the stern expression on my face. I look from the crowd, back to Biff. I give her a gentle hug and turn to leave the stage, while Biff stays put, basking in the joy.

I look like I'm in a hurry to get going.

There is work to do.

7

A NATIONAL APPETITE FOR CHANGE

After the March4Justice was over and the crowd in front of Parliament House in Canberra had melted away, rally organiser Peta Swarbrick looked around at the detritus: discarded banners, posters, water bottles, bits of rubbish. Having delegated herself the unglamorous job of cleaning up, she began with the dog poo ('Well, someone's got to do it!'). As she scooped, she also collected a stack of scattered banners and soon had several dozen piled high.

Reading through their messages – punchy, powerful, hilarious, angry and everything-in-between – Peta realised this was no pile of ordinary rubbish. It was a heap of history – feminist gold:

I am Woman hear me ROOAARR

It's OUR TIME NOW!

I CAN'T BELIEVE WE ARE STILL
PROTESTING THIS SHIT!

Home of the BIG SWINGING DICKHEADS

IF IT WAS YOUR DAUGHTER
Jen would call for an inquiry ScoMo

Ditch the PRICKS!!

I'm with her ®

CUNT SHIT FUCKERY

I will not be lectured about sexism and misogyny
by this man. I WILL NOT!

We will NOT BE SILENT #ENOUGHISENOUGH

Unsure what to do with these piles of profundity, Peta rang
the National Library of Australia and asked if anyone would be
interested in archiving the stuff. They were. In what sounded
like a cartoon comedy, Peta had to find a way to get the loot to
the NLA before it closed, and she called the 'Dead Piano Man'
– someone Bethany found online – who had an empty truck
normally reserved for transporting retired pianos. Happy to be
of service, DPM stacked the booty on board and off they raced
to the library, where they were met by a line-up of librarians
with trolleys at the ready. With the goods delivered and history
preserved, Peta went home. Exhausted.

Other members of the organising committee headed across
Lake Burley Griffin to the Q Hotel, where a hundred or so
women gathered around the bar to toast the day's success. Kate
Walton, who by now had convinced her parents she hadn't fallen
in with a cult, settled into a corner with the rest of the Canberra
crew. Worn out but jubilant, they sat on the outskirts of the
larger group, which included a number of high-profile national
women leaders and well-known feminists.

'It was quite odd,' says Kate, reminiscing about that afternoon. 'No one knew who we were – that we were the organisers.
It was quite funny.' Other than journalist Margo Kingston,

whose investigative nose sniffed them out, no one ruptured the happy obscurity of this bunch of women who had pulled the event together and made it happen. This organising crew saw no need for personal prominence or celebrity leadership. It was all about the 'we', not the 'me'. They were in it for Everywoman.

Kathryn Allan had set up a small volunteers' table at the march, with a pile of petitions calling on the government to invest more in women's safety. Within an hour or so, she'd collected thousands of enthusiastic signatures. That night Kathryn posted the petition online, asking women to share it around. In a few days the petition amassed over 23 000 names. In the following weeks Kathryn ran a series of 'activism and campaigning action workshops' to teach young people how to build a political protest. Her workshop model was later adopted by volunteer groups across Australia. The happy surprise for Kathryn was not just the numbers willing to politically engage or sign a feminist petition, but how quickly the March4Justice rebranded 'feminism' as a mainstream concept. 'For years, "feminism" was almost like a dirty word,' Kathryn told me. 'But immediately after the march, that changed. When I said the word "feminist", people would start to listen. It was just so quick. I do a lot of work with kids at schools – and now everyone wants to talk about feminism.'

Another of the Canberra organising crew, Blair Williams, a feminist academic who was in her late twenties, says the rally 'radicalised women' who may have been sitting on the periphery of the feminist agenda. The week after the march, Blair and Kathryn decided to continue the protest by staging their own two-woman 'sit-ins' outside Parliament House. Every Monday, during their lunch break, they'd sit on the ground outside the public entrance and sing women's protest songs while engaging in a bit of craftivism. Occasionally Peta joined them too. Security would move them on if the singing got too bawdy, but mostly they were ignored. The point of the action was to keep the spirit of the March4Justice alive and – importantly – to chat with any member of the public bold enough to ask what they were doing. With their knitting, feminist embroidery and song sheets, it was a quaint throwback to Women's Liberation–style sit-ins – but without the police rumble and arrests.

The feminist history in our DNA

I interviewed numerous women involved in the March4Justice, initially to simply document what happened, how and why. As I sat down over weeks and months to speak with them, I was struck by the passion with which every woman continued to talk about the 'moment' and what it meant. The speed and scale of the event fascinated me, along with the anonymity of the organisers. But it was the uniform expression of women's rage that intrigued me most. I could feel that rage and women's response to it rooted in our feminist history – and I needed to know if others felt that too. Was it a direct link – a line of connection with our recent feminist past – that gave form and power to the national consciousness raising we experienced in 2021?

Even without asking such lofty theoretical questions, the answer quickly emerged. References to our feminist foremothers echoed throughout every single conversation I had. Connection to those 'on whose shoulders we stand' – second-wave feminists and the Australian Women's Liberation Movement – were referenced in the language, stories and actions of all the women I spoke with. From some it was a direct nod of acknowledgment; for others it was little more than a hint, or an echo of the past. But no matter how they expressed it, an underlying connection and gratitude ran like an unbroken thread through all our talk, knitting new patterns of 21st-century feminist response and action.

Like many women who came of age during those noisy Women's Liberation actions of the 1970s, Marilyn Lake was thrilled with what she witnessed on 15 March 2021. 'It was an amazing example of women Australia-wide, including younger women, being moved again, passionately and politically,' she told me later. Most amazing is the fact that it happened at all. Lake says collective mobilisation of women is always challenging given our myriad differences, and the March4Justice was even more remarkable because, overwhelmingly, the action and anger around the country was directed at the Australian parliament.

What struck Lake as truly unique about this movement was the fact that the organisers were anonymous, which is highly unusual in the history of women's activism. 'None of us knew who they were. And they remain more or less anonymous. They didn't become household names.'

For Biff Ward, the movement propelling the nation-wide action in 2021 demonstrated a profound shift in Australian women's thinking about themselves and their agency as individuals, as well as a new shared understanding of women's collective power. A few weeks after the march, Biff's eyes were still alight with astonishment at what just happened. 'In the 1970s, when we started Women's Liberation, we had a huge focus on recruiting,' she remembered. 'We knew we couldn't change the world until there were a lot of us. We did all sorts of things to grow the movement, but we didn't reach anything like what we have now – this new explosion in women's consciousness!'

Biff was moved 'to tears' at the power of the movement she had witnessed. 'I really didn't think I would live to see this new way of thinking right across the land,' she says. 'Whether it's situations of sexual predation or workplace discrimination, finally women are being believed. That is extraordinary.'

The fact that Janine Hendry faded from view after the March4Justice speaks directly to the unique impetus that drives successful feminist movements. While public activism might rally around a timely call to action – like a tweet that zings the zeitgeist – the March4Justice was not about Janine. Nor was it about a singular world view. Instead, the enormous surge of power was found in a shared sense of purpose and solidarity that coalesced in a moment of time – a critical moment that breathed new life into women's activism and feminist consciousness.

Helen Dalley-Fisher, a veteran of protest marches and rallies, says she has never experienced the sort of respectful listening, along with moments of joy and laughter, that she experienced at the March4Justice. 'People had come with such full hearts,' she said. 'You could feel this wave of emotion. There were people crying, people clearly reliving their own trauma, but standing there in such unified solidarity with people, other women, they didn't know.'

Not only was Janine Hendry new to feminist protest, but a large majority of the tens of thousands of women who joined the march had never attended a protest rally before, much less a feminist-led one. I had never before spoken at one. For so many of us, this was new. This was a movement for all women. Inspired by Everywoman. Enduring friendships were also forged during the March4Justice and powerful connections remain, as a thread of new sisterhood weaves through women's lives.

Across Australia, hundreds of women were motivated to volunteer and support the March4Justice for myriad personal reasons within the rabble of rage. But there was a universal unifying factor: timing.

Renee Jones was still breastfeeding her first baby when she answered Fiona Scott's call-out for skilled women to join the organising committee. She was a veteran of feminist protests – back in 2012, before the ACT Government introduced safety zones around abortion clinics, Renee staged months of daily one-woman protests to ward off the aggressive shaming tactics used by anti-abortionists. But by March 2021, despite the distraction of new motherhood, Renee was stung with a sense of urgency. Like many of us, she watched Janine Hendry's call to action gather speed and it kicked her into gear. 'It felt like this was the moment. There was no woman in my life who just wasn't absolutely furious – including women from my conservative small-town background, who would never call themselves feminist, and probably still don't. I just knew that it was *now* for something big to happen.'

Renee befriended Kate Walton on Twitter and the two of them got talking. 'It was opaque as to who was making decisions and how they were making decisions. But we could see that something was going to happen, with or without us,' Kate says.

They both opted in. Kate took her knitting to virtual meetings. Renee took her baby.

For Kathryn Allan, the youngest of the Canberra organising committee, the March4Justice was not only transformative for the nation – it was a personal game changer. 'For me, everything changed in that moment. It was when I woke up and understood that my body and my voice was powerful. And it matters. And I don't think we can take away from what that means to women. It's just so powerful.'

Fiona Scott compared the staggering momentum of the March4Justice to the vibe of an election campaign heading for victory. 'Once people start to think you can win, it just takes off. And once people started to think [the March4Justice] was going to be a big deal, it completely snowballed … There was such a strong sense that people wanted this to succeed. They wanted it to be a "moment".'

Fiona went on to run the office of independent senator and political 'kingmaker' David Pocock, so her life is subsumed by work, but when I ask her, six months later, if she still catches up with any of the other women, her eyes glisten. She looks up at the ceiling to stop tears rolling south. 'I know every single one of those women are there for me. And I would do anything for them,' she says. One of Biff Ward's old besties from their Women's Liberation days once told me that the friendships forged during times of political protest and activism are among the strongest relationships in a woman's life. I took that as a lesson in nourishment for the feminist soul.

So, what changed at the pointy end?

So what really changed – beyond us, beyond women? What changed in law?

You might recall in the lead-up to the March4Justice that Sex Discrimination Commissioner Kate Jenkins said that in her 30 years focused on sexual harassment and discrimination of women in the workplace, she had 'never seen any moment like this'?

Three years later, when she had finished her term as commissioner, I asked her to describe 'that moment'. With the distance of time she went even further, saying that 'March 2021 felt like a long-awaited turning point for progress.' Noting that 'the pace of change' for women had 'stagnated or plateaued since the 1980s', Jenkins described early 2021 as characterised by 'widespread appetite for change' across politics, business and the community – built on the back of advocacy and action by women's rights groups.

Jenkins' name was synonymous with reviews, reports and 'fix-it' solutions around the time of the March4Justice. Back in 2018, as a highly regarded arbiter, Jenkins was commissioned by Kelly O'Dwyer, then Minister for Women in Malcolm Turnbull's government, to conduct a world-first national inquiry into workplace sexual harassment. It was a huge undertaking with massive implications. While the focus was on the 'cost' of harassment and the economic impact of bad behaviour at work, thanks to Jenkins, the review also shone a bright, almost blinding light on the alarming rates of 'normalised' sexism, abuse and harassment. By the time Jenkins handed her devastating report to government detailing the 'endemic' nature of sexual harassment, Scott Morrison was in charge; a burnt-out or perhaps disillusioned Kelly O'Dwyer had fled politics altogether, citing family reasons, and the Jenkins report, *Respect@Work*, was shelved. It sat under wraps, gathering dust, for a year. But the March4Justice and the almighty commotion it created throughout the country rang a piercing alarm along parliamentary corridors.

Veteran feminist Wendy McCarthy, who has spent five decades working at the coalface of feminist activism, particularly around childcare policy and abortion rights, thinks the March4Justice shocked politicians across all parties. A short ten days before the march, the Morrison government was showing signs of being rattled. The women's movement was clearly building, and Janine Hendry's social media call-out was rapidly gaining traction. Morrison called the diplomatic and obliging Kate Jenkins back to parliament and asked her to do a full, independent review of Commonwealth parliamentary workplaces. Until the march, says Wendy McCarthy, women 'had just been white noise in the background. But the politicians could never have predicted that there would be an organic uprising, in over 40 centres, across Australia. Now they'd have to be very anxious!'

And they were. With its feet to the fire, the Morrison government blew the dust off the Jenkins report and three weeks after the March4Justice, on 8 April 2021, it released a flimsy response with the quaint title *A Roadmap for Respect: Preventing and Addressing Sexual Harassment in Australian Workplaces.* In it, the government committed to implementing six of the

55 recommendations Kate Jenkins had made.[1] If the Minister for Women, Senator Marise Payne, was embarrassed by this pathetic and deeply inadequate response, she certainly didn't show it. But then Payne was a ghost in this portfolio, rarely seen and even more rarely heard. Which was odd, given her government's escalating panic about how to respond to its now well-known 'women problem'.[2]

In November 2021, eight months after the March4Justice, Jenkins handed the government her *Set the Standard* report on parliamentary workplaces. By now, feeling the weight of shame heaped on it by angry women, and with the nation now awake to its appalling record of ignoring and dismissing women, the Morrison government knew it needed to at least look like it was treating the report with due respect. Unlike the *Respect@Work* report, this one they read – perhaps with fingers covering their eyes. It was a scorching assessment of power imbalances and patriarchal structures that not only disadvantaged women working in parliament but exposed a toxic culture in which sexual harassment, bullying and abusive behaviour had been normalised.

In her foreword to the report, Jenkins championed the 'global #MeToo movement and associated momentum for reform' for encouraging 'numerous brave women' to share their stories. She also singled out Brittany Higgins for 'courageously' sharing her experience, which Jenkins acknowledged was fundamental in forcing the government to establish the review. (Although Jenkins worded the 'Higgins effect' much more demurely than that.)[3]

Now, several years after the Jenkins report and implementation of all its recommendations, including a parliamentary code of conduct and a powerful new Independent Parliamentary Standards Commission (IPSC), the Australian parliament is a very different workplace. The IPSC sets out a clear independent mechanism to investigate complaints about bad behaviour, bullying, harassment, discrimination and sexism by politicians, or indeed anyone working in Commonwealth parliamentary workplaces. It also has the power to impose tough punishments. On the day the new IPSC legislation was tabled in parliament, I found myself smiling at the churning wheels of change, as television news bulletins referred to the establishment of the new body as 'a recommendation in the wake of Brittany Higgins'.[4] That's it. No more explanation needed. The use of Higgins' name was media shorthand for women's fightback and the power of women's collective voice.

A gendered media shift in the centre of gravity

As we row forward looking back, the role of the media in shaping cultural change draws into sharp focus. So too does the media backlash that tried to thwart it.

It took Australia several years to absorb #MeToo and tap into the new female power that began sweeping the globe in 2017. But once we did, once women stepped up the political and workplace fightback – individually at first, then collectively – countless acts of female courage lay the groundwork for an unprecedented national shift in how we understand gender discrimination. By the time the March4Justice exploded onto the streets, very few Australians were unaware of the anger felt by women right around the country. The role of the media in this profound period of awakening has been pivotal – as well as complex and fraught. At times the media coverage of women's anger in general, and Brittany Higgins in particular, was disarmingly destructive. Yet, ironically, Australia would not have reached our New Now if it weren't for the news media's institutionalised misogyny and bedrock of sexism. It forced a show of hands.

It is undeniable that the Australian media has been central in shifting the public narrative around women, workplace cultures, violence, harassment and power inequity. This is primarily what media does – frame the story and curate the narrative. But in recent years, particularly in the lead-up to the March4Justice and its aftermath, the muscular work in pushing the slow-moving dial on public attitudes was done primarily by women journalists. This alone was quite remarkable and indicated a new level of female seniority and editorial clout. Remarkable too was the blatant and unreconstructed blowback from male colleagues, unnerved by this new focus on women – by women.

In early 2021, in what became a rather spectacular 'chorus of sexism', female journalists were accused by male commentators of everything from having 'hissy fits' to failing to comprehend that 'women are better off than ever'. They were said to be throwing 'tantrums' and 'exceeding the traumas' they were reporting on; slammed as 'subjective' and 'emotional'; criticised for being too focused on 'outrages rather than solutions'; and shouted down for being 'angry journalists'. And to reinforce how much men hate angry women, some of the strongest commentary by women was slapped down as 'hysterical'.[5]

In one particularly nasty piece, *Australian Financial Review* former senior correspondent, Aaron Patrick, did a classic media 'hit job' on news.com journalist Samantha Maiden, who would go on to win a Gold Walkley for her coverage of the Brittany Higgins story. In a dig for dirt on Maiden, whom Patrick said had a reputation 'as a difficult colleague and spiky competitor', Patrick trawled through Maiden's childhood, claiming with gawking irrelevance that Maiden's family lived in 'fear of debt collectors', and 'her single mother struggled to pay the fees' for Maiden's schooling. You could almost hear the well-practised scoff as Patrick explained Maiden was expelled from school for 'disobedience'. (Good lord! A spirited, independent-minded woman in journalism? Whatever next? Soon these crazy media sheilas will be destroying the joint!)[6]

While the point of this muckraking was far from clear, the overt sexism was less ambiguous. Cartoonist Jon Kudelka tweeted: 'Did the AFR seriously just run a comically transparent hit job on Samantha Maiden for being a journalist while female?'[7]

Muddled and disjointed, the long feature, titled 'PM caught in crusade of women journos', was not only an attack on Maiden but an attempt to round up all the angry women – who were writing about angry women – for a sheila slapdown. Patrick namechecked the members of this new 'female media leadership' responsible for 'angry coverage that often strayed into unapologetic activism', all of them highly respected journalists: Laura Tingle, Louise Milligan, Katharine Murphy, Amy Remeikis, Lisa Wilkinson, Karen Middleton and Jessica Irvine.

The AFR's editor, Michael Stutchbury, defended Patrick's article, insisting the attack on these women for being 'angry' activists 'was not an attempt to demean their journalism'.[8] Well, that's not what it felt like to me, or to many other women.

Louise Milligan returned a volley via social media, tweeting that 'No-one commissions snarky profiles of male investigative journalists. No one cites "activism" when men relentlessly, admirably pursue stories on war/casinos/finance. No-one explores their irrelevant childhood/calls their old school. Male investigative reporters aren't the story.' Karen Middleton, veteran press gallery journalist and political editor of *The Saturday Paper* at the time, didn't hold back either: 'Pathetic, irrelevant & sexist hatchet job in the @FinancialReview on @samanthamaiden, who broke the Brittany Higgins story & is a ferociously competent journalist.' Katharine Murphy, a press gallery doyen and then political editor of *The Guardian*, added: 'I do want to make the following clear. @samanthamaiden is doing stellar work with these critically important stories.'[9]

Journalism is a fiercely competitive business. It's rare for senior journalists at rival news organisations to take a public stake in supporting a competitor against another journalist's commentary. Men almost never do it. But women do. Well drilled by the sting of gender-based attack from our own colleagues, women journalists are quick to support one another. In a heartbeat.

So what was really irking the blokey bureau of the *AFR*? The giveaway was Patrick's complaint that the women's reportage 'cleaved a schism through political journalism, exposing a shift in the centre of gravity from the male perspective to the female'. There is your problem right there. Embedded in this profoundly sexist remark is confirmation that the natural order of things – the 'male perspective' in media – has been wildly and unnaturally disrupted by the emergent female perspective. Women are right to sense a seething edge of male resentment in this creepy and creeping sentiment.

As one of Australia's most prominent and respected political journalists, Katharine Murphy – who later went on to be media adviser to Prime Minister Anthony Albanese – set a powerful tone of feminist fightback. Writing in *The Guardian*, she called out the Morrison government's abject failure to comprehend the cultural shift happening in the lead-up to the March4Justice. Acknowledging how both the press gallery and parliament – back in 2012 – misjudged the power of Julia Gillard's Misogyny Speech, and misunderstood how deeply it reflected cultural sentiment and women's truth, Murphy wrote:

> Every woman I know is following the events of the past three weeks in politics very closely …
>
> They are watching for one purpose.
>
> They want to know if anything can, or will, change.
>
> …

What this all boils down to is simple. Standards are changing. Expectations are evolving …

[T]he world outside has knocked hard on the door of the Australian parliament.[10]

Powerful and pointed, it was commentary such as this that got under the skin of some ballsy types who like to think of themselves as the serious media muscle. Men have always feared women's intent as they rise to positions of power or influence, and nowhere more so than in the media.

Fitting women into masculine media frames

The ramped-up sexism and attacks on women journalists we witnessed during this period need some unpacking.

Journalism is a peculiar industry in which to work. People drawn to it, regardless of gender identity, share a few common-alities: a love of story, in both the hearing and the telling; an insatiable curiosity; a hunger to be at the centre of what's happening; a healthy bit of ego; and a fierce competitiveness (which we try to hide behind a touch of charm). Good journalism is hard work and occasionally brutal. Personal blows are common, and one quickly learns to be robust and resilient. Most of all, journalism is all-consuming. It's not a job – it's a lifestyle.

In my experience, women and nonbinary people bring greater empathy, more compassion and a broader world view to the complexities and contradictions that are so often knotted at the heart of many stories. However, traditionally news journalism does not comfortably accommodate emotional intelligence. There has been no real place for it in the masculine and, until now, limited framework for news reporting.

Everything we have come to expect from mainstream news media – what makes a good story, what works as a headline, which details are important to include and which aren't, who should be interviewed and whose voices are prioritised – all of this is shaped by male values. Traditionally, men owned and told the news: therefore, it was men who fundamentally got to decide what mattered. As women have joined the ranks of journalism – slowly over the past century, then vigorously and in vast numbers in recent decades – women have had to learn 'what makes news' and 'how news works' according to a rigid masculine frame. News templates have been constructed by and for men. Women have had to fall in – or get out.

Naturally, as the commercial benefit of attracting women as news consumers became increasingly apparent, women's pages became 'a thing', and slowly but surely, through an ill-defined osmosis, along with guts and grit, women moved into mainstream news roles. Yes, even as editors. But while media workplaces are now heavily populated with women, and digital technology along with AI have changed how we work, the fundamental framework that dictates what we do as journalists has nevertheless remained largely unchanged since early last century.

For the first 15 years I worked in television journalism, there was not a single woman over the age of 50 working on air in a senior reporting or presenting role. I was first put on notice about 'female temporariness' in broadcast journalism when I graduated as a news cadet and used the moment to tell my boss I had just got engaged to be married. One of the newsroom's senior reporters loudly announced that, once hitched, I would quit my little 'hobby job', with only a collection of old VHS tapes as memories of my time as a journalist. Women weren't expected to last. If we did, we knew – thanks to our own instinctive survival skills – that we had to toe the man-made media line.

Around the time I began my role as ABC News anchor in Canberra, in 2001, a prominent female current affairs host turned 50, which I took as great encouragement, given she was in her career prime. Yet the birthday was kept strictly secret: I was told she didn't want anyone at work to know she was 'getting old'. There is now a sizeable handful of women over 50 in on-air roles, with many compelled to spend inordinate sums of money and time on 'self-maintenance' to disguise their age. (Cheating age and body remain a constant burden in media. In my twenties, days after signing a new contract with a commercial TV network, I was told my breasts were too small and could do with some 'adjustment'. It just so happens I liked my flat breasts, so I kept them.)

The sort of criticism levelled at women journalists at the height of our awakening in 2021 exposed a deep fear that media, most importantly the powerful press gallery, might indeed be 'fracturing along gender lines', as academic Denis Muller put it.[11] The existential threat felt by media men was that women might just come out on top.

Very soon, they did. And not just in the media.

Winds of change blast the ballot box

In the year following the March4Justice, a discernible shift in public mood was evident. Institutional and cultural forms of women's oppression and silencing were exposed. And, as any feminist will attest, once you see it, you can't unsee it. Sexism, misogyny and brute disrespect had been outed en masse.

Riding this wave of elevated consciousness, a bunch of women with media muscle and clout ganged together to press home the point. Together they wrote, produced and self-funded a video campaign titled 'Safety. Respect. Equity', which ran on television and across social media a month before the critical 2022 Australian federal election. This was not an election advertisement and it made no mention of the upcoming poll, but the intent was clear: *Think power, think politics, think women.*

The video featured a formidable intersectional and inter-generational group of 12 women, some of whom by then were household names: Brittany Higgins, Grace Tame, Chanel Contos, Julia Banks, Christine Holgate, Wendy McCarthy, Indigenous academic and activist Larissa Behrendt, Paralympian Madison de Rozario, youth leader Yasmin Poole, Georgie Dent from nonprofit The Parenthood, philanthropist Lucy Turnbull and union boss Michele O'Neil.

The three-minute video opens with a now famous one-line message from Tame: 'Australia, we need to talk.' From there, each woman stares straight down the barrel of the camera and eyeballs the viewer: '2021 was different. It wasn't the first year women were harassed, unsafe, violated, dehumanised, ignored, disrespected. It wasn't the first year that women spoke up ... But 2021 was different. More Australians started to listen.'

With each line overlaid to feature many voices in a staccato rhythm, every word was delivered to pack a punch: 'The collective voice that roared in 2021 is not going away ... When we work together, this movement is unstoppable. We will turn that wave of women's anger into a tsunami of change.'[12]

Although not billed as such, the video campaign was an unspoken celebration of Australia's awakening. It drove a digital stake into the ground, marking women's claim on the New Now.

So, did it work?

The 2022 election emerged as an undeclared referendum on women, and women *smashed* it. More women won seats in 2022 than in any previous federal election in Australia's history. Ten independents were elected, nine of them women, six of them first-time politicians. Dubbed the 'Teals' by the media, due to their similar shade of campaign colour – a mix of the blue Liberal electorates they were contesting and their green-tinged environmental policies – some of these women won by enormous margins. Each of the new Teals knocked off men in what were considered safe, conservative seats. Even the popular federal treasurer, Josh Frydenberg, the man expected to be the next Liberal leader and possibly prime minister, was knocked out by Monique Ryan, an independent who – like all the Teals – had never run for political office before. ABC political commentator Patricia Karvelas didn't mince her words on election night when the nation-wide results became clear. At 10.11 pm, she tweeted: 'One overwhelming story. Do. Not. Ignore. Women.'[13]

However, as academic Camilla Nelson, from the University of Notre Dame, wrote, 'Women were everywhere and nowhere in the 2022 federal election.'[14] It was the sort of paradox we have come to expect from the Australian media. Despite the obvious community demand for greater integrity and accountability in government, and the wariness of voters about political patronising and patriarchy, mainstream media either misjudged the appeal of women independents and ignored them, or chose to openly ridicule them.

One of the most prominent curmudgeons of the male commentariat, Paul Kelly, used his column in *The Australian* to warn aspiring prime minister, Anthony Albanese, not to be distracted by 'the 2021 zeitgeist – the emotional demand by women to re-set the norms of respect and justice'.[15] There is much that could be said about the misogyny inherent in that statement, and plenty of argument as to why 'respect and justice' are not emotional demands, but rather moral ones – a natural expectation in any reasonable democratic system. How easily flag-wavers of the patriarchy dismiss women's valid demands by belittling them as 'emotional'. One can only wonder if Kelly has ever stopped to consider why it is left up to women to do the demanding when it comes to 'respect and justice'?

The closer the election drew, the nastier some of the conservative media commentary became. Independents were called 'fakes', 'frauds', 'sewer' and 'spewing'. And it wasn't just shouty men on Sky News working themselves into a lather over these uppity, opinionated women, who prioritised gender equality, climate action and political integrity. Shouty female hosts on Sky also had a crack. Queen-bee commentator Peta Credlin didn't like these 'fake independents' one bit. 'Their sheer impertinence made her cross,' wrote Denis Muller, suggesting that News Corp had 'gone rogue on election coverage' and was engaging in 'truth distorting.'[16]

Most conservative commentators refused to believe these remarkably well-credentialled women – all professionals – could be acting alone. Surely there was a sugar daddy or 'puppet master' somewhere in the background, pulling the strings, setting the strategy and providing the finance? Soon they unearthed philanthropist Simon Holmes à Court as the wizard ventriloquist who was supposedly controlling the women's words and actions. Holmes à Court, a fierce climate-action advocate and founder of the not-for-profit organisation Climate 200, donated money to 23 independent community candidates – including the Teals – who prioritised climate action and were chosen by their local communities to contest the election. A somewhat shy, hands-off bloke who wanted to support new talent but stay in the shadows, Holmes à Court was hounded by mainstream media who simply didn't want to believe this new crop of women running as independent political candidates had agency of their own. Disbelieving journalists insisted the Teals were 'fakes': fake conservatives (they're secret Greens); fake politicians (it's all marketing); and fake independents (they're a secret women's party and will vote in a bloc).

Despite their struggle to provoke thoughtful, well-informed national debate on issues such as climate change and gender equality, the Teals were kept on the margins by mainstream media. Unperturbed, they worked hard in their own communities and prioritised local media, steadily building voter recognition and trust. Soon each of these women amassed a huge army of volunteers. That alone should have been enough to attract serious media attention, along with the growing evidence of a women-led community fightback against government failure and political insincerity. Yet national media gave the Teals little more than novelty coverage.

Once again, it was mostly senior women journalists who applied a gender lens and took a broader view of what was really going on. Katharine Murphy, Karen Middleton, Annabel Crabb, Fran Kelly and Niki Savva were among a handful who looked beyond the novelty and saw the deepening community appeal of these women candidates. One of the few male commentators to do the same was Mark Kenny (the Mark Kenny with whom I share a dog and a marriage), writing in *The Canberra Times*. Struck by the intellect and political savvy of these women, Kenny was fascinated by how and why such women were drawn to politics, at a time when the Australian parliament was infamous for its toxic masculinity. Why too, he wondered, were communities so open to engaging with these women who openly admitted to being semi-conservative, yet proud feminists? The group included a former journalist and foreign correspondent, a paediatric neurologist, a business executive with expertise in renewable energy, a communications executive and former CEO, a GP, and a lawyer. Kenny argued:

> You might think the emergence of highly credentialed female competitors to the major parties is a hell of a news story, right? You might even imagine it is a potential source of news yarns if they succeed in injecting fresh vim into a discredited public discourse – journalism included.
>
> Yet many journalists seem lazily inclined to adopt the sneering tone of government.[17]

As Patricia Karvelas called it on election night, the singular story to emerge in that election was a story of women. It was a nation-wide story about pissed-off women stepping up, fighting back and claiming public space and a right to leadership. A story about women saying, 'We can do better. We *will* do better.'

The new 47th Parliament had a record number of women: 38 per cent in the House of Representatives, and 57 per cent in the Senate. Most importantly, as always happens when the ground shifts for women, everyone benefited. More culturally and linguistically diverse Australians won seats that year than in any previous election, including people with Indian, Vietnamese, African and Chinese heritage. We also witnessed an increase in Indigenous Australians and those identifying as LGBTQI+ in parliament. In sum, the 2022 election was a powerful story of women's progress – and a community's coming of age.

Critically, the story of the feminist fightback in our New Now is a story of continuous forward motion. The 2022 election sweep that ushered historic numbers of women into political power was no aberration, no blip. The May 2025 election with its *new* 'record-smashing' numbers of women storming into parliament was so stunning, so emphatic, that calling it an 'historic high' barely describes it. With women in the new government dominating both houses of parliament, and for the first time in history also federal cabinet, the winds of change felt like a cyclone. Back in 2021, before the March4Justice, Australia was ranked a shameful 73rd out of 193 countries for women with ministerial power. In 2025, the nation had moved well up the global ladder to a forecast equal seventh place.[18]

A radical pathway forward ...

Is our feminist future written in the past?

Sometimes the answer to what feels like a tangled riddle, an impossible puzzle, is staring us in the face.

As I left the stage at the end of the March4Justice, Biff still beaming with joy, and me wearing my worried face, I looked down at that cluster of older women sitting in plastic chairs at the front, or on their picnic rugs – the 'memory keepers', as historian Sharon Crozier-De Rosa calls them. Elizabeth Reid was among them. Like Biff, she looked utterly elated. These women were almost levitating with joy. They were the women who had given their lives to the revolution. Their holy grail was never equality with men. It was *liberation* from them. They have done the work. They've paid it forward. They have gifted us a rich and rebellious history – fabulous feminist foundations – from which to shape a stronger future.

What happens next is up to us. You. Me. Your daughters, their daughters, our granddaughters.

In the years since the March4Justice, geopolitical forces around the globe have accelerated a tidal wave of anti-women sentiment and state-sponsored backlash against women's rights. The speed of this change is dizzying. It is also seriously dangerous and not to be underestimated. Australia is not immune, nor free from increasingly overt expressions of misogyny and the push for male supremacy. It is seeping into our politics; bleeding into public discourse; and clogging up our social media. It is even parading onto our streets in occasional neo-Nazi – 'Australia for the White Man' – marches, with black-clad, faceless thugs on recruitment drives.

Perhaps most alarming is the significant regression in male attitudes towards women that is showing up repeatedly in national and global surveys. In 2025, a substantial 45 per cent of

Australian men said women's equal rights 'have gone far enough': that was a 14 per cent increase on the previous survey, in 2019.[19] Most terrifying is the nexus with violence against women. A 2024 survey by researchers at the University of Melbourne found that nearly 20 per cent of Australian men believe that 'feminism should be violently resisted, if necessary'.[20] I shudder to think what that 'necessary' might mean.

This is not where we thought we would be 50 years after International Women's Year in 1975, when a 'spontaneous awakening' swept feminist consciousness around the world and shook Australia to its cultural core. That was the year in which Australia was hailed internationally as a gender equity authority and seen by some as an emerging feminist utopia. For a very brief moment, it almost was.

In his 2025 International Women's Day message, the Secretary-General of the United Nations, António Guterres, confirmed what we all knew: that 'women's human rights are under attack'. His speech was a rousing clarion call: 'Centuries of discrimination are being exacerbated by new threats ... We cannot stand by as progress is reversed. We must fight back.'[21]

In Australia – thanks to our New Now – we are highly attuned to misogyny. We're on the hunt for it. Ready to call it out, expose it and take it on. Our awakening seriously strengthened our pushback against the 'pushback'. Women have collectively flexed feminist muscle. There is no doubt about that. Now, we need to go in harder – much harder – if we are to tackle the increasingly formidable and insidious forms of backlash gaining momentum around us.

The unprecedented display of energy and rapid organisation we saw in early March 2021, when women who hardly knew one another pulled together the largest, loudest women's rally in Australia's history, in towns and cities around the nation, proves we have exceptional power to activate. Anger is a tremendous motivation. But to use that anger to finally and thoroughly dismantle patriarchy, and prevailing patriarchal attitudes, we must be strategic. It takes a sustained women's movement to build transformative change.

The task facing Australian women now goes beyond connecting the dots between women's activism and admiring the linkages. It is time to draw on the idealism and rebellion of the women before us – those feminists and Women's Liberationists from feminism's second wave.

Australia's feminist foundations run deep and the roots are radical – more radical than you might imagine. Not content just fighting for reform, these women wanted a revolution. They demanded it. A revolution in people's heads. An explosion in people's brains.

The actions of women five decades ago changed everything. For all of us.

So, did they win the revolution? Or are they still living it? How did they do it? What did they do? And why was the Australian Women's Liberation Movement celebrated and applauded internationally, yet so shockingly ridiculed at home? What were the men in power – and mansplainers in the media – so very afraid of?

Women. That's what.

PART 3
FEMINIST FOUNDATIONS

In 1970 I had no idea just how subversive the ideas
of women's liberation would turn out to be.[1]

Anne Summers

Ours was a radical feminism.
A commitment to a feminist revolution.[2]

Elizabeth Reid

8

THE GREAT 'SPONTANEOUS AWAKENING'

Before I rang Elizabeth Reid's doorbell, I caught a glimpse of her through the side glass. She was sitting at the end of a large dining table stacked with papers and manila folders. Bathed in afternoon sunlight and bent over a laptop writing, she seemed fully and utterly absorbed – a woman at work. The room was busy with books. A walking frame lingered close by, pushed into the shadows. I could see right through a back window to the lush garden outside. This peaceful yet industrious tableau caught me off guard and for a moment I couldn't help but stare. This woman has had a profound impact on the story of Australian women's lives over the past 50 years, yet there she was, living alone in quiet suburban obscurity.

Until recently, I knew little about the role Reid played in pushing and cajoling Australia towards embracing the liberation of women. As the first woman in the world appointed to advise a head of government on women's affairs, Reid had the ear of prime minister Gough Whitlam, right when Australia was spinning through the most intense political reform and social change in its history. It was Reid who led the charge on policies to benefit and support women, while also forcing a fundamental shift in gender attitudes across the country. She took on a deeply sexist media that ridiculed her as the 'PM's Supergirl' and fixated on the substantive gender questions – 'Did she wear a bra?'

Most importantly, Elizabeth Reid prised open myriad opportunities for women to challenge and change the way they viewed themselves. Although her tenure was brief, Reid catapulted some of the most important cultural shifts in relations between men and women Australia has experienced. Yet her impact remains surprisingly unheralded.

As I stood staring through the window at this extraordinarily accomplished and humble woman, now in her eighties, I was struck by how vague we are as a nation about our fierce and radical feminist past.

A watershed year like no other, my dear

1975 was the year the United Nations declared International Women's Year.

It was the year my grade 6 teacher, Miss Lidgett, stopped wearing a bra. The year Germaine Greer talked about orgasms on telly and lesbians appeared on talk shows. It was the year 'Women's Libbers' ran riot in Parliament House in Canberra, demanding both revolution and reform, draping placards on the statue of King George V and writing slogans in lipstick on mirrors in the loos.

It was the year Gough Whitlam urged women to take control and change the 'man-made world' in which they lived and give it 'a shove in the right direction'.[1] It was the year the male press pack mocked budget spending on women as 'money for the sheilas!' and a big fat 'joke'. It was also the year thousands of ballsy women activists from across the globe gathered in Mexico for the first United Nations World Conference on Women – the biggest and rowdiest political gathering of women ever seen before.

It was the year Australia's Elizabeth Reid was hailed an international feminist rock star as she lectured the United Nations on dismantling patriarchal power structures and changing social attitudes towards women. Most importantly, she urged global leaders to face up to the crippling reality of 'sexism': a new concept that, like 'sexual harassment', didn't exist in the lexicon back then. It was the year the world witnessed what historians now call 'the greatest consciousness-raising event in history'.[2]

This landmark year turbocharged the women's movement in Australia and feminist action around the world. It ignited at the precise moment in which women across the world – from the global north to the global south – were ripe for radical change. Despite myriad differences – amid perceptions of privilege, imperialism and cultural relativism among women in the north that butted up against the experience of colonialism, development disadvantage and economic injustice in the south – astoundingly, women found some common ground. In Australia, where the intersection of racism and class divisions struggled for space on the feminist agenda, Indigenous women staged a Speak Out in Canberra, and added their voice to the global Tribune conference in Mexico.

The United Nations gender agenda for 1975 was bold, ambitious and fiercely fraught. Which, frankly, made it all the more fabulous. Like most historic 'big bangs', it was all in the timing. International Women's Year landed just as women were collectively waking up to the systemic forces of female oppression working against them. Consciousness raising among Western feminists was having a flow-on effect, reaching out to women across diverse communities.

Then, as if a global-sized penny had dropped like a meteor from outer space, women everywhere were part of what Elizabeth Reid calls a 'spontaneous awakening'. The vibes of this awakening would soon reverberate around the planet and give birth to an 'array of global feminisms' that eventually changed everything.[3]

What happened in 1975 laid the foundation for the gender freedoms – both personal and professional – that we take for granted now and rarely stop to think about. International Women's Year was a wild ride – yet it remains broadly unacknowledged as the fuse that lit the fire of feminist revolution around the globe. A revolution we are still living. Every. Single. Day.

Here in Australia – like all good revolutions – the plotting began a few years earlier. The sexual revolution of the 1960s had shaken out bigger issues than free and fun sex: questions of female power and autonomy were bubbling to the surface of women's expectations. Many embraced a radical fashion freedom as tweed skirts gave way to jeans and floaty cheesecloth; beehive hairdos collapsed; and the jangle of bangles, beads and knee-high boots was the new soundtrack of women on the move. But beneath it all was a foundational shift in mood. The new vibe was raw, edgy and open to challenge.

The story of how women arrived on the threshold of International Women's Year primed and pumped for radical change begins in those critical few years leading up to '75. This important period is when an unprecedented shift in women's collective thinking exposed systemic gender inequity and women's oppression in ways not previously understood. As we know, revolutionary action can begin around a kitchen table – or, as was the case in the early 1970s across suburban Australia, with women sitting in circles on cushions, beanbags and on living room floors.

Excuse me, Miss, is that a bomb in your bag?

The chaps from ASIO were hiding across the road from the old brick-veneer home in Canning Street, Ainslie, a quiet pocket of suburban Canberra, in June 1970. None of the eight women arriving, or the three hippie dudes who lived there and were now leaving, suspected for a moment that they were under government surveillance – which was odd, really, given the cameras were probably clicking from a car parked directly opposite them. Among the group were a couple of political activists, two schoolteachers, a 'Catholic follower of Liberation theology', a psychologist, a sociologist and a peace activist. Most of them were young mums.[4] It didn't occur to the women that ASIO might be interested in this meeting, even though some of them were self-declared Marxist revolutionaries.

The late 1960s and early '70s proved a busy period for government surveillance in Australia. Active factions of the political left were competing, plotting and generally agitating. Many had been involved in anti–Vietnam War actions. But this 'new' group gathering in suburban Canberra had the spy agency fixated. It was strictly sheilas. They had not encountered this before in sleepy Canberra. Sure, women in the political left had participated in the various Marxist, Trotskyist, communist and anarchist gatherings ASIO monitored. And women were certainly active in the anti-war movement. But why was this meeting a women-only gig? What were they up to?

It was 6 June 1970, the very first meeting of the Canberra Women's Liberation Group. Of particular interest to the government spooks was a woman who arrived in a woolly cardigan and dark sunglasses, her hair in a short ponytail and carrying a highly suspicious, bulbous hessian bag.

The woman was Julia Ryan. The bag contained her knitting.

Daughter of feminist trailblazer Edna Ryan, Julia was both a prolific knitter and note taker, and she quickly became the unofficial scribe at these meetings, taking copious notes and chronicling her astute observations. She would diarise and write illuminating commentary about the Women's Liberation Movement (WLM) for several years.[5] Her list of discussion topics in the early days of the Canberra group was comprehensive. Everything was up for exploration, as they sought to define and untangle women's oppression: feminism, patriarchy and anarchism; sexuality, lesbianism, abortion and contraceptives; women in the Russian Revolution, Cuba, China and Vietnam; 'Tolstoy, Monstrous Patriarch'; work, housework, trade unionism and equal pay; prison and criminal law reform … and so it went on. Nothing, it seemed, did not warrant a feminist critique, as these intrepid and deeply curious women debated and theorised their way out of their old lives and into something entirely new.

'For those who came regularly, we were rewarded with exploding brains, lives turned topsy-turvy, and energy we had never known before and the sense of what we came to call sisterhood,' remembered Biff Ward, a fixture of the Canberra group meetings.

> We threw all the elements of our lives into the air so that we could examine the underbelly of everything. We shared our own experiences, then picked out the common patterns from among our stories, thus developing theories about why things were the way they were and what we had to do to change them.[6]

At that first meeting, Julia positioned herself with a view out the window directly onto the street, but didn't notice the spooks parked outside or peeking through the venetians from the house opposite. As the women settled onto beanbags and cushions, Julia opened her bulging bag and pulled out her knitting. What did the trenchcoat brigade make of that? Knit one, purl two. During World War II, the Belgian Resistance recruited women whose houses overlooked railway yards to note the comings and goings of German trains. Purl one for one type of train, drop one for another. Was the clack of Julia's needles tapping out some devilish communist code?

Two of the women present, including Julia's sister Lyndall Ryan, had driven down from Sydney to talk about the Women's Liberation group established there. Within a year or so, similar groups had sprouted across Adelaide, Melbourne, Brisbane and Hobart, all holding weekly meetings and attracting new attendees. The meetings were busy events with highly structured discussion agendas, in which women took turns to lead. From the outset, the Australian Women's Liberation Movement was fiercely anti-hierarchical. Some of the women became committed regulars; others came and went. The Canberra group conducted recruiting drives, extending broad invitations to any women even remotely interested in this women's discussion group. There was nothing clandestine. Their flyers and advertisements in newspapers gave dates and addresses of meetings, including the phone numbers of women to contact. With seemingly nothing to hide, they were easy to find. So what had ASIO so interested and alarmed?

Years later, Biff and Julia decided it was time to see what ASIO had on them. Three decades had passed, and the 30-year secrecy rule on ASIO files from the early 1970s had been lifted. The reception staff at the National Archives of Australia were delighted when Biff and Julia requested to view their files. More staff gathered in awe when they discovered that not only were these two sweetly polite, rather ordinary-looking older women the subject of government spying, but their files were big. Biff's was nearly 12 centimetres high, filling numerous folders.

It turns out that ASIO was rather obsessed with the Women's Liberation Movement. They kept 'extensive files' on the WLM and 'heavily monitored' its members, particularly in Sydney, Melbourne and Canberra.[7] They tracked who came and went from meetings, bugged women's phones, and possibly even inserted the occasional 'plant'. Several years into their regular meetings, Biff had been contacted by a Melbourne woman from the extreme political left, who'd said she was keen to meet with a few women in Canberra to discuss 'an important project'. 'Only invite women you really trust,' she told Biff. Julia and

Biff phoned around and selected a few women to join them. On the allotted evening, a woman they knew from the women's movement but hadn't directly invited turned up. They were a little surprised, as they didn't consider her to be particularly politically active.

Once the meeting got underway, it became clear the so-called 'project' was well outside the Canberra group's style of activity, so they rejected it outright. When Biff and Julia later tracked down the uninvited woman to quiz her, she broke down in tears and said she had been blackmailed by ASIO into attending and forced to report back. Needless to say, she didn't appear at any further meetings.

ASIO, it seems, were worried that the WLM's well-publicised slogan, 'the personal is political', might in fact get too political, and feared that the various WLM chapters sprouting around the country might join up and become some kind of overwhelming force that would strain social cohesion and threaten the Australian way of life. It seems ASIO was desperate to know when this 'revolution' the women kept talking about was going to blow![8]

It didn't take long for the women to realise they were under surveillance. Biff had grown up as the daughter of a prominent left-wing academic, Russel Ward, who hosted Communist Party social gatherings at home, and had many friends actively involved in socialist politics. As a kid she was accustomed to the idea that the family house was under surveillance. So when her own home phone started to hum with roomy echoes and strange sounds, she knew it was bugged. After she registered a complaint with the telephone company, a serviceman arrived to fix the phone. He pulled the big old dial phone apart and innocently announced that the phone seemed to be connected to a 'third-party line'. He headed back to HQ to investigate and later rang Biff, sounding very chastened, insisting he had made a mistake. There was nothing wrong with her phone; there was no third-party connection. Then he hung up.

Yet, there they were some 30 years later, bulging out of her ASIO file – two years' worth of phone transcripts of every single phone call Biff ever made or received from 1970 to 1972 (the spying had stopped when Gough Whitlam took power). Biff had been the contact person for the CLM, so there were literally hundreds of conversations that had been transcribed by some poor ASIO lackey, word for word. They were meticulous in detail, noting dates, times and precisely who was doing the talking. But what they didn't include was any serious effort to analyse what the WLM discussed and what the women were in fact trying to achieve.

Subversives in skirts

Many of the women drawn to developing feminist theory though the intellectual funnel of Women's Liberation arrived with a Marxist mindset, which gave them an understanding of power relations and a notion of revolution. At a feature event I moderated at the 2023 Canberra Writers Festival, with an all-star cast of women who had played central roles in the feminist reforms and activism of the early '70s, Biff Ward took the opportunity to remind the audience of those Marxist ideological beginnings.[9] Gail Radford, a founding member of the Women's Electoral Lobby and the inaugural Director of Equal Employment Opportunity in the public service, told the audience she was, and always will be, an anarchist.[10] Elizabeth Reid suggested she was more anarchist than Marxist. But in a rollicking and at times wild discussion that traversed the highs and lows of Women's Liberation and the driving ideology of women's revolution, all generally agreed that Women's Liberation first sprang from a Marxist springboard.

In the 21st century, such descriptors perhaps seem a little obscure. After all, for all his powers of insight, Karl Marx never appeared to land a realistic understanding of the reasons behind women's oppression, beyond a belief that women were too beholden to reproductive labour within the family unit, which left them unpaid and undervalued. That much seems blindingly obvious, even to the non-philosophers among us. Marx's solution was to get women fully participating in the 'productive' labour force alongside men. As to who would pick up the slack back home, do the chores, raise the kids and teach men how to play an equal role in domestic life, well, none of that seemed to figure in Marx's consideration of gender inequality. As British psychoanalyst Juliet Mitchell wrote in her famed 1966 essay 'Women: The longest revolution', Marx wrote about women as 'an anthropological entity … of a highly abstract kind'.[11] It took his co-philosopher Friedrich Engels to deepen the thinking about women, after Marx's death. Engels embraced an ancient truth – one that was well understood by women the world over – when he identified the depth of gendered grievance embedded in humankind. As Mitchell explained it, Engels understood that 'the inequality of the sexes was one of the first antagonisms within the human species'.[12]

Juliet Mitchell suggested Women's Liberation posed feminist questions and gave Marxist answers.[13] Yet that was inadequate. Marxism went some of the way to help explain the structures of women's oppression, but it did not offer the solutions. They had to work that out for themselves. Anne Summers – journalist, energetic activist and once a key member of Sydney Women's Liberation – was frank when she admitted the movement's efforts to reconcile their new thinking with old ideology wasn't easy. Nor was it fruitful. In her early memoir, *Ducks on the Pond*, Summers wrote:

We knew the theory of revolution as articulated by Marx and Lenin, and later by Mao and Ho, but we had also had to face the limitations of Marxism when it came to the position of women. An awful lot of tortured prose was devoted to trying to reconcile Marxism and feminism, but many of us had become impatient with this exercise. We were fired by a strong sense of outrage at what so many women were enduring at the hands of men, be they disdainful gynaecologists, violent husbands or men who would not take no for an answer when it came to sex. Once we recognised that we could do a lot about these problems ourselves, there was no reason to hang back.[14]

Debates over Marxism were not new among Australia's political left in the 1960s and '70s. But what had ASIO really baffled by the Women's Liberationists was why women were collectively applying Marxist thinking to their own lives in this new, gendered way. As far as the government agency could see, there was something dangerously subversive about this kind of intellectualising. They just didn't know what.

Given the movement was steadfastly anti-hierarchy, there was no clear set of leaders to keep under constant surveillance. Instead the WLM was like an amorphous pack of wriggling parts – incessantly moving, amplifying and expanding in number. They wanted to dismantle institutions and the committed Marxists among them also wanted to wage war on capitalism. But the more radical core of the movement looked beyond Marxism to a full-scale social upheaval and direct challenge to patriarchy – all of which appears to have panicked ASIO. Unlike those ballsy and fearless first-wave feminists, the suffragettes – who blew stuff up, destroyed buildings, smashed shop windows, attacked members of parliament, chained themselves to grilles in the House of Commons and endured torture as prison guards beat and force-fed them – women from what became known as the 'second wave', the Women's Liberation Movement, were innovating a whole new way of doing revolution.[15]

As members of what Marilyn Lake calls an 'intensely literary movement', the women of the WLM read the few feminist texts in circulation – works by Simone de Beauvoir, Betty Friedan, Robin Morgan, Kate Millett, Germaine Greer, Shulamith Firestone, Sheila Rowbotham – along with essays by Juliet Mitchell, Anne Koedt, Carol Hanisch and Pat Mainardi.[16] Later, Anne Summers' *Damned Whores and God's Police* added a critical Australian perspective to the feminist canon. Women's Liberationists mined their own lives, exploring deeply, as they developed radical new social and political theories around what it meant to be female and how women's oppression featured in every aspect of their lived experience. Their vision called for a total transformation of society. As far as the chauvinistic security organisation ASIO could see, that posed a pervasive threat to the status quo – they just couldn't work out what. Some within the government agency believed lawlessness was afoot, but others feared that female political consciousness would tear at the 'moral fabric of Australian society'.[17]

In hindsight, it is staggering how much taxpayer money was wasted on this surveillance, given files such as Ward's and Ryan's – along with numerous others – indicate ASIO didn't appear to know what they were looking for. They just kept looking ... or was it gawking?

Historian Michelle Arrow has spent much of her career unpacking Australian life in the 1970s and the WLM in particular. Her take on ASIO's targeting and tracking of women within the movement politely suggests the surveillance reports were often 'persistently sexualised and voyeuristic'.[18] Put less politely, it's as if the men doing the watching and tracking were little more than government-funded perverts. For example, Isabelle

'Coonie' Sandford, a member of Sydney Women's Liberation, caught the spying eye of ASIO very early on. The Sydney group began in January 1969, not long after Coonie had returned from a trip to the United States, where she had met some of the key players in this new women's movement. She quickly became an enthusiastic convert to the revolutionary ideas of liberationists, and it was Coonie who travelled with Lyndall Ryan to Canberra to spread the word. ASIO recorded her as follows: 'Approximately 23 years of age ... 5'2" tall, with shoulder length straight dark brown hair ... weighs approximately 8 stone. She has a good figure, is neat and well groomed.'

So thorough were they with their powers of scrutiny, I'm surprised the scribbling men of ASIO didn't guess her bra size and hip measurement. Their further notes on Coonie suggest they either pieced together snippets of information and made creative assumptions, or they had an informant on the inside: 'She is not popular with the other members of the Women's Liberation Group as they consider she talks a lot of rot, and has in fact been accused on occasions of being a liar.'[19]

Another young woman who caught the lascivious eye of ASIO was Melbourne medical student Liz Elliott. A member of both the Carlton Women's Liberation group and the Communist Party, Elliott was officially recorded as a 'very attractive girl'. But, alas, despite the young woman's beauty, according to ASIO she was a bit of a slob when it came to her lack of a decent frock. ASIO described her as 'untidy in her general appearance'. I can almost hear them joke: *That's commies for you. Even the sheilas.*[20] Pity they didn't actually consider some of what Elliott had to say. Biff Ward vividly recalls seeing her for the first time in 1971, when she gave a paper at a Women's Liberation Trade Union Conference in Melbourne. Elliott's thesis was about male supremacy in the working class, and the role of the housewife as a duped consumer cog in the wheel of capitalism.[21] However, it was Elliott's outspoken and highly personal account of the trauma she had experienced that stuck with Biff, and no doubt others listening: 'She spoke so movingly about how very attractive women had to live with always being lusted over by men and isolated from women who were threatened by it. It was something we had never thought about before and really illuminating.'

This was new territory for the emerging women's movement – how women treat other women as competitors in the quest for male attention. Naturally, this too became a serious subject for WLM discussion. As for ASIO's interest in these revelations? None recorded.

As members of Women's Liberation became aware they were being bugged by government spies, some played with the opportunity 'to stir them up'. In her book, *Brazen Hussies*, about the radical activism of women in Victoria in the 1970s, Jean Taylor details how some WLM members would deliberately discuss subjects to shock the men listening in. Alva Geikie and Zelda D'Aprano – who had, along with Thelma Solomon, famously chained themselves to the entrance of Melbourne's Arbitration Court in 1969 after a test case for equal pay – regularly discussed D'Aprano's abortion, in 'gruesome' detail, when they suspected ASIO was listening in.[22]

D'Aprano was a well-known agitator. The equal pay case that had triggered her anger was instigated by the meat workers' union and the Australian Council of Trade Unions (ACTU), and as a union member D'Aprano quickly became infuriated by a legal process in which women sat in the commission hearing 'day after day as if mute, while men presented evidence for and against their worth'. The eventual 'win' only allowed equal pay for women performing exactly the same job as a man, and only in the meat industry. For D'Aprano, that simply wasn't good enough. She became quite expert at chaining herself and her feminist comrades to the doors of government buildings.[23]

Kate Jennings and 'that' speech

Ironically, it was not just the outrageous sexism of old white men that was the problem for Women's Liberationists in the 1970s. It was the sexism of the very men the female hippies and political activists of the '60s and '70s hung out with – and the men they loved – that pushed these young women to build a revolution of their own. The sexual revolution of the 1960s was a fabulous moment in history – for men. But not so liberating for women. Thanks to the pill, the earth-shifting medication that arrived in Australia in 1961, women finally could take control of their own reproduction and have as much sex as they pleased without the fear of pregnancy. But there was no pill capable of rewiring male supremacy or castrating male chauvinism. Male arrogance and appetite for domination remained at large, and women remained available and on call. This is how the acerbic Germaine Greer put it: 'The sixties was the hey-day of male display; the most successful sixties women were scented, decorative and slender, voluptuously dressed in diaphanous chiffons, old embroideries, baubles, bangles, beads and boots, and spoke in blurred voices – if they spoke at all.'[24]

But as history has proven, women have plenty of voice. And when we are angry beyond redemption, we can use it to eviscerating effect. On 8 May 1970, at a packed anti–Vietnam War moratorium on the lawns of Sydney University, 22-year-old poet and writer Kate Jennings gave one of the most blistering feminist speeches in Australian history, later credited as the nascent Women's Liberation Movement's first major public 'outing'. Jennings and her sisters in the Sydney Women's Liberation Glebe Street hub were sick of being pushed to the margins of left-wing political debates, in which their cocky male lovers and comrades played lead roles, doing all the talking, pontificating and theorising. This was the first day Women's

Liberation had taken the mic at a public rally.

Racked with nerves yet propelled by the heat of female rage, Jennings began at full throttle, her speech notes laid out on paper like pulsating visual poetry:

watch out! You may meet a real
                              castrating female
                      or

you'll say I'm a MANHATING BRABURNING LESBIAN MEMBER OF THE CASTRATION PENISENVY BRIGADE   which I am

I would like to speak.

I would like to give a tubthumpingtablebanging emotional rap AND be listened to, not laughed out. You don't laugh at what your comrade brothers say, you wouldn't laugh at the negroes, the black panthers. Many women are beginning to feel the necessity to speak for themselves, for their sisters.

I feel the necessity now.

And on she pushed, with unrestrained fury in her voice, lecturing the men who 'think with your pricks' and view women as second-class citizens. She attacked her 'brothers' for their hypocrisy: their outrage at the killing of Vietnamese people at the hands of imperialist oppressors while they failed to notice the deaths of their 'sisters' back home from illegal abortions. Jennings wrapped with:

I feel hatred

I feel anger

Without indulging in an equality or marxist argument
I say all power to women

Because that's what I feel

ALL POWER.

There were a few more lines about telling men to 'go suck
their own cocks', and suggesting women buy weapons to 'kill
the bodies that you've unfortunately laid under often enough'.
Then she finished with a rousing, final, 'ALL POWER TO
WOMEN!'

It was stunning, game-changing oratory, brisling with
raw power and long-harboured resentment – a frenzied poetry
aimed at verbally castrating every male in the thousand-strong
crowd. And it worked. 'Ugly bitch!' they yelled. 'You belong on
your back'.

It had the 'men of the revolution in full throat', she said
later – 'they went berserk'. They booed, laughed and yelled
obscenities. Women in the crowd were stunned and drop-jawed.
Over three decades later, when rereading the speech for the first
time, even Jennings was gobsmacked by her audacity: 'Holy
shit! Blistering!' Nevertheless, back in 1970, an army of women
agreed with her. 'Everything changed that day,' she said.[25]

The times called for a genderquake, and Jennings had just
helped pull the trigger.

9

BUILDING THE WOMEN'S MOVEMENT

They entered the 1970s as young mothers, wives and graduates, some of them active in the anti-war movement – most assuming they were modern and liberated and that the world was theirs. Until they found it wasn't.

Radical consciousness raising prised open their eyes, recalibrated their thinking and caused a seismic shift in the ground beneath them. Once they saw the sexism and systemic patterns of women's oppression all around them, they couldn't unsee it.

In their quest to unearth the primary source of female oppression, members of the Women's Liberation Movement uprooted lives, ended marriages, split families. Everything about what it meant to be a woman was ripped apart and restructured anew. 'In 1970 I had no idea just how subversive the ideas of women's liberation would turn out to be,' Anne Summers wrote, much later, as she looked back on those years.[1] 'We had changed our world – and so very much more,' recalled Julia Ryan in the mid-1980s. Later, when she was asked if second-wave feminism was worth the struggle, Ryan was unequivocal: 'Absolutely, yes. We had no choice. Once our awareness was heightened and our consciousness raised, we had to change.'[2]

But first women needed to grasp the need for change. Why change at all?

Who needs liberating, and from what?

Who needs liberating when life seems good – or good enough? When you're young, in your twenties, maybe thirties, racing forward, building that life you've mapped out in your head. You're educated. Independent. You have friends, a community, a job, maybe even a partner you love. Your sex life is pretty good. You might be married, possibly with a young kid or two. Other than the usual issues – income, rent or mortgage, job promotions – there is nothing getting in the way of living the life you choose. No obvious gender inequity holding you back. Some women might have it tough – restrictive parents, conservative family cultures, unreasonable expectations about wifedom and motherhood. But not you. You've got it worked out. Nothing stands in your way.

Maybe this describes you. It certainly describes me in the 1980s and '90s – minus the kids. Ironically, it's also how women a generation older than me, in the 1960s and early '70s, described themselves too.

Liberation? Who needs it?

Anne Summers published her first book, *Damned Whores and God's Police*, in 1975, when she was 30 years old. A forensic, historical exploration of the oppression and marginalisation of women in Australia, it still stands as one of our most important feminist texts. Yet, in the years leading up to writing it, Summers assumed she was as liberated as she needed to be. She describes her surprise when in 1967 she first read Juliet Mitchell's iconic essay, 'Women: The longest revolution': 'I did not see being female as any kind of handicap; as far as I was concerned, I could do anything I wanted.'[3] Ironically, at that time Summers had just got married and taken her husband's name, and was aware that until the marriage bar was lifted in late 1966, a new 'wife' would have had to resign her job if she'd worked in a bank or the public service. But she wasn't interested in that kind of work, so dismissed the draconian marriage bar law as something that didn't personally affect her. She could not have taken out a home loan on her own. But that wasn't an aspiration either. She couldn't have got maternity leave if she fell pregnant, nor a legal abortion; she could not have driven a train, piloted a commercial plane, or led a top ASX-listed company. There is a long list of 'could nots', but if they didn't directly impinge a young woman's immediate life aspirations, these sorts of issues remained somewhat opaque. Women were yet to connect the dots between entrenched, deliberate systems of female discrimination and the role of the patriarchy.

Like Mitchell, when writing and theorising about women, Summers still referred to 'they' and 'them', not 'we' and 'us'. It was all a little abstract. Women's oppression seemed to be happening to 'them', 'over there' somewhere. But not to 'me'. Not to 'we'. Interestingly, Summers notes that around this time American feminists 'seemed to be less disciplined, more emotional and they were starting to get very personal', whereas in the early days of the Australian movement, women's equality was often viewed as 'an objective problem, one that could be dealt with by the usual political methods'.[4]

Such thinking was about to change dramatically, once the practice of consciousness raising took hold. But before that could happen, women first needed to open their eyes – and minds – to their need for liberation. Surprisingly, back in 1970, it wasn't immediately obvious.

Julia Ryan was initially lukewarm on the idea. Her dear mate Biff Ward had just returned from a trip to Sydney, where she'd attended yet another anti-Vietnam War talkfest. Buzzing with excitement, she couldn't wait to tell Julia about an amazing session she'd been to where she heard about this new 'Women's Liberation'. Totally energised by a shift she was feeling in herself,

Biff said they should set up a Canberra discussion group. Julia wasn't so sure it was necessary. She wrinkled her brow and said, 'Well, I suppose there's still a way to go with equal pay.'[5] Which, in hindsight, was such a wry understatement, given it was only a year since Zelda D'Aprano and her mates had chained themselves to the Arbitration Court in their protest about equal pay. And job ads still stipulated 'male' or 'female' applicants, with salaries listed according to sex.

For Biff, the realisation that women needed to focus on liberating themselves came in a light bulb moment. Ironically, she had attended the 'women's session' at the Sydney anti-war event for the singular purpose of making a complaint. She viewed the gender segregation as divisive and wrong. Vietnam was the focus, not themselves. However, that rush of protest stopped short when she listened to the speakers. One of them, Julie Gibson, gave a very personal account of how she felt she wore a mask through life, trying to be someone she wasn't. She said she worked in a male environment and worked extra hard to 'fit in' by doing what men did. She explained she was always striving, yet failing, to properly assimilate into a world made by and for men. The penny dropped for Biff. She suddenly saw herself in Gibson's words.

Soon, Julia Ryan also had one of those 'awakening' moments. During the first Canberra Women's Liberation meeting, she listened as the women who had come down from Sydney outlined the social status of women in Australia: 'Yes, we've had the vote and legal emancipation in this country for generations, but how many women are in powerful positions?'[6] Julia had thought it was just a matter of time before that changed, but the speakers challenged that. 'In some spheres women are less represented than they were 40 or 50 years ago. We're either standing still or going backwards,' they said. The open question to the group was, 'Why?' (If this is sounding uncomfortably familiar. It should. It's become a Groundhog Day conversation still playing out today.)

Later, Julia wrote in her diary:

> I lay down my knitting, bent my head, spread my fingers over my eyes. I, who argued loudly for women's equality, was secretly puzzled by my own and other women's failure to push forward when legally the opportunity was there. I began to distinguish between emancipation and liberation. Emancipation was legal equality, the vote, entry to all spheres: liberation was acceptance as a social equal by the culture.[7]

The more women dug deep into their own lives, investigating their own experiences, and the more they talked and shared how they felt, the more they understood the links and connections in their stories. Very soon the quest for liberation became overwhelming. It wasn't equality with men that they wanted. It was liberation from them, and from the cultural attitudes and social norms of patriarchy that entrenched and maintained female inferiority. How to achieve it was unclear and unsettling. But once they started down that path there was no going back. Ever.

The Canberra Women's Liberation group met weekly on Wednesdays. According to Julia's diary notes, they initially decided to keep the group small 'until we'd worked out the details of our oppression'. A few months later, they opened up to new recruits and in November 1970 held their first public meeting.

Elizabeth Reid, a young single mum and philosophy tutor at the Australian National University, saw the advertisement in *The Canberra Times* and decided to go along. She joined another 60 women and men at a local public hall in the early evening. A rotation of speakers covered topics such as 'Women's conditioning', 'The difference between liberation and emancipation' and 'Suburban neurosis'. That last subject was a nod to Betty Friedan's searing critique on the role of the housewife. Her 1967 book, *The Feminine Mystique*, was claimed to have kickstarted second wave feminism, and Friedan herself was lauded by some as the 'mother' of the movement. But with their Marxist-socialist inclinations, some in the Australian movement found Friedan 'too bourgeois' and her theme too middle class.

Reid listened intently to the discussion. A 28-year-old Oxford-trained philosopher, with a steel-trap mind and insatiable appetite for ideas, she found that much of what she heard that night resonated deeply:

> I had lived the silencing, the sexual innuendos, the
> trivialisation of my thoughts and concerns, the 'no' means
> 'yes's ... These social constructs, these assumptions about
> the way the world should be, obscured the reality of
> women's lives, obscured the silencing, the violence, the
> indignities, and more, which made up this reality.[8]

Reid had travelled abroad and was appalled by the Australian mateship ethos, which she says badly 'twisted' the national psyche. She viewed the narrative around Aussie men as larrikins, tough, resilient, hypermasculine and 'manly' as a 'shocking, debilitating narrative for women to grow up with'. Compounding this was the stereotype of being 'just a housewife' that women carried around in their head.[9] At the Canberra meeting that night, Reid was struck by the commonality of women's feelings. Others shared her fermenting feminist frustrations. At last, she'd found her tribe. Others had too. Beryl Henderson, a 68-year-old, 'straight-backed' Englishwoman with glossy white hair, leapt out of her seat and famously called out, 'I've been waiting all my life for you girls!' The Sydney WLM group had a similarly aged woman, Bessie Guthrie, burst into their Glebe meeting saying the same thing. Clearly, Women's Liberation was intergenerational from the get-go.

Back at the Canberra meeting, when it came time for questions, a man raised his hand and asked if the women speakers would mind standing on their chairs. He wanted to see if they had anything worth looking at – perhaps their legs? Another chap present who thought that was a marvellously clever suggestion – at the ladies' expense – was columnist Alan Fitzgerald, who followed up the next day with a proud writer's flair for top-rate misogyny and sublime arrogance when he wrote about it in *The Canberra Times*. Fitzgerald was a well-known regular columnist – someone today we'd call an 'influencer'. He viewed the women's mission to change social attitudes and end female subjugation as deserving the full force of male mockery. He scorned the idea of a future in which women would have access to 'birth-control clinics, abortions on demand and free creches for children'. He mocked their call for women to participate in 'the responsibilities of citizenship', and the suggestion that husbands and wives could share household duties. Most of all, he was appalled by a 'future in which no job would be linked with sex or anyone discriminated on the basis of sex'. This was feminist Armageddon and Mr Fitzgerald was having none of it. He smugly told his readers: 'From the back of the hall, I asked Madam chairwoman whether, "the panel's denigration of the role of woman as a sex object would not carry more weight if even one of the panel was a passable sex object." There was a hush.'

Revelling in self-congratulation at his withering wit and the power of clichéd chauvinism, Fitzgerald ends with, 'The time had surely come to go. There was a lynching in the air.'[10] His article was published with a photo – not showing the dozens of women attending the meeting but a small handful of women outside who called themselves 'Anti-Women's Liberation Movement members'. They faced their sign towards the camera lens: 'We like being dominated', it read, stamped with a hand-painted upside-down peace symbol.

This was an important moment for the Canberra Women's Liberation group. There would be no lynching, just a razor-sharp slash of reality. This is what they were up against. Julia Ryan noted the moment in her diary as 'Our first group experience of the trivialising, sex-objectifying media attitude.'[11]

These women had grown up smothered by sexist objectification. Australian media reeked of it. They were used to it. But this very personal attack, mocking their new ideas and refusing to treat them seriously, was a swipe at all women attending the meeting. It was felt collectively. These were early days, but the personal was about to get very political. Beryl wrote a stern letter of complaint to *The Canberra Times* and told Mr Fitzgerald 'you have unwittingly done the movement a service'.[12] He had.

Media manipulations: 'Ain't we all sexy now!'

To fully understand the depths of anger and rage that stirred women to join the WLM, motivating them to rethink their lives and rearrange how they lived them, it's essential to climb into the belly of the beast and examine Australian media at the time. If you can bear it. For all its retro glow and tie-dye cheesecloth, 1970s Australia was in fact what Anne Summers would later call a 'thoroughly masculine construct'.[13] And that's putting it ever so politely.

The iconic gender theorist, Judith Butler, says we learn to perform our gender from a very young age. We learn what's expected of us – in a binary sense – from the moment we are born and declared 'girl' or 'boy'. From there we are named accordingly and then every message we receive about how to behave is gendered: boys do this, and girls do that. If you were a young, impressionable girl growing up in the '70s with a fascination for media, as I was, the message was clear: all the cool, groovy women, the women who got all the attention, were sex kittens and temptresses. They were voluptuous and curvy, and they wore short skirts, high boots and bikinis – or sexy aprons with frilly bits. They lay sprawled over cars, purred over perfumes – or ovens, eggbeaters or vacuum cleaners. Women and their bodies were used to sell everything, from boxes of matches to electric drills. The shameless mass-media titillation was full of tits. Whether you liked it or not.

Australian feminist magazines and newspapers – such as *MeJane*, *Refractory Girl*, *Mabel*, *Scarlet Woman* and the various WLM newsletters that countered and pushed back against the outrageously overt sexism of the Australian media – never surfaced in my little world. Nor did the wildly sexy and deliberatively provocative nakedness produced and published by prominent feminists associated with the Sydney Push, a progressive subculture active in the 1960s: women who, according to academic Catharine Lumby, were 'a loose alliance of libertarians and anarchists'.[14] Fired by sexual freedom, they celebrated the raw power of women's bodies and cunts. They whipped body shame with sexually liberated autonomy and cutting-edge creativity. While I was way too young to encounter this niche stuff, the participation of leading feminists such as Germaine Greer in producing and promoting it ultimately served to encourage and even inadvertently endorse the hypersexualisation of women's bodies in 1970s mainstream media.

In the summer of 1970, Greer was commissioned to guest-edit a special issue of *Oz* magazine – a provocative, counter-culture mag set up by a small band of Australian men in the early 1960s, and later expanded to London. Greer's issue was titled 'Female Energy/Cuntpower Oz'. She saw it as a ripe opportunity to indulge in sexual shock and awe – from a woman's perspective. Greer wanted to go hard: 'If I had been able to cover *Oz* with strong-scented pubic hair I would have done.'[15] (Alas, there were limits!) Twice during production of the issue, the London *Oz* office was raided by what Greer called 'Scotland Yard's Obscenity Squad'.

A quarter of a century later, when Greer reflected on the 1970 issue, I sense a faint hint of regret in her words as she notes the wild pace of the times meant 'there was no time to develop a visual language of female energy'. *Oz* readers, she says, were accustomed to women with 'dewy eyes and perky tits', and all she had time to do was turn them into creatures of 'springing hairs and thundering thighs'. In what she called an 'anti-fashion spread', Greer featured female bodies with 'crocheted stick-out nipples and an enormous bush on a modest bikini … modelled for the photographs by a girl-child – not my idea at all', she lamented later. Greer went on to argue the 'principal difficulty facing the feminist creator of propaganda images in 1970 was that so little of the process of producing, publishing and placing the images was controlled by women'.[16]

In short, Greer had just nailed the fundamental problem. While women remained outside the media machine, absent as leaders and controllers, during this heady time of social change and rapidly increasing consumerism, masculine norms led the charge. The rise of women wanting to flout female sexuality and the liberation of their bodies – along with their minds – opened market opportunities that were ripe for exploitation. Thus began the commodification of 'feminism' as a commercial brand. It enabled a hypersexualisation of female bodies that was sold back to women as a form of empowerment.

Media options in Australia in the early 1970s were exceptionally limited. In the major cities, three commercial TV stations, along with a well-funded ABC, formed the bedrock of entertainment and our primary sources of news. Most states had a couple of widely read and influential daily newspapers, with morning and afternoon deliveries. Local radio was a staple in many households. For housewives like my mother – when she wasn't on the phone – radio was a trusted companion. But while the choice of media was profoundly limited, the consumer appetite was huge. Everyone in my community read and watched the same thing. We kept pace with the same sitcoms. If there was a big story on the TV news, we all knew about it. We saw the world through the eyes of those intrepid men in safari suits, reporting from across the globe for the ABC, and later Channel Nine's *60 Minutes*. Back home, men dominated the airwaves. They read the news, hosted the TV chat shows, and wrote all the big, important stories in the papers. The few women on air, such as Caroline Jones, Claudia Wright and Margaret Throsby, were like rare, exotic birds in a forest of dark tree trunks. You always got the impression they were there with special permission.

Ultimately, every bit of information, entertainment and media stimulation was filtered through a male lens. The default setting was the male gaze. News values were male values. (And yes, they differed profoundly from female values at the time.) Men owned the media and controlled the output. Men decided what mattered and what didn't. In essence, it was a single-sex industry, with women on the sidelines. Other than exercising a choice about what TV or radio shows we might tune into, or what newspaper we might graze, Australians simply consumed what we were fed.

As a young suburban schoolgirl, growing up in a cloud of mindless media passivity while indoctrinated in the superiority of men, I absorbed the gender stereotypes that flooded my world. My father didn't buy the rude newspapers that had topless girls on page three, and near-naked women illustrating stories as diverse as the arrival of springtime to the opening of duck-hunting season. But our local newsagent was full of this stuff. It was impossible to miss. Like all the kids around me, I was imbued with this sort of stereotyping by osmosis. So ubiquitous was the hard sell of females as slavishly sexy, I don't ever recall anyone commenting on it. As kids, we weren't allowed to watch the racy TV favourites *The Box* and *Number 96* – replete with full nudity, sex scenes and shots of Abigail's bare breasts – nor that hypersexist British romp *The Benny Hill Show*. The issue wasn't that they were exploitative and dreadfully demeaning of women; it was that they were considered 'adult TV viewing'. We kids would just have to wait until we were 'grown up'.

By the time I was at primary school, the United Nations had turned its attention – for the first time – to the power of the media and its unrivalled ability to create and reinforce negative and damaging stereotypes. The 1972 Commission on the Status of Women (24th Session) passed a resolution acknowledging the role of the mass media in shaping perceptions of gender and influencing attitudes towards women. Energised by this, academic Pat Edgar and writer Hilary McPhee published the first comprehensive feminist survey of Australian media. It was a cracker. Titled *Media She*, it zoomed in on the 'chief stooge of the media man – the "sweet and simple" feminine stereotype, the women who "lighten" the pages of even our most responsible newspapers'.[17]

Similar international studies reported by the UN exposed a mass media out of control. It found 'discrimination and the perpetuation of an image of women as sex symbols and inferior beings' was the staple of media output. *Media She* focused on Australian advertising where, unsurprisingly, there was no shortage of wildly offensive material. Large bare breasts, fig-leaf nudity (one with a gorilla's hand in place of the metaphorical leaf), idiotic and infantile taglines spilling from the lips of housewives, secretaries, 'career girls', mothers – they were everywhere. Luscious women in bubble baths with protruding nipples sold bath salts; others, squatting in skimpy bras and pants, sold diet pills ('Now you can achieve the figure men admire'), or they lolled about in satin sheets ('Great in bed'); one advertisement showed a naked nymphette having skin cream erotically massaged on her body, under the headline 'Skin care starts at school'. Even a new brand of Magic sticky tape 'does for sticky what Women's Lib has done for women – it takes you out of hiding'. While I have no idea how women hide behind sticky tape, the super-sexpot secretary selling it, sitting at her desk wearing what looks like a leopard-skin negligee, makes the eye linger on the ad – out of confusion if nothing else.

Taken from television, cinema advertising, magazines and newspapers, the *Media She* survey's random selection of advertising represented what the authors called the stuff of 'our daily lives'. They argued (with good reason) that despite the clear exploitation and debasement of women – 'seen every day' – media sexism remained 'unrecognized for what it is'.[18] In what their male colleagues saw as 'harmless', the authors saw undercurrents of violence enacted on women. To prove their point, Edgar and McPhee conducted a very clever photoshoot experiment in which they flipped the genders. They took the highly sexualised, near-nude images of women flaunting their bodies and substituted the female model for a male. Then they showed the results to those men who earlier 'could not see what we objected to'. The reaction was embarrassed shock – and barely disguised revulsion. Seeing men adopt the infantilised poses used by women in regular advertising suddenly illuminated how extreme the media portrayal of women was, and how much it enfeebled and demeaned them. The degradation was seen more clearly for what it was – a manipulated, covert form of gendered violence. Edgar and McPhee insisted the photo flip was 'not a gimmick'. They were worried media might make light of this experiment – as if it were a joke – and repeat it. But they didn't. The ugly violence wreaked upon men was too profound.

So, did the *Media She* survey stop advertisers debasing women in this way? No. That wouldn't change for a long while yet. But as the first study of its kind in Australia, it kickstarted further investigation of media manipulation and exploitation of women.

Perhaps most fascinating and appalling in equal measure is the fact that women were exploited as both the 'seller and the sold'. Juliet Mitchell raised this in her book *Woman's Estate* when she unpacked the role of housewives as 'the main agents of consumption', while men were considered the agents of 'production' – the creators of wealth. Mitchell writes: 'Appealed to as consumers, women are also the chief agents of that appeal: used aesthetically and sexually they sell themselves to themselves.'[19]

Selling glossy sex to women

The explosion of sexual liberation gave rise to a swathe of new commercial media opportunities, and a new line of magazine publishing specifically targeting the 'new liberated' woman. Women's mags such as *Cleo*, *Cosmopolitan* and *Pol* hit the stands in the early 1970s. *Pol* – with a radically progressive publisher and a female editor – published the first Australian male centrefold in 1972, featuring Germaine Greer's new husband Paul du Feu. *Cleo* followed months later with a pale, hairy-chested Jack Thompson sprawled in the manner of Titian's *Venus of Urbino*, but lacking her eroticism or sex appeal. Nevertheless, the issue was a sellout.

But when is selling sex actually sexy, and when does it become sexist?

What these mags sold women was highly dubious. Dunked in the language of 'liberation', there was plenty of freedom for the body but little for the brain. Worse than 'housewife' magazines that promoted traditional roles for women, Edgar and McPhee in *Media She* argue these new glossies were 'more seriously sexist because they pretended to offer liberation'.[20] The feature article in *Cleo*'s male centrefold edition was a multi-page spread: '*Cleo*'s sensual and sensible guide to keeping a sexy house'. *Cosmopolitan*'s tagline was 'Even if you're not glossy, the least you can do is think and feel glossy.' I was never sure what that meant. Are we talking lip-gloss glossy? Or wet-vagina glossy?

Flying high on the booming market for women's magazines, Helen Gurley Brown, editorial director of *Cosmopolitan* in 13 countries and queen of the glossy scene, arrived in Australia from the US in late October 1975 and was whisked into the ABC TV studios in Sydney for a live recording of *Monday Conference*.[21] A serious chat show hosted by Robert Moore, *Monday Conference* was regular viewing in my house. But to my ten-year-old way of thinking, the topics discussed were dull 'men's business': politics, public policy, economics. In the lead-up to 1975, less than a handful of women had appeared on the show as expert speakers or panellists. The few who did were mostly international women with outstanding expertise, which fed a sense of female exceptionalism. The message to my young mind – and no doubt to thousands of other females watching – was that you only get to talk about serious matters on TV if you are an incredibly 'exceptional' woman. (As for ordinary, unexceptional men talking on air, that was a given.)

But 1975 saw a distinct effort by the all-male editorial team at the ABC to include more female speakers in their *Monday Conference* line-up. A month earlier, the show had featured an all-women cast, including Elizabeth Reid, for one of the most substantive discussions on women's liberation ever broadcast in Australia. But now, with a few feminist runs on the board, the prime-time show wanted to explore women's liberation and 'sex appeal'. Sort of. Host Robert Moore was keen to dig a little deeper into what the media glossies such as *Cosmopolitan* sold as 'liberation'. Here's his opening question to Gurley Brown:

> It does seem to me there is something of a conflict in the psychology or the psyche of the magazine itself. I mean, on the one hand you're saying, as I take it, 'Women, live for yourselves, don't live through men, don't just be the mere appendage of a man.' And yet on the other hand, you're also telling women how to be prettier, smarter, even richer in order to catch a man.

Gurley Brown sat to attention, excited by the provocation. Oblivious to the exposure of her own sexism, she told Moore that those two things are not incompatible:

> To be a sex object, so to speak, to be desired sexually by a man, is a fabulous thing to have happen to you. But there generally are more available women than there are attractive available men. And men are so valuable and we need you so much [close-up camera shot of Gurley Brown batting her eyelids] that we should do everything we can to have one of you in our lives for our very own.
>
> And to do that you have to beat out the competition. At the same time you want your own career: you can be ambitious as anything and do everything you can to get on in the world on your own terms professionally.

Moore points out that this ridiculous and contradictory suggestion sounds like something his grandmother might say, minus the bit about a career. But Gurley Brown digs in. It's 'wonderful to look as pretty as you can and to be healthy and attractive and to have your hair, body and face look as beautiful as possible – that's partly for a man', she says. 'But a lot of that is your own wellbeing and happiness, and I must say that I think you are more appealing to men when you look good and sound good, and we promote doing a great many things to be alluring.'

Baffled, or perhaps bemused, Moore asks, 'So, where does *Cosmopolitan* fit into the … women's movement or feminist movement?' Gurley Brown smiles broadly and insists that *Cosmo* is very much part of the women's movement – 'We just have a different way of going about it.'

By now the audience can smell a fake. Not your regular ABC *Monday Conference* suited audience, this lot look a little less like Gurley girls and more like Reid rebels. We'll never know if the audience was stacked with Women's Liberationists, but soon Gurley Brown is ducking for cover.

An audience member attacks her over *Cosmo* advertising that suggests women should 'talk less and listen more to their man'. With a broad smile, Gurley Brown defends the campaign, suggesting that 'a woman who doesn't have a brain, who isn't articulate, can't talk to a man, doesn't understand what he's talking about' is better off being a passive listener. The audience member lobs straight back: 'All women have brains, and *Cosmopolitan* seems to be trying to make them forget that.' Another asks Gurley Brown what *Cosmo* thinks 'femininity' means. Once again, Gurley Brown runs the train off the rails: 'Femininity means you love being a woman … you love turning on for men and having them sexually attracted to you.' When another young audience member says she has no interest in polishing her husband's shoes and wants to know if that makes her 'unfeminine', Gurley Brown looks baffled until she is reminded that *Cosmo* had run an article about the joy of polishing men's shoes. 'Oh sweetie, I don't think that would have anything to do with femininity,' she coos.

While Moore must have felt like he was watching a women's ping-pong match, the women in the audience kept hurling accusations of absurdity at Gurley Brown. One pointed out that while *Cosmo* told women it is 'a very lovely thing to be a sex object', what if 'you don't want to be objectified?' A hailstorm of questions followed – about older women, single women, poor women, plain women, migrant women. Where did the kaleidoscope of women's lived experiences fit into the *Cosmopolitan* view of feminism?

While Gurley Brown kept her composure and sweet smile, we will never know what she really thought of these combative Australian women. This was a tough gig. The questioning was intended to unsettle. Admirably, however, the antsy audience did not attack the glossy queen personally. Instead, they targeted the substance of her inherent sexism and exploitation of women, and resisted her claim that a woman's power resided in physical beauty and talent to compete for male attention.

Often in a live studio broadcast, it takes a few outspoken audience members to embolden others. However, on this occasion, the steady stream of pushback fired at Gurley Brown suggests women were accustomed to thinking and talking about these issues, and were unafraid to call out nonsense when what was masqueraded as 'liberation' didn't add up – in ordinary women's lives.

The timing is important here. It was late 1975, when the frenzy of sexist and negative media coverage spawned by International Women's Year had infiltrated every corner of the country. No matter where you stood on women's rights, or Women's Liberation, by this stage few Australians were unaware of the rumble of change. And despite the derision they copped, women themselves were increasingly asking questions.

When it came to the issue of race, a beautiful model in the audience landed a bullseye on Gurley Brown's forehead. As a woman of colour, she asked why *Cosmopolitan* in Australia had never had a black woman on its cover. Gurley Brown deferred to the Australian editor, Sylvia Rayner, who was sitting in the audience and who stumbled indignantly. Rayner explained that cover models were chosen mostly from women who come into the office and leave a portfolio of shots. 'I've never seen you in the office so I wouldn't even know you exist,' huffed Rayner.

'But I'm not the only black lady in the country,' the model shot back.

'Well, I've never had a black lady come in,' snapped Rayner, adding, 'I can't go and look for them, I'm too busy.'

'Oh, well,' said the model, 'I'll see you in the morning.' The audience exploded with laughter and applause.

While the female audience members weren't holding back, it was a man who raised the issue of female nudity in the magazine. He admitted he liked nude pics, but said, 'I can't see why a woman would enjoy looking at them.' On this, Gurley Brown was emphatic. 'Women do!' she enthused. 'Women like to look at other women naked.' Now, here was an opportunity, an opening for Gurley Brown to earn herself a dab of redemption: nudity is natural, it's healthy, the female form is beautiful to behold, women enjoy female eroticism, *anything*. But instead, she sank all women into the melting pot of female competition as she happily chirped: 'It's partly narcissistic. When you're looking at other women, you're comparing yourself with her and saying, "How do I measure up?" … When you see women in a room … you're looking to see what they're wearing and what kind of bosoms they have.'

It was all downhill from there. Exasperated by her Australian audience's unapologetic interrogation, Gurley Brown threw the switch to romance. 'I absolutely believe that romance is going to resurface,' she said brightly, 'because we've gotten so unmysterious and so flagrantly frank about everything, I think people are longing for another *Gone With the Wind* chapter.'

I wish I could end here with a line about 'quaint' musings from the former US queen of women's magazines, musings that are today blurry and lost in sepia sentiment. But I can't. Because 50 years later, here we are, in the thick of a mainstream magazine culture – played out online – that is obsessed with romance, marriage, weddings, couplings, bachelorettes and beauty. If you squint while watching this old footage and perhaps throw in a few 'trad wives' to sit on set with Helen Gurley Brown, we could well be watching a contemporary chat show. Morning breakfast TV, perhaps?

But it is worse than that. It is not just trad wives, steeped in domesticity and subjugation, who personify Gurley Brown's 1970s media creation of 'femininity' and warped version of 'liberation'. Today our pop culture and social media is awash with women who would make Gurley Brown proud. Women for whom adornment and physical attraction – 'hotness' – is paraded as the pinnacle of female power. Their highly curated presentation may be wrapped in the lingo of women's self-empowerment, perhaps with a dash of diversity thrown in for virtue-signalling, but at its core this is little more than market-encouraged narcissism, driven by alarming levels of commercialised sexism.

I am utterly perplexed and dismayed by how thoroughly women have become 'the seller and the sold', as Juliet Mitchell put it half a century ago: women selling themselves to them-selves. Never have we had so many tools that demand we play this game. From the moment we wake in the morning, our social media feeds urge us to rate one another: to like, love, applaud and repost, in an endless endorsement of competitive envy, aspiration and judgment.

But this too is where lessons from the past, from the Women's Liberation Movement, have the power to steer us beyond our contemporary media malaise and our obsessive on-line marketing of brand 'me' – towards a stronger, truer, feminist future.

Bra burning and other media misdemeanours

No one loves an enemy as much as the media. Mainstream media loves to hate. To that end, the Women's Liberation Movement proved a perfect foil. Liberation was super sexy when there was gloss to sell and new revenue streams for male proprietors, but it was presented as immoral and dangerous when the patriarchy needed some propping up. Mainstream media has always been a critical tool for entrenching patriarchal dominance and ideology – which is why Donald Trump's inner cabal at his 2025 inauguration was a posse of social media tech bros and media barons, with elected members of Congress shuffled out of camera shot.

Back in the early 1970s, as soon as women's voices began to emerge as part of a collective movement pushing back against male dominance, the patriarchy wasted no time in pulling the power levers on information control. The Women's Liberation Movement made no effort to hide or operate in secret. It welcomed all women, everywhere. But its overt presence, while inclusive and broad, also made it an easy target for unchecked media attack and wild ridicule.

From the outset, Women's Liberation was blamed for all manner of social evils. According to breathless media reports, it was destroying the family, creating a spike in crime and respons-ible for 'the increasing suicide rate among women in Western societies'.[22] To combat the latter, Professor Peter Sainsbury, a British psychiatrist, told a Brisbane audience that women should return to housework, arguing that the 'security and sense of belonging generated by a housewife's life, while sometimes boring, reduced the possibility of suicide'. (Clearly he hadn't read Betty Freidan's data on the epidemic of housewives' addiction to tranquillisers.) A visiting US 'futurologist' warned Australian husbands that 'Libbers' would be anti-booze, and 'when [the wife] gets more educated she won't stand him going off drinking like that'.[23] Media headlines proclaimed that 'Women's Lib frightens the men', after 'Mizz' Gloria Steinem railed at US 'press men' for not reporting women's activities seriously.[24]

The obsession with bra burning across the media of the Western world began in 1968, when angry women, fed up with the parading of female flesh like juicy meat, staged a demonstration against the Miss America pageant in Atlantic City. Bra burning, of course, never actually happened. US feminist writer and journalist Robin Morgan was one of the pageant demonstration organisers, and she later reported: 'The demonstrators mock-auctioned off a dummy of Miss America and flung dish-cloths, steno pads, girdles and bras into a Freedom Trash Can.' She says the 'act of bra-burning' was 'totally invented' by 'the male-controlled media'.[25] But the titillating tool of denigration stuck. In 1970, when reporting a large women's demo held in Washington, D.C., Australian headline writers couldn't help themselves: 'Bras burnt: Thousands of women march for equality.'[26] Yet not a single bra was brandished, binned or burned at that march.

While American members of Women's Liberation insisted on speaking to female reporters, their Australian sisters didn't have that luxury. There were too few women on the beat. A similar but smaller demonstration through the CBD of Sydney in 1970 was met with a hail of questions about the 'aim' of the women's movement. Was it all about 'equality' the reporter wanted to know? The response, from an unnamed woman, was, 'There is no one main aim – there is a whole complex of aims.'[27]

This was perhaps the first whiff of what would become a theoretical point of departure from the US as the Australian Women's Liberation Movement carved out its own unique place in feminist history. They were thinkers, talkers and theorisers. On occasion they were also great pragmatists. At times there were considerable tensions, as women theorised their way into a new form of revolutionary practice. While the aims and methods were a source of debate, there was one thing clear across the Australian WLM – the endgame was not 'equality'.

Equality is not the goal

If you have become increasingly irritated by bland and often baseless bureaucratic references to 'gender equality' and the sort of corporate posturing we see around International Women's Day, when company directors boast how many women they've employed, you can take heart from the Australian Women's Liberation Movement's concerted lack of interest in 'equality'. As I have noted, 'equality' with men was not the aim – which is an idea some readers may find surprising. Equality was not ambitious enough, nor an accurate reflection of the full and complete transformation that Women's Liberation wanted.

As far as Germaine Greer was concerned, 'equality' lacked edge. It was tepid. The quest for 'liberation', though – well, that was something entirely new and radical:

> The idea of women's equality threatened nobody, for
> it took the status of men as the ultimate that women
> could aspire to; the question of liberation was far more
> disturbing in its implications. An unfettered woman could
> be increasingly redrawing the limits, redefining her own
> nature and the relations she might have with others.[28]

When she was visiting Australia in 1975, British feminist Juliet Mitchell was blunt about equality being too limited a concept. It was a wasted ambition, she told an audience in Canberra, 'and we're not going to get it'.[29] Elizabeth Reid went further. She argued equality was not only unambitious and narrow in scope, but dangerous – a blinding distraction. In mid-1975, Elizabeth Reid lectured a somewhat stunned audience at the United Nations on why 'equality' was counterproductive to women's progress. 'Equality is a limited and possibly harmful goal,' she declared. Although the struggle for equality had produced 'some needed and just reforms: equal pay, equal access to formal education and vocational training, equality under the law, and equal rights to vote and to run for public office', she argued that hitting equality 'targets' would not solve the greatest problem plaguing women's lives the world over – sexism:

> We can no longer delude ourselves with the hope that formal equality, once achieved, will eradicate sexist oppression – it could well merely legitimise it. For there is a real danger, a very real danger, that satisfaction with the achievement of formal equality will encourage the belief that all problems are thereby solved. However, even if formal equality would be achieved, all else still remains to be done.[30]

Reid was not only dead right but ahead of her time. Current debate about feminism's 'solvedness' speak to the direct danger of using equality as the key measure. When we believe that all legal barriers to women's full participation in public and professional life have been dealt with, we are encouraged to think the job is done, that feminism is finished, and that any remaining issues must be either an individual matter of 'personal choice' or evidence of 'natural differences' between genders.[31]

As prime minister John Howard put it in 2002, 'the feminist battle has been won, it's over' – it was no longer 'an issue'.[32] Which of course was utter tosh back then, and total tosh now. It is intellectual laziness and precisely what Reid was warning about back in 1975. Legislating to enable women access to opportunities they were previously denied, is a mechanism for gender equality, and a very necessary one, but such mechanisms and legal enablers do nothing about changing fundamental attitudes and beliefs. They have little or no impact on the deep-seated sexism that fuels belief in male superiority and continues to empower patriarchy.

Interestingly, a couple of decades later, Reid deepened this analysis to provide a powerful critique of our current-day practice of 'institutionalising gender analysis'. Put simply, gender analysis is a systematic approach to assessing how policies, laws and practices, in any given context, may impact men and women differently. It is supposed to help root out gender biases that are so baked into organisations that no one has stopped to ask – for example – why there are no women in the executive leadership. Unfortunately, however, many workplace attempts at 'gender analysis' are little more than counting exercises, and Reid argues that this approach treats what is effectively a tool for mapping gender as a type of human resources fix-it. She argues that such analysis does little to transform the *quality* of women's lives. Instead, it simplifies binaries and ultimately disempowers rather than empowers.[33] All the while, the core problem remains: the dominant presence of sexism that is deeply embedded in our social and cultural norms, directing our behaviours and responses.

Now, well into the 21st century, while we may have a more sophisticated understanding of how sexism threads through society, drives consumerism and dictates media algorithms, sexism nevertheless remains a fundamental part of our gender conditioning. A neoliberal pimping of post-feminism might argue that an 'empowered' woman – a 'girl-boss' imbued with 'girl power' and independent agency – is not susceptible to sexism, that she won't fall 'victim' to it and can somehow rise above it. But women know this is not true. No matter how strong and empowered we purport to be, we cannot live in this world without internalising sexism. The unwritten rules about how we are supposed to perform our gender and what is expected of us are so deeply ingrained in our psyches that we continue – perhaps unwittingly – to shrink ourselves to fit in. Reid again:

> This fitting of oneself into a smaller space, an enfeebling space, cannot be captured in a gender analysis, or through pro-diversity or pro-equality initiatives.
>
> Sexism works against the emergence of a sense of self in solidarity ... A politics of access, or opportunities, does not reach anywhere near the social and psychological condition that marks the lives of women more profoundly than those of men.[34]

Reid's take on the contemporary use of gender analysis as an overused workplace tool helped me understand why my own focus on building an institution dedicated to improving the numbers of women in leadership was a folly – a busy distraction that failed to create any fundamental shift in men's attitudes towards women. In fact, our research indicated the opposite – a correlation between women's workplace progress and increasing male backlash. Our work identified what has now become a clear trend: the greater number of women in leadership roles in workplaces, the greater the sexist, 'anti-women' attitudes among men.[35]

Perhaps the last word on equality should go to Germaine Greer, who, strictly speaking, never attached herself to the

Women's Liberation Movement. Instead, this global media megastar styled a more individualistic approach to liberation. While the WLM was full of radicals and rule breakers, all members shared one golden rule: no leaders. No hierarchy of voice. No 'stars'. A precocious intellect and independent libertarian, Greer could never abide by such confines, so she flew straight through the feminist radar rather than under it.

The publication of *The Female Eunuch* in 1970 shot Greer to international fame and was considered mandatory reading among Australian members of the WLM. While expressing many of the same concerns that troubled Elizabeth Reid, Greer closed her famous book by urging women to free themselves from guilt and shame and their own 'tireless self-discipline'. Liberation, she wrote, demanded a self-styled personal transformation: 'It does not understand the phrase "equality of opportunity" for it seems that opportunities will have to be utterly changed and women's souls changed so that they desire opportunity instead of shrinking from it.'[36]

Greer's final words insisted that 'reforms are retrogressive', and that 'the old process must be broken, not made new'. While many radical feminists within the WLM agreed with that (arguments about the value of reforms aside), it was Greer's final sentence – 'What will you do?' – that was a key point of departure. Those classic closing words implied personal responsibility. A singular challenge. The message was 'it's now up to you'. Where the WLM used collective solidarity and sisterhood to help one another transform from 'shrinking' woman to flourishing woman, Greer's view was 'you're on your own'. She never diverted from insisting the path to female freedom and liberation was a solitary one. Her consistency on that made me laugh out loud when, nearly 40 years after *The Female Eunuch* had shocked the world, Greer snapped at an audience at Adelaide Writers' Week: 'Don't follow my flag.

I'm not a tour operator … All those women who say to me, "You changed my life" … no I didn't. You changed your life.'[37]

With no intention of being tour operators, the Women's Liberation Movement nevertheless did hold up a flag, of sorts. A welcome flag to all women. As Reid put it:

> To become a feminist is to begin to identify how what happens to me, happens to others, and that this 'happening' is part of a social structure … But to bring about feminist revolution, we needed to (collectively) understand what changes were necessary and how these changes could be brought about.[38]

To end patriarchy, these young Women's Liberationists knew they first needed to understand it. To do that, they had to develop a coherent platform that was accessible, transformative and inclusive. 'We knew that how we did things was as important as what we did,' Reid later wrote. 'Our task was to create a revolution in the act of living it … It was not a case of reform versus revolution, but of working out how we could create a revolution that would unfold alongside our reforms.'[39]

Now, 50 years since that first meeting of the Canberra Women's Liberation group, Biff Ward smiles warmly when I ask about 'living' the revolution. She tells me that in the 1980s, when the noise of Women's Liberation had faded and the weekly meetings had stopped, people would still mockingly ask, 'Aren't you liberated yet?' Her answer then was the same as it is now: 'Our belief is that until every woman is liberated from sexism, no one is.'

10

SISTERHOOD AND STRATEGY

Across the nation, Australian women's lives were fundamentally changed or challenged by the Women's Liberation Movement, whether they were involved in it or not. The
movement mounted a full-scale disruption of the status quo
with an aim to smash assumptions about gender divisions. Social
constructs were ripped apart in efforts to peel back the restrictions
that had kept women sidelined and inclined to shrink. Systems
of gender control were identified. Patriarchy was unpacked and
exposed. (Not dismantled, mind you. Not yet.) Afterwards,
nothing remained the same. Women most of all.

Even my mother Joan, a conservative, Catholic woman,
secreted a clandestine copy of *The Female Eunuch* in her wardrobe,
wrapped in a brown paper bag (yes, as a child I was a prize snoop).
I have no idea if it helped my mother 'humanise the penis'. I
doubt it. But, if nothing else, at least talk of women's liberation
made her curious enough to perhaps try. My primary school days
were punctuated by my mother's endless meetings – gatherings
of church women. I was too young to connect the dots, but since
inheriting Mum's faded 1972 copy of Greer's bestseller – billed
on the front cover as '#1: The Ultimate Word on Sexual Freedom'
– I've long suspected that book was the subject of many long
afternoon discussions in the lounge room. Those ladies certainly
weren't talking gospel as they emptied all those casks of Moselle
and smoked Alpine cigarettes.

Unlike the women's movement in the US and the UK,

Australia managed to effectively embrace both 'revolution' and 'reform' in the early 1970s by creating a unique and exceptionally powerful platform of action, knowledge and influence. So, how did they do that? Where did they start?

'We needed a theory but there was no theory with which to frame our work, no accumulation of feminist literature,' says Elizabeth Reid. 'Mostly we developed our theory little by little by listening to and then reflecting on the stories that poured out of the women in small group discussions.'

Women's Liberation meetings varied from group to group, with some more informal than others. But the connecting thread that wove throughout the movement was the fundamental centrality of women's own lives and bodies. According to Anne Summers, the insistence on centring women was a hallmark of the radical feminism they developed, and a point of their ideological departure from socialist feminism.[1] 'We were our own evidence,' says Biff Ward.[2] While a 'women-centred approach' might seem an obvious strategy to contemporary minds, the fact such emphasis was a deliberate and concerted shift from the norm and considered radical at the time says a great deal about how invisible women's lives, experiences and concerns had been.

The weekly meetings were a critical way of changing that. Discussions strengthened women's confidence, empowering them to become their own change agents as they worked out new ways to live their lives. Although famously – and occasionally infamously – 'anti-hierarchical', the meetings required some level of rules. Some groups distributed speaking tokens to determine when and how often women got to speak. Others chose topics a couple of weeks in advance and women took turns to write or deliver papers and lead the discussion. Over time, the Women's Liberation Movement developed a core set of practices around 'Voice', 'Consciousness raising' and 'Sisterhood'.

Voice

Once upon a time, women were reluctant to talk about themselves, and they avoided using pronouns such as 'I' or 'me'. Imagine that! Social media has now shaped a world in which our lives are 'performed' more than consciously lived, and oversharing what we do, eat, wear and think, suggests an anxious need to be 'seen'.

According to Elizabeth Reid, the practice of 'Voice' began with the difficult task of encouraging women to simply speak up:

> The approach was one of theorising through autobiography or through storytelling. This was a conscious strategy since, for many women, using the personal pronoun, 'I', was so difficult. Instead we might say, when talking about our own experiences, 'Women say ...', or 'I have heard it said that ...', or 'We ...', but to use 'I' was often to reveal too much.[3]

Seemingly straightforward, the practice of Voice was – and still is, as I've recently discovered – rather tricky. The idea was to ensure every woman participated equally. Given the movement was strictly against any form of domination, the practice meant those accustomed to normally taking charge – the educated and articulate, or highly opinionated – couldn't. They had to learn to put a sock in it. Women could not appropriate other women's stories but instead spoke from their own experience. Each woman's story was listened to, respected and reflected upon. The idea was to make space for every woman without interruption. 'The theoretical basis for this practice lay in the collective experience of women being silenced. This was such a common experience there was a shared sensitivity to women becoming themselves the silencers,' Elizabeth Reid explains.[4]

I recently joined a small intergenerational group of women writers who use this practice. In addition to deep listening, we have also adopted the WLM courtesy of not plying the speaker with questions as she talks. As someone who grew up in a noisy family where six kids fought to speak over the top of one another, verbally muscling in to be heard, I was shocked at how hard a formal respect for Voice proved to be. Initially I tried to excuse my interruptions by explaining that as a journalist I'm plagued by curiosity – hence I can't help but volley questions at the speaker. The women were impressively patient, until eventually a senior member of the group stopped proceedings and drew an invisible zip across my mouth. Chastened – but warned – I got it. It took serious effort for me to learn to shut up, but with concerted effort and practice at staying silent, I have become astounded at how much more I not only hear but comprehend.

Consciousness raising

Half a century after the Women's Liberation Movement peaked in Australia, it is hard to imagine how extensively the practice of consciousness raising (CR) changed and rearranged lives – particularly for young women in their twenties and thirties. But it did. Whether we are aware of it or not, we continue to inherit the benefits of those radical social shifts in women's psychology.

Consciousness raising didn't just 'happen' by osmosis. It was something women worked at together, usually in small, private groups among women they trusted. It was a grassroots practice in which women shared their individual experiences with a group, in order to unravel the patterns and see the connections. It was about learning to understand the true nature of women's oppression. Through questioning their own circumstances, women quickly saw how their personal struggles were in fact political: rooted in systemic sexism and deliberate, well-organised forces of discrimination.

Not long after sitting with Biff Ward as she explained the profound impact of these 'brain-exploding' CR sessions women held in the 1970s, I had coffee with a young student I admire who excitedly told me how the discovery of a new style of coffee had 'absolutely changed her life!' (The previous time we'd met, it was macarons.) With declarations of 'awesome' and 100 per cent infatuations aside, I love her enthusiasm. I really do. But it got me mulling over how it is even possible to convey the sort of epoch-changing shift our feminist foremothers experienced, when these days we eat superlatives for breakfast.

'It is difficult to exaggerate the magnitude of these changes, just as it is almost impossible to remember that women were once quite different,' reflected Anne Summers, decades later.[5] American academic Elisabeth Jay Friedman, an international expert on CR, is more blunt: 'Humans are humans, but women are no longer women in the same way as the seventies.'

Friedman laughs uproariously when I tell her the first I ever heard of 1970s consciousness-raising sessions were whispered stories about women sitting around in circles, on beanbags and cushions, using hand mirrors to check out their vaginas. 'Yes,' she says, 'there was a bit of a fad' among some groups to do this, but it wasn't as big a thing as some suggest. Friedman says those particular sessions occurred in response to the publication of *Our Bodies, Ourselves* by the Boston Women's Health Book Collective in 1970. The first book of its kind, it encouraged women to get to know their bodies and reproductive organs, and provided information about women's sexuality, lesbianism, abortion, sexual identity, birth control and a list of issues that, until then, were simply never discussed beyond whispered, private conversations.

Although the CR-style genitals inspection originated in the US, like many of the movement's practices it quickly hit Australian shores. I hesitated when asking Anne Summers about it, assuming the Australian Women's Liberationists – who were astute theorists and perhaps a little more politically inclined and policy focused than their US sisters – may have ignored this rather confronting group practice. But not at all. Anne delighted in telling me how she and a small bunch from the Sydney Women's Liberation group squatted down at journalist Liz Fell's house, in Paddington, and got to work with mirrors and plastic speculums to become intimately equated with their own vaginas. She recounts this one-off event in her memoir *Ducks on the Pond*, saying that it was 'the first time in our lives [we] saw what our cervixes actually looked like'.[6]

Intimate inspections aside, the deep value of CR was the opportunity it gave women – usually for the first time – to question the assumptions and conditioning they grew up with, identify the patterns of oppression in their lives, and ultimately build new forms of independent identity. 'Its premise was that women could come to understand societies and their structures because of the lives that each woman had led, not despite them' is how Elizabeth Reid puts it: 'The aim of the WLM was, among other things, to end all forms of patriarchal oppression. But we were not just against the shackles of oppression; we were struggling towards a new sense of positive identity for women, both individual and collective.'

To understand just how radically new this thinking was at the time, Biff Ward says it's important to understand the extent of political radicalisation sweeping through Australia in the late 1960s and '70s. 'It was as if a whole lot of different forces came together and created this huge, historic moment, which was also happening in America and other Western countries,' she recalls.

The anti-war protest movement in response to Vietnam, along with the powerful civil rights movement in the US, created a very radicalised generation powered by the sort of radicalised thinking their parents would never have dreamt of, such as questioning authority and social structures. And then there was this intervention about gender, about sex roles, and suddenly we were talking like we'd never talked, telling stories we would never have told.

American writer Kathie Sarachild – one of four women who infiltrated the US Miss America pageant in 1968, unfurling a banner proclaiming 'Women's Liberation' – wrote extensively about consciousness raising in the US, and viewed the weekly discussion sessions as one of the primary 'educational, organizing programs' for Women's Liberation. By the early 1970s, she said, 'women who at first didn't think they needed it [were] all doing it'.[7] According to Elisabeth Friedman, the beauty of consciousness raising was that it could take place wherever women came together, whether it was women who worked together, met for kids' playgroups, volunteered at the school tuckshop or lived in the same street (or perhaps even gathered for church meetings). She says it was as simple as women hearing about it and deciding to have a discussion themselves, 'without having to wait for instructions from some central organisation'. In Australia, Elizabeth Reid says, 'By International Women's Day 1974, there were small consciousness raising groups all over Australia, even in rural and remote Australia.'[8]

Critically, the repeated word, almost to the point of being a mantra used by every woman with whom I've discussed CR, is the word 'trust'. With revealing insight, Anne Summers explains it like this:

Trust was essential in consciousness raising because women had been taught to be competitive with and suspicious of one another. It felt strange and often frightening to be telling your innermost secrets, something you might once have told only your closest girlfriend, to a room full of women you scarcely knew. Yet if mistrust were replaced by solidarity – by sisterhood – men would be less able to dominate by divide and conquer tactics.[9]

Perhaps unsurprisingly, what Summers calls 'this new solidarity among women' became increasingly 'unsettling for many men'.[10] Julia Ryan's husband eventually felt so threatened by the change she was undergoing and the solidarity she felt for the sisterhood that he accused her of 'emotional adultery'. Soon after, they split.

Consciousness raising today

Far from being a fad, or a practice that women outgrew, Elisabeth Friedman says CR not only 'undergirded the extra-ordinary explosion of the Women's Liberation Movement', but it was fundamental in creating what we now call 'feminist consciousness'. The practice of CR provided the infrastructure for analysis and action which we continue to use today, even though we may not directly identify it as radical feminism, or acknowledge the feminist legacy in what we are doing.

As discussed earlier, we saw feminist consciousness erupt in Australia in 2021, in the lead-up to the March4Justice. Inter-estingly, it was the first time in decades that the word 'feminism' had been used broadly without cringe – including in the media. The term itself connected women to a sense of solidarity in our collective fury at the government's mistreatment of women and failure to treat allegations of sexual violence seriously. The very personal experiences shared by women – Brittany Higgins, Grace Tame, Chanel Contos, Saxon Mullins and dozens of others – were the trigger. But the personal resonance felt by women across Australia beamed a blindingly bright spotlight on the patterns of oppression, dismissal and belittling that all women experience when they complain. The rush of conversations around this time – the personal sharing, intimate disclosures, connections made and systemic discrimination exposed – were consciousness raising on a national scale. The power of the patriarchy to control the narrative and shut down women's voices became demonstrably evident in prime minister Scott Morrison's initial – some might say instinctive – response.

Globally we witnessed a very 21st-century version of consciousness raising when #MeToo erupted in the US in late 2017. Unlike the protected privacy and intimacy of the CR sessions developed by the women's movement, #MeToo used individual experiences of sexual abuse and rape to build collective solidarity by effectively shouting through the megaphone of social media. Elisabeth Friedman likens this to a sort of 'CR 101', but on a mass scale: 'That's a very different place to start, to go public with your experience, rather than [first] use your experience to build solidarity and identity. And then theorise why this is happening and strategise what we should do.'[11]

Despite #MeToo's 'shout first' method, the fundamental driver nevertheless remains the same – it's all about the politics of women's own experiences. Most importantly, lived experience is not only valued as primary evidence; rather it is valued because *it is* primary evidence. Friedman believes a renaissance of consciousness raising is occurring among young women now, in the mid-2020s. Her sense is that this is happening with a return to the more intimate, private, face-to-face style of gatherings first developed during the Women's Liberation Movement.

The story shared by Chanel Contos, when she went public back in late February 2021, is a classic example of a contemporary consciousness-raising experience (no hand mirrors or plastic speculums needed). I happened to be researching CR in the Women's Liberation Movement at the time the story broke, and I was still trying to get my head around how feminist awakening worked in a group setting. When aging Women's Liberationists told me about their 'exploding brains' while sitting in CR sessions listening to other women share their intimate truths, I struggled to understand how the so-called 'aha moment' happened. Was it extreme ignorance, or social complicity, or a mix of both that meant women were genuinely shocked to learn of other women's degrading experiences, particularly around sex?

Then I heard Chanel Contos speaking on radio and I got it. Here was the scenario being played out all over again.

I later contacted Contos and interviewed her on my podcast *BroadTalk*. Living and studying in London, she was in the early days of her advocacy journey and still coming to terms with the enormous impact her moment of 'awakening' had had. We spoke at length about her shock at realising how deeply entrenched rape culture was in her social circles, to the point where it was not only normalised but 'romanticised'. Contos repeatedly blamed herself and her friends for allowing this to happen: 'We made it. It's the culture we've created. Girls just want to be the cool girl and want to be accepted by the boys and [so] they opt into it. We're taught to internally be competitive with other women, to bring them down and to rate them.'[12]

In all this self-flagellation was a very concerted attempt to unpack and understand their own oppression as women and girls. How had it come to this? Did the boys – most of whom were their friends, or part of their wider social circles – have any idea how much their demeaning and selfish sex acts traumatised their female schoolmates?

Contos explained how she had been staying with a small bunch of girlfriends, sitting up late one night talking, when the subject turned to sexual assault. Initially it took the form of gossip, and then – as she later detailed in her book *Consent Laid Bare* – the young women began naming names of the various boys, now men, who had assaulted girls they knew. Names and stories were swapped and very quickly a pattern emerged. These weren't one-off incidents. Forced, unwanted sex and sex acts without consent had been rampant in their social circle throughout their teenage years. 'It is fucking unbelievable,' Contos writes:

> Eventually, we share our own stories with each other. For one of the girls, it is her first time telling anyone. When I name my perpetrator, one of the girls tells me that this same boy did a very similar thing to a mutual friend of ours … What if I had reported him? But then, how could I have done? I didn't even know it was a sexual assault.[13]

The following day, still processing their shock over the group's revelations, Contos and her friends spent six hours in a car travelling home. 'Lots of time to chat,' she wrote. 'We share more stories, and brainstorm about what can be done.'

The rest is history.

With the help of friends and family, Contos mounted one of the most successful public advocacy campaigns in recent history – 'Teach us Consent' – to get the Australian school curriculum rewritten. It now includes guidelines for sex education at all school age levels. This was a phenomenally successful outcome from what began as an informal conversation among a small bunch of young women who gave space and deep trust to one another. It was indeed classic contemporary consciousness raising – they just didn't know it.

She's no longer with us, but I reckon Julia Ryan – the chronic chronicler of Canberra Women's Liberation meetings – would have loved Chanel Contos' story. I can almost hear her madly applauding these young women and whooping with joy at their contemporary version of what Ryan dubbed the feminist 'Mode' of action. The Mode was a way of women working together to reach transformative change. Her dear friend Biff Ward says Ryan spent years developing her theory of the 'Mode'. 'In essence it was our way of operating,' Biff explains. 'As we saw it, the purpose of feminist action grew from first understanding how you were "feeling". It was about asking and exploring your experience. From there, you begin to work out what you want to do. And then you work out how you are going to do it. All of this happens collectively, although it doesn't mean everyone had to do everything. And out of that process, somehow, enormous trust grows.'

Something else that grew, too – well beyond any woman's expectation – was what they soon came to call 'sisterhood'.

Sisterhood

Some years ago, I scored an old, fat, fading copy of the classic 1970 anthology *Sisterhood is Powerful: An Anthology of Writings from the Women's Liberation Movement*, edited by the iconic American feminist writer, poet and civil rights activist Robin Morgan. Inside the front cover is a handwritten message: 'For Pam – some of this is fascinating – with love from Noeline. New York, 1971.' It made me laugh. This is 600 pages of the most radical feminist writing of the times, and Noeline is warning Pam that only 'some' of it is fascinating.

For a reader today, more than half a century later, the whole tome is a fascinating insight into how raw, new and deeply confronting many of the issues being discussed for the first time were, even to women who considered themselves radical, such as Morgan herself. She opens the book with an admission that before collaborating with dozens of women to produce it, she had 'shied away from admitting' that she was oppressed in any serious way. (Can you hear a familiar echo here? 'Liberation – who me? What for? I'm as free as I need to be.') With startling honesty, Morgan writes:

> I also nurtured a secret contempt for other women who weren't as strong, free and respected (by men) as I thought I was (that's called 'identifying yourself with your oppressor') ... Especially threatening were the women who admitted that they were simply unable to cope with the miserable situation we were all in, and needed each other and a whole movement to change that.
>
> Well, somewhere during (this) year, I became such a woman – and it's been a radicalising experience. I still don't fully know how it came about.[14]

The clue to how 'it came about' is embedded in the title of the book – 'sisterhood'. The phrase 'sisterhood is powerful' was first coined in a Women's Liberation flyer written by Kathie Sarachild. Sarachild, along with Morgan, was part of a small gang of women known as the New York Radical Women, who viewed radical activism as central to dismantling the patriarchy. But it was the work of collective consciousness raising and developing a powerful trust in sisterhood that ultimately led Morgan to fully experience the true depth of her unacknowledged feminist anger: 'The history we learned, the political sophistication we discovered, the insights into our own lives that dawned on us! I couldn't believe – still can't – how angry I could become, from deep down and way back, something like a five-thousand-year buried anger.'[15]

The groundbreaking feminist publication *Ms.*, founded by Gloria Steinem, was first introduced to the public in late 1971 as a lift-out in a special edition of *New York Magazine*. It opened with an essay boldly titled 'Sisterhood' by Steinem, in which she wrote about the impact of sisterhood as 'the exhilaration of growth and self-discovery, the sensation of having the scales fall from our eyes'. She argued that 'women understand' one another in a way that men just don't: 'The odd thing about these deep and personal connections of women is that they often ignore barriers of age, economics, worldly experience, race, culture – all the barriers that, in male or mixed society, had seemed so difficult to cross.'

Steinem went on to describe the enormous sense of liberation she felt now that she could 'admit anger, and use it constructively, where once I would have submerged it and let it fester into guilt.' She concluded with what read almost like a personal prayer:

I no longer feel strange by myself, or with a group of women in public. I feel just fine.

I am continually moved to discover I have sisters.

I am beginning, just beginning, to find out who I am.[16]

Sisterhood became a precious mantra among Australian members of Women's Liberation. For journalist Anne Summers, who would go on to become editor-in-chief of *Ms.* in the late 1980s, the notion of 'sisterhood' seems to have emerged as an unexpected by-product of women's collective toil:

As we met and talked and planned and did things together, something surprising began to happen. It became apparent that we were leaving behind our traditional, instilled competitiveness with and even dislike of most other women and were learning to value and appreciate each other. We began to seek out and take pleasure in each other's company, often in preference to men's, and to hold women-only social events. Not just conferences and meetings but dances and parties too. This was more than friendship. It was – there was now a word for it – sisterhood.[17]

Sue Jackson was just 18 years old when she joined Women's Liberation in Melbourne, and quickly becoming a celebrated activist. Like most Libbers, she found that spirit of sisterhood stuck with her for life, and her description of it is magical. She said you can see the effect of sisterhood for yourself by just looking at photos of the era. 'From Margaret Whitlam on ... all the women of that time, there's a look on the face. That wide-eyed sort of bright and hopeful look ... this sense of joy and power coming from this working together and working it out and the scales being taken from the eyes.'[18] Elizabeth Reid smiles when I ask about sisterhood and recalls a favourite comment by journalist and Canberra Women's Liberation group member, Helen Shepherd, who said sisterhood 'was like a petrol pump: it kept you going and going'.[19]

While sisterhood in Australia was felt by many as an open embrace, Indigenous women did not experience it in the same way. Unlike the women's movement in the US, the Australian movement was not founded on the back of a powerful civil rights movement and broad-based black activism. Consequently, issues of race and class were not centred or understood as they were in the American context. In 1987, Indigenous academic Jackie Huggins wrote: 'Unfortunately, despite all the rhetoric about sisterhood and bonding, white women are not sincerely committed to bonding with black women to fight sexism.'[20]

A foundational member of the women's movement, Indigenous woman Pat Eatock, traversed a nuanced path when speaking of sisterhood. Eatock arrived in the capital as a single mother with a baby in arms. She became a key player in the Aboriginal Tent Embassy, and an active participant in the Canberra WLM group. In 1972, Eatock proudly became the first Indigenous woman to run as a candidate for federal parliament (with Elizabeth Reid as her campaign manager). Later she joined the Australian delegation to Mexico to participate in the Tribune conference in 1975.

After her death in 2015, Eatock's daughter Cathy carried on her advocacy work and in 2023 joined me on stage at the Canberra Writers Festival, for a special event celebrating the 'radicals and rebels' of International Women's Year. 'There was a tension for many Aboriginal women and the feminist movement,' Cathy told the audience. 'Many perceived Women's Liberation as middle class and not addressing the source of their oppression, which they attributed to colonisation, dispossession and of course white violence, which has been targeted on Aboriginal women since invasion.'[21] These tensions would flare during the landmark Women and Politics Conference, held in Canberra in late 1975. The experience of Indigenous women has been critical to developing a more intersectional understanding of feminism and the development of sisterhood in 21st-century Australia.

Standing in the wings:
Sisterhood and the feminist continuum today

As a young woman starting out in my journalism career, I always felt a twinge of envy when I heard older women speak of female solidarity and 'sisterhood'. I had female friends I loved, and women I worked closely with, but claiming a sense of sisterhood seemed too much of a stretch. Almost as if sisterhood was a club for which I hadn't earned the rights to membership. But as I grew older, wiser, more worldly and politically astute, the depth of my feminist anger against relentless patriarchal power ballooned into something quite overwhelming. Gradually my sense of connection to sisters everywhere took hold. It's now part of who I am: an inextricable, philosophical and emotional link to all women. But can I boldly proclaim this 'sisterhood'?

Around the time I was pondering this, I received an unexpected note.

It's uncanny, isn't it, how sometimes, just as we stand on the brink of a question, something – or someone – comes along to nudge us over the threshold towards our answer. Here's what happened.

Early in 2025 I found a card in my mailbox that struck at my heart. Chewed by the snails – because I rarely check for mail – it was an old Christmas card. The woman who sent it had had a stinker of a time with a philandering husband, a broken heart and a family in collapse, so I was surprised she was sending out cards at all. She is younger than me and we are not close friends, although we meet up at various events and occasionally fangirl each other on social media. But it's what she wrote in signing off that caught my breath and reminded me of how important the use of 'we' has come to be: 'I can't pretend that this past year or so has been good. I have been broken. [But] I have been touched by kindness and solidarity. This year I have learnt just how much the sisterhood is real. Thank you for being a part of that.'

Perhaps it is like buying a new red car – suddenly it seems as though every other car on the road is red. Once you start looking for sisterhood, you see it everywhere. It's a shame we don't acknowledge it more often, because it is so affirming when we do.

After the tumultuous year of 2021 and the eruption of

consciousness raising that swept Australia, I noticed a deepening of women's relationships all around me. We took greater care in looking out for one another, taking the time to talk and to listen. When Grace Tame and Brittany Higgins shared the podium at the National Press Club in early 2022, in another powerful performance from both, I was struck by the gentle space they held for one another, despite their differences. Here were two women with vastly different backgrounds: Higgins a political conservative, an apparatchik who viewed working for a Liberal government as her 'dream job'; Tame an edgy progressive who doesn't shy away from making political statements on prime ministerial turf, like a strategic side-eye to Scott Morrison in front of news photographers, or sporting a 'Fuck Murdoch' T-shirt when visiting prime minister Anthony Albanese at The Lodge. Yet, political and character differences aside, there was a vibe of solidarity between these two women as they faced the national press.

There is something profound and powerful that stirs in women when they recognise another victim-survivor. At such times, that shared connection activates an innate sense of sisterhood – one that has the power to override all else, even if it's just for a short time in their lives.

At face value, the concept of sisterhood can seem quite straightforward, perhaps like the Australian use of the word 'mateship'. But it is more than that. It is not simply about friendship forged through shared and perhaps profound experience. Sisterhood is multidimensional. It has deep empathy and respect for all women at its centre. But the glue is the purpose – support and solidarity. This is where seeing ourselves as part of a continuing lineage of feminist energy is the most empowering thing we can do.

The late, great Australian feminist Dale Spender was relentless in urging young women to understand that they are part of a long feminist past and collective continuum. Spender was one of the most prolific feminist writers in our history, and her 1983 book *There's Always Been a Women's Movement This Century* argued that the historic practice of forgetting and erasing women's contributions and achievements – as well as their rebellion – means each generation of women is left feeling they are starting from scratch.

In my first year at university, I stumbled upon her massive and brilliant tome, *Women of Ideas and What Men Have Done to Them*, published in 1982. In the years since, Spender's work helped me see more clearly the everyday sexism around me – in language, in work practices, in the TV news program I worked on. I had read my way through de Beauvoir and other international feminist texts, but reading Dale Spender was different. She was Australian and an authority on feminist linkages: linkages that hadn't occurred to me previously. Her driving theme of women's connections and the feminist continuum has since become an enduring theme in my own work. Not just out of respect for history, but because it helps make sense of our 'now' and fortifies our feminist future.

'If we believe we are without a past … our collective strength is undermined, and the idea that we are inferior takes hold of our minds and helps to construct the bonds of our oppression,' she wrote. Women must do the important work of making connections and building bridges where there are gaps in our knowledge of feminist lineage, she believed. 'Unless we take matters into our own hands and actively make those links we are just as effectively divided from older women, as we are from women of the past.'[22]

Acclaimed feminist historian Sharon Crozier-De Rosa takes up this theme in earnest when arguing the case for ditching talk of feminist 'waves' – such as the 'first wave' of suffragettes back at the turn of last century who won women the vote; the 'second wave' in the 1960s and '70s that turned full focus on women's liberation; and the 'third wave', with which I loosely identified, a somewhat vague connection of Gen X women who in the early 1990s thought we were redefining feminism by putting the word 'post' in front of it. As for the 'fourth wave', there is no agreement on when it started but the development of social media, Facebook, MySpace and similar platforms saw a new feminist generation emerge around 2010. Marked by technological savvy and prominent digital activism, this wave is perhaps best identified by its broad intersectional embrace of diversity and fierce fight against gender-based violence and sexual harassment.

I must admit, I initially resisted Professor Crozier-De Rosa's argument. I believed that acknowledging feminist 'waves' was a way of honouring the women and the work that distinguished those periods. But Crozier-De Rosa has convinced me that speaking of these waves 'seems kind of rude'. Rude in that it overlooks – or, as Dale Spender says, forgets – the huge amount of women's activism and energy in between those waves, which is instrumental in bringing about the next crest. Focusing on waves also suggests feminism only exists in blocks of time, and that in between those waves it disappears altogether. It doesn't.

'I think younger feminists and other activists feel like they're starting anew, and they have to find all this energy to begin anew,' Crozier-De Rosa tells me. 'But no. There is a legacy, a momentum to continue. You are not alone … you are in fact part of a long and strong history of women's activism and you should draw strength from that.'

Spender's book *There's Always Been a Women's Movement* is a 'radical' book even today, says Crozier-De Rosa, 'Not least because of its potential to inspire feminist consciousness-raising, which is vital if we are to address a form of alienation that some younger generations of feminists profess is prevalent today'.[23]

What young women yearn to learn

If the suggestion that young women might feel 'a form of alienation' seems like a big call, Crozier-De Rosa has good cause to say it. I first met her at an event held by the Whitlam Institute in late 2023 to celebrate Elizabeth Reid, marking five decades since her appointment as Whitlam's women's adviser. Crozier-De Rosa was one of a panel of speakers I hosted, along with Reid, the star of the occasion.

At the conclusion of speeches, when taking questions from the audience, an ANU student stood up and asked a question of Reid that melted the hearts of feminists in the room. Zoe Mitchell explained that she was interested in the role of 'personal story' in contemporary feminist debate and wondered if Reid had any advice on how young women's voices can be 'leveraged to help create change'. The real melting moment was when, fumbling for the right words, Zoe said, 'I was wondering how to merge the disconnect felt on social media and a post-capitalist perspective on feminism?' Apologising for her nervousness, Zoe continued to outline what Crozier-De Rosa later described as 'a pervasive feeling of disconnection and aloneness as an emerging feminist'.[24]

Days afterwards, I met with Zoe over coffee to hear more. She explained that while she and her friends had experienced what she described as, 'a consciousness raising when sharing our stories and anecdotes in small groups', she was left frustrated that 'there is not really any forward momentum. It's just kind of like the sisterhood stops there'. It was a heartfelt conundrum about feminist connection. Back at the Whitlam Institute event, Elizabeth Reid responded to Zoe by urging her and her colleagues to make a concerted effort to return to physical gatherings and face-to-face encounters. She assured the young woman that the unique experience of being present, along with the practices of deep listening and holding space for others, has a transformative power.

This was certainly not the only time I had witnessed women seek some form of solace about sisterhood from Elizabeth Reid. A few months earlier, at a packed event at the Australian National University, Elizabeth was quizzed by another young audience member. 'How have you maintained the rage?' the young woman asked. Then, in reference to the older feminists and members of the Women's Liberation Movement in the audience, she added, 'And how has this group stayed together and stayed motivated?'

The question came from Renee Jones, one of the organisers of the Canberra March4Justice. Back in 2021, a week before the march, Renee and another member of the Canberra crew had joined Elizabeth Reid and a dozen women from the Women's Liberation Movement for lunch, and spent a glorious couple of hours listening to these energetic women – some of them octogenarians – share their laughter, their stories and their excitement about the upcoming rally. 'We had very specific goals for meeting with them,' Renee told me later. 'We wanted to tell them about what we were trying to achieve and ask them if there were any things we should consider [ahead of the rally]. And I also wanted to thank them and let them know that we were standing on their shoulders.'

At the panel in 2023, for a moment Reid looked flummoxed over the source of the group's enduring motivation. 'That's a very important question,' she said. 'I've never thought it through.' Then she looked down at the front row of the audience to Biff Ward: 'Biff, have you thought about it?' The audience laughed. Forty years after they had met, Reid said she and her Women's Liberation sisters still shared what she called 'a gross passionate outrage'. They have been meeting monthly for the past decade and will for the rest of their lives. The message was clear –

sisterhood is solid. It sustains all of life's various chapters and changes.

As we charge through our busy lives, building careers, families and friendships, we don't often stop to consider those who came before us as much as we should. Yet, if we heeded Dale Spender's advice, and sought out stories of the countless women who have traversed the path we think we are building afresh, I have no doubt we would feel less lonely on our journey and absorb tremendous strength from what we learn.

The 'tyranny of structurelessness' and the odd mini-tantrum

These days I'm an out-and-proud champion of the sisterhood. But it would be remiss of me to be dewy-eyed about sisterhood and fail to mention that our feminist foremothers, back in the 1970s, gave it a fair old battering when strong opinions differed – when women radicals were radically uncooperative with one another and radical lesbians even more so. Of course it happened. No revolution can occur without internal biffo. And the Women's Liberation Movement was no exception. There were tensions, hostilities and fallouts. A couple of key national women's conferences held in January 1973 highlighted how things occasionally went awry – even among the sisters. At a residential weekend conference held at Mount Beauty in the Victorian Alps, arguments over sexism and perceived persecution of lesbians by non-lesbians within the movement derailed the conference agenda entirely. Some very personal attacks left lingering scars.

In the twilight years of Women's Liberation, historian Silvia Kinder wrote, 'The concept of sisterhood became the theory of unity.'[25] But such unity was always going to be problematic, when insistence on anti-hierarchical, flat structures meant sometimes the talk went in endless circles. Literally. Prominent member of the Hobart Women's Liberation group, Kay Daniels, left a WLM conference in Sydney utterly exasperated at what she called the 'non-organisation' and 'time-wasting'. She later wrote in the feminist newsletter, *Liberaction*, that the Sydney women were too 'mellowed by sun and sisterhood' and that 'the interminable introductions around the circle made me feel like a brownie on my first day out'.[26] Ouch! American feminist Jo Freeman penned her famous essay 'The tyranny of structurelessness' in the early 1970s, warning this would occur: 'Unstructured groups may be very effective in getting women to talk about their lives; they aren't very good for getting things done.'[27]

The essay was circulated in Australia in numerous formats and the fundamental argument absorbed. Women who were dominant in the WLM, such as Anne Summers, later admitted that the movement did have leaders, 'we just didn't admit it'.[28] The Women's Electoral Lobby (WEL), on the other hand, was more overt about its leadership, with named 'founders' and elected convenors. As for 'structurelessness', WEL was the antithesis of the WLM. But that didn't stop the 'sisters' within WEL from spitting out a few expletives occasionally.

A week before the conference at Mount Beauty ended sourly, the Women's Electoral Lobby had held a conference in Canberra. It too had descended into bitter argument – not over theories around sexism and lesbianism, but over process, governance and how centralised the organisation should or should not be. Journalist Julie Rigg had been billed to deliver a concluding paper on 'The future of feminism'. Ironically her core argument was to be that sisterhood was 'one of the most valuable things to emerge from the new feminism'. But the day's angry disputes and open rivalries made her ditch that speech, which would have seemed 'farcical'. Reporting on this for the feminist publication *MeJane*, Anne Summers wrote: 'The conference itself was characterised by a degree of distrust and even acrimony that totally belied the notion of much sisterhood within the ranks of WEL.'[29]

Summers was not a member of WEL and it should be noted that, although it was a powerful and successful lobby group, it operated very differently from the Women's Liberation Movement. They were 'reformers', not 'revolutionaries'. WEL members weren't necessarily looking for transformative changes in social attitudes, or even in women themselves. With a focus on what was practical and possible, they lobbied directly for policy changes, such as childcare, child endowment payments, equal pay and reproductive rights – which were also of concern to the women in the liberation movement. But WEL's style of hierarchical leadership – in order to get things done – set it apart from the revolutionary ambitions of the liberation movement. Nevertheless, both groups were grounded in sisterhood, imperfect as that might be. Indeed, a significant number of WEL women got an additional fix of sisterhood by also joining their local Women's Liberation groups.

The party and the PM's 'Supergirl'

Ahead of the Australian federal election in 1972, WEL conducted a groundbreaking survey of all the political candidates to ascertain their views on issues and policies affecting women. It was certainly radical in concept: until then, politicians had never been asked about women's issues. The survey's value as a strategic feminist tool to build public awareness was outstanding, even though it didn't result in getting a single woman elected to the House of Representatives. What it did achieve, however, was solid data that proved an overwhelming majority of political candidates held deeply sexist and misogynist views.

The only candidate to receive a score of 40 out of 40 for positive attitudes towards women was Pat Eatock, running as an

ACT independent. Despite their exhaustive efforts, Pat didn't win. It took another 41 years before Australia was ready to elect an Indigenous woman into federal parliament.[30]

It's unthinkable now, but neither the Liberal nor Labor parties included any specific women's platform in their 1972 election campaigns. Not only was the women's vote assumed to be influenced by the male values of husbands, fathers and boyfriends, there had been no national research on what women wanted from their political representatives.

By the time Gough Whitlam had his victory in December 1972, the Women's Liberation Movement was agitating for serious radical change. It was time. They didn't know it on election night, but a radical, militant feminist from Canberra Women's Liberation was about to step up and make national and international history.

On a Saturday night in late March 1973, 18 shortlisted women candidates for an intriguing new job as the prime minister's special adviser on women arrived at a highly bizarre job selection soirée. Held at the home of Labor Party heavy Gordon Bilney in the Canberra suburb of Hughes, it was a pleasantly warm evening, with the doors thrown open as women kept arriving. Anne Summers remembers the party. So too does Biff Ward. And Elizabeth Reid – as she should; she was one of the star job candidates circling the room. Dany Torsh, a journalist who later founded the Media Women's Action Group, was there too. Like Reid and Summers, Torsh was one of the shortlisted candidates, there to impress and circulate. But Torsh doesn't remember much about it, other than she had a great time. Did she chat with the new prime minister, Gough Whitlam, or his wife Margaret? 'Oh, I don't know,' Torsh laughs when I ask her. 'I just got stoned.' She wasn't the only one.

There was music and laughter as women weaved through the packed rooms of this small family home. Biff can't recall who invited her. In fact, other than the shortlisted candidates, no one seems to know who invited the other 50 or so women who turned up. But no one seemed to mind. The beer and wine flowed. A few sneaky joints blew a sweet scent across the garden. And the street was jam-packed with cars, little Beetles, Holdens, a few family station wagons and a bunch of official Commonwealth cars, there to ferry the government ministers and various Labor luminaries home. But no one was in a hurry.

Biff recalls sitting on the kitchen sink, drinking wine, 'as you did in those days', when a rather striking woman in a 'wild lime green pantsuit strode through the kitchen like a panther'. Some years later they'd become great friends, but that night Deborah McCulloch, who had set up a branch of WEL in Adelaide and went on to become women's adviser to South Australian premier Don Dunstan, was one of the few women at the party Biff didn't know. Yet all the women present were linked by an unspoken, singular force. 'We were a tribe,' is how Biff describes it. 'There were invisible threads connecting us as we moved among these men, a sure and certain knowledge that we and our new agenda were the reason we were all there and that we had these men ever so slightly on edge.'[31]

There was a palpable frisson in the air. It was nothing to do with sex and everything to do with sisterhood. Most of the women were young, in their twenties or early thirties; many were in their first jobs, or the first women in their families to have jobs. Nearly all of them were committed advocates or activists within the women's movement. The 'party' was part of a week-long job selection process that was not only unprecedented but utterly novel. It's hard to imagine today, but the applicants themselves partly determined how this process would run.

The creation of the job had taken the women's movement by surprise. They hadn't lobbied for it. No head of government in the world had appointed a women's adviser. This radical idea came from Peter Wilenski, the principal private secretary to Gough Whitlam. Wilenski was married to Gail (now Radford), a self-proclaimed 'anarchist' and active member of the WLM. Wilenski urged Whitlam to appoint an adviser with a background in the WLM, arguing 'it [is] the most important social movement of our time'.[32] Whitlam didn't need convincing. When the United Nations had proclaimed 1975 as International Women's Year, Whitlam had embraced that idea. He was a strong internationalist and valued the opportunity such a focus on women could deliver.[33] Domestically, he saw the political brilliance in appointing someone with a background in the women's movement to the inner sanctum of his ambitiously progressive government. But finding the right person would mean a bit of guesswork.

Around 420 people applied for the job, including around 20 men. Those who made the shortlist were flown to Canberra and put up in the same local motel, near Parliament House. Soon the candidates got together – most knew one another – and decided to draft a joint media statement to emphasise their sisterhood and confirm their collective commitment to work with whichever one of them got the job. In addition, the group demanded the new Whitlam government set up an inquiry into the status of women. In recent years, I've seen a few collaborative gestures among women applying for the same senior role, but never anything quite like this. It was, well, *radical*. There's a famous photograph, published in *The Australian*, that shows six of the leading candidates – Dany Torsh (before she got stoned), Eva Cox, Suzanne Baker, Anne Summers, Elizabeth Reid and Lyndall Ryan – all squashed together on a motel-room bed, photographed after issuing their press release. It looks more like a Women's Lib project meeting than a group of candidates vying for the same job. The Canberra Women's Liberation group printed T-shirts brandishing the now famous symbol –

the clenched fist – on the front, and the word 'Superwoman' on the back. Dozens of women wore them to the party. Anne Summers wore hers to the job interview.

While this extraordinary solidarity among the job applicants might seem unfathomable today, it was completely in sync with the way the Women's Liberation Movement operated. When I ask Dany Torsh how serious she was about getting the job, we both laugh. I tell her I doubt I would even drink a glass of wine, much less get stoned, if I knew I was being assessed for the role of prime ministerial adviser. 'I was really stupid,' she laughs. 'I couldn't really speak very cleverly. I ruled myself out. But, you know, I sort of half-wanted it, but I also half didn't want it.' I find this fascinating. For what was clearly a fabulous job opportunity of a lifetime, none of the candidates seemed too fussed about getting it. Anne Summers wrote, 'Many, perhaps most of us in all honesty, did not think it mattered which of us got the job.'[34]

Taken at face value, such seemingly blasé attitudes to this newly created and potentially powerful position could be read as either career ambivalence or even doubt about the value of the role. But neither of these was the case. It's important to remember how novel even the concept of a 'women's adviser' to a prime minister was back then. No other government leader in the world had viewed the systemic discrimination and oppressions women face as worthy of specific executive government attention. Women's miserable lot as secondary citizens was 'just the way things are' and, presumably, the way they would stay, with a bit of natural, trickle-down progress along the way. Of course we now have amassed enough ring binders to circle the globe full of evidence that there is no such thing as 'natural progress' for women. Women have had to fight for every single legislated right and social advance in history. When it comes to power, nothing – *nothing* – is ceded.

So, back in 1973, the move by Prime Minister Whitlam to install a women's adviser within his inner sanctum of four senior advisers, someone who would have direct access to him, and whose advice he would take and act upon – well, it was no small thing. While the applicants can't have foreseen how big a role it would become, given the lack of precedent, those on the shortlist of candidates were nevertheless smart enough to value the revolutionary potential it offered. That's why they were there. But as evidenced in the joint press statement and proclamations of support for the appointee, whoever she might be, they understood the women's adviser role was a product of the success of the women's movement. It was about all of them. Not just one of them.

The media lampooned and ridiculed the candidates from the outset, dubbing them 'supergirls'. Cartoons depicted them as contestants at a crass beauty contest. The women hit back. In one of the only press articles to actually interview the women about the role, candidate Suzanne Baker – a journalist herself – lashed her colleagues for treating them like 'media freaks'. Elizabeth Reid, however, gave a detailed account of 'some of the areas the job might entail', which included issues such as childcare and abortion law reform, trade union attitudes to women, and various other subjects debated at Women's Liberation meetings over the previous couple of years. She told journalist Jacqueline Rees that whoever got the job 'must reach those women not in women's movements, too. She should be able to let all these women – black and white – know that there is someone representing them. For the first time in the history of Australia there is a real chance to do something for women.'[35]

Elizabeth Anne Reid's appointment as adviser to Gough Whitlam 'on a range of domestic issues, especially those bearing on the welfare of women', was announced on 8 April 1973. The $10 000 annual salary was considered substantial – for a woman.

The next day, Reid agreed to an 'all-in' press conference at her home. It was a train wreck from the moment that one of the dozens of men crammed into Reid's living room said, 'Let's make sure our cameras are rolling, chappies. Okay Eric? We're on.' Reid, dressed in an attractive shirt dress and possibly sporting a dab of lipstick and mascara, was physically backed into a corner of the room, up against a wall, with ten or so reporters squatting at her feet, shoving mics at her, firing inane questions and making outlandish accusatory statements like: 'You disagree with marriage and only just tolerate children' (which was news to Reid's beloved five-year-old daughter Kathryn).

Dubbed the 'PM's Supergirl' from that day on – with all its overtones of sexist ridicule and trivialisation – Reid was asked about abortion, prostitution, rape, lesbianism. Not a single question was asked about the job, what she intended to do, or what she viewed as the problems facing Australian women. Given her media inexperience and with a philosopher's training to take questions at face value, Reid simply answered what was asked of her, providing considered arguments around the morality of an individual's right to choose. The next day's front page of Sydney's *Daily Mirror* ran a screaming headline: 'PM's Supergirl says: LEGALIZE POT, ABORTION'. Numerous articles referred to Reid's lack of bra and, frankly, little else. Others butchered quotes from student lectures she'd given years earlier on masturbation. The prime minister was immediately tackled in parliament about his new adviser's 'views and attitudes of womanhood'. According to Reid, one MP even stormed across the parliamentary chamber and tossed media articles at Whitlam, saying, 'Is this the woman you say can represent the women of Australia?' Another asked if Reid intended to advocate 'legalising prostitution and homosexuality'.[36] With the tone set, it was all downhill media muckraking from there. A Melbourne *Herald* columnist who began, 'Would the sisterhood please stand still for a moment and stop wobbling under their T-shirts?' devoted column inches to the difficulty of pronouncing 'Ms'. Was it 'M stroke S'? He settled on 'Miz'. The same bloke spat with mockery when hearing about Reid's intentions for International Women's Year in 1975. 'Elizabeth Reid wants to … somehow bring together CWA sponge-maker and Women's Lib shrieker.' His final line was pure sneer: 'Out of a year of women's talk, meetings, exhibitions, may emerge the new Australian phenomenon – the female individual. But that's only if they ever stop talking.'[37]

Throughout history, women with steely spines and super-strategic minds have been seriously underestimated. Australia's Elizabeth Reid was one such woman. But those around her knew what she was capable of. Julia Ryan mused that Prime Minister Whitlam probably 'valued her quiet intellectual demeanour' when he chose her for the role, without realising that she was in fact the most radical among them. What's more, she had a plan! As Ryan saw it, 'She took the pure Women's Liberation method of operating as guiding light in that job.'[38]

When it was all over, Gloria Steinem asked Reid the question no one else had dared. 'Why were you, a radical feminist, chosen for this position in the first place?'

Reid's response: 'Who knows?'[39]

What Elizabeth Reid achieved, and the extensive reach of her radical influence, has never been fully understood or appreciated in Australia. But international experts laud her success in shaping radically new feminist thinking at critical global forums. When it came to International Women's Year and its all-important UN World Conference on Women, Elizabeth Reid emerged as a global 'feminist rock star', whose message back then has not diminished with time.[40] Indeed, in the face of increasing global backlash against women's progress – fuelled by expanding misogynistic theocracies and Trump-style tech-bro fascism and male supremacism – the overarching message Reid took to the world stage in 1975, about the insidious power of sexism, has alarmingly urgent resonance right now.

PART 4
INTERNATIONAL WOMEN'S YEAR, 1975

The women's movement in Australia has now entered
into the decision-making world, not merely in order to
be equal with men, or to learn to play tired old games,
but in order to change the world.[1]

Australian National Advisory Committee
for International Women's Year

It is a story about people looking at the world from
what appeared to be the brink of revolution and trying
to imagine their places in a world made anew.[2]

Jocelyn Olcott

11

EYES ON '75 AS THE SHEILAS SHIFT THE FOCUS

In 1975, our world switched to colour. On 1 March, Australian television flicked from black-and-white to colour TV. The historic moment was kicked off by a ludicrous Aunty Jack sketch on the ABC, in which a fat man dressed as a woman stomps on green jelly and asks Norman Gunston, parading as a pirate, 'Where are your tits?' He then sounds an alarm as colour bleeds onto the screen and he yells at children that he'll 'rip ya bloody arms off' if they dare watch black-and-white television ever again. (And to think that conservative commentator Bob Santamaria was worried about the 'intellectualised garbage' that he claimed had been spoken about International Women's Year'!)[1]

I'd like to think Australia introduced colour TV just in time to celebrate International Women's Year (IWY). After all, television first arrived in suburban homes in 1956, to coincide with the opening of the Melbourne Olympics. But watching women from around the globe debate and shape the future of half the world's population doesn't excite ratings as much as the punch-up in the men's water polo semi-final. That said, International Women's Year was wild with colour. And there were plenty of verbal punch-ups, even a famous physical tackle on stage in Mexico, at the United Nations World Conference on Women, in June 1975. But unlike the men's 1956 water polo semi-final, no blood was spilt.

The United Nations – an overwhelmingly male bastion – battled to get the idea of a year devoted to women through its General Assembly. Those firmly against it didn't believe a World Conference on Women was necessary. Or even made sense. Why a special focus on women?

While not explicitly anti-women, the United Nations was certainly pro-men. In 1975, among the top 35 executive roles at the UN there was only one woman, Helvi Sipilä of Finland, who naturally was appointed head of International Women's Year. Not because she was an obvious choice, but because she was the only choice. Unless, of course, the UN appointed a man to oversee a year dedicated to women's issues. And given what we know of the UN back then, I wouldn't doubt they considered a male appointee at the time. Among the United Nation's top 300 jobs, only eight were held by women.[2] Now, some 80 years after it was first formed, the United Nations has still never appointed a female secretary-general.

In 1972, under pressure from anti-sexist activists among UN staff, the Secretary-General had agreed to review his office's promotions policy and appointed eight people to the UN Appointments and Promotions Board: all men. No doubt all exceptionally meritorious, marvellously brilliant men, who outshone all the exceptionally meritorious, marvellously brilliant women – who didn't get a look in. Two years later, ahead of the 1974 World Conference on Population and Development in Bucharest, the secretariat released a draft plan which failed to make any reference to women's role in population questions. When this was pointed out, it was revealed they 'forgot to consult women'.[3] The patriarchy can be very funny at times. If this was in a movie, we would probably laugh. How can a bunch of men who think they speak for the world sit about and discuss population without including the human beings without whom population is impossible – women? More than just women's lady bits, women's rights, choices and views, as well as their bodies, are pivotal to population growth, decline or stagnation.

But the men of the UN didn't think of that, and unfortunately this wasn't a movie – it was real life. No one laughed. But women like Elizabeth Reid got very angry. In a mad scramble, the Population Conference secretariat put out a call asking all UN member states to send a woman of 'high public office' to a quick women's forum, to ask the ladies a few questions. Australia sent Reid. This would be her first encounter of the UN in operation.

It didn't go well. 'I was shocked to my feminist core by the sexist and discriminatory attitudes of the senior UN officials who spoke at the opening sessions,' Reid says. 'One senior man who said that he had come to learn about the "mysterious problem called the status of women" and also "to find out what were the latest fashions".[4]

I suspect Reid's neat shirt and flared jeans didn't cut it. But her feminist fury did. With help from the Australian mission to the UN, Reid called a press conference and let rip. According to historian Jocelyn Olcott, the articulate and sharp Australian 'set off a firestorm',[5] blasting the UN men at the forum for their condescending attitudes and for wasting women's time.

The New York Times ran the story of women's outrage, quoting Reid. A UN staffer, who smelled an ally, sent her a private note: 'Needless to say, your comments in the New York Times caused an unprecedented commotion amongst the UN men – beginning in the secretary-general's cabinet meeting. You really shook the men up – they were furious and indignant and, incidentally, interested. International Women's Year suddenly became an object of interest.'[6] The Mexico World Conference on Women would not only provide women with an international space previously denied them, or thought unnecessary; it would crack open women's deep-seated anger at being dismissed and patronised. One thing became clear: women could no longer be ignored and viewed as undeserving of the full weight of UN attention.

By the end of International Women's Year, the UN had designated 1976–1985 as 'The Decade for Women', with two other World Conferences on Women to be held in Copenhagen (1980) and Nairobi (1985). The fourth UN Conference on Women was held in Beijing in 1995. It drew more than 30 000 delegates, making it the largest global gathering of women in history. Famed for Hillary Clinton's speech insisting that 'human rights are women's rights and women's rights are human rights', Beijing was groundbreaking.[7] It launched the most comprehensive blueprint for gender equality the world has ever produced – the Beijing Declaration and Platform for Action. This foundational document remains one of our most important tools in the global battle for women's rights and recognition. Yet it didn't emerge in isolation. The Beijing Declaration had its genesis in Mexico, at the first UN World Conference on Women. It all started in 1975.

In March 2025, marking 30 years since 189 nations signed on to the Beijing Declaration – including Australia – Hillary Clinton urged women to take stock of where we are now, by looking back to 'understand where we have come from, where we are today, and what we need to do together ... [to] push back the pushback'.[8]

As you and I know only too well, and perhaps the reason you picked up this book in the first place, women are not where we had hoped – or dared assume – we would be by now. Our own pushback against the pushback against women's rights, autonomy and liberation demands a great deal of us. But we are not alone, and we are not without a fabulous feminist legacy to drawn upon.

Australia's IWY agenda

Back in Australia, ahead of 1975, Elizabeth Reid had persuaded Gough Whitlam to endorse a full year national focus on IWY. He didn't take much convincing. Whitlam famously stated, 'It is a sobering thought that women throughout the world have to be granted an opportunity to be heard.'[9]

Prime Minister Whitlam set up the International Women's Year National Advisory Committee (NAC) in 1974, to establish themes and set the agenda for International Women's Year, and – importantly – to allocate funds to community projects. The NAC, headed by Elizabeth Reid, was a diverse group of nine women and two men who included representatives from regional Australia, Indigenous communities, child welfare, media, trade unions, and women's rights activism. Government departments and agencies were also instructed to develop IWY programs within their portfolios and direct funds accordingly. State premiers were on board too, with enthusiasm spilling into local councils. From the outset the government was clear that it was not up to the NAC to 'impose' an IWY program. Rather, it was up to the women of Australia 'to speak out their thoughts, their needs, their worries, their hopes and their dreams for the future'.[10] And they did, with the applications for funds flooding in.

The UN themes for the year were 'Equality, Development and Peace'. Laudable, but lofty and loose. Australia, under the guidance of Elizabeth Reid, took a more nuanced approach that was both radically ambitious, and overarching. The intention was to create genuine, transformative change, using a three-fold framework. This is how Reid described the objectives in a cable to *Ms.* magazine in late 1974: 'Firstly, to change the attitudes of both women and men towards women, their skills and potential. Secondly, to lessen distress and suffering, and to overcome areas of discrimination. Finally, to present the joyous aspects of being a woman, to look at women as creators both of art and of life.'[11]

Celebrating creativity and reducing discrimination against women took on a variety of innovative and challenging forms. A total of 687 submissions for IWY projects poured in from around the country. Funds were distributed for projects in the arts, theatre, music, film, literature and feminist publications. Money also went to health and welfare programs, women's centres, women's homelessness and education programs, including efforts to stimulating young women's interest in technology and engineering (sound familiar?). The Australian Council of Churches received funds to establish a large-scale inquiry into the ordination of women, which included regional conferences in the Pacific. Various women's conferences, forums and seminars mushroomed around the country. The diversity of programming was impressive. But by far the biggest and boldest challenge was to change social attitudes. In its final report to parliament, the NAC stressed that it regarded changing attitudes as 'most fundamental': 'while legislative and institutional reforms are essential, they will not be sufficient or permanent without a significant alteration in the attitudes of society to women, and of women to themselves'.[12]

Elizabeth Reid's ambitious vision to change how women and men thought about gender and sex-role stereotypes – while identifying how sexism entraps and oppresses – was pivotal to Australia's agenda. Indeed, 'changing attitudes' became the mantra for International Women's Year. But sexist social attitudes were so deeply baked into the nation's DNA that attempting to change them would prove a herculean task. Yet that didn't stop Reid and her team trying.

Reid's ability to envisage a better future in which women were elevated out of subordination and all forms of discrimination into a life of liberation – in the full sense – was a powerful motivator for those working immediately around her. Including the prime minister. Whitlam clearly shared many of Reid's progressive views about women. A towering intellect himself, Whitlam must have been impressed by Reid's ability to meticulously decipher a social problem and construct meaning out of what looked like a muddled mess. Her decisiveness instilled confidence. But most of all, her solid theoretical and practical grounding in the principles of the Women's Liberation Movement meant she had a well-considered framework informing her decisions. She knew what she wanted.

But what has drawn me most deeply into this story is the unshakable sense of *hope* that Reid and Australian feminists had. This was a rare, unprecedented moment in time, and they knew it. They stormed forward with an agenda that was both radical and reform-driven. It was proactive rather than reactive. There was plenty to be angry about – and they were – but the powerful, forward momentum was not energised by complaint as much as a clear sense of purpose and possibility.

Australia – thanks to Reid – not only grabbed the global spotlight during International Women's Year, but was praised for delivering one of the best IWY programs in the world.

'The Year of the Bird': Onya, luvs!

International Women's Year Down Under turned out to be a wild ride. It's a story that is rarely told, despite it being absolutely pivotal to the lives and liberation of women living in Australia today. As a journalist, I was shocked by how much of our strong and proud feminist legacy I didn't know. And, as you'll see, it's a story that needs to be shared.

From the outset, the United Nations was acutely aware of 'the tremendous potentialities that the mass media have as vehicles for social change'.[13] This was diplomatic technojargon for saying what anyone with a vested interest knew too well: media would be the main battleground in International Women's Year. That proved to be true, and nowhere more so than in Australia. 'The media ... are the most insidious and powerful force for creating and maintaining attitudes in Australian society,' noted the NAC in its final report.[14]

International Women's Year was a bonanza for the Australian media. There was so much manly muckraking to do. Thrust into the spotlight, women were fair game. The year-long focus gave media men – and a few women – a daily excuse to openly ridicule, trivialise and infantilise women throughout the year. 'Giving the girls a go', blared *The Australian* (11 January). 'Mum's the word as the big yak-yak begins', sneered *The Daily Telegraph* (17 June). 'No chicken, but feted at hen party' was *The Age*'s descriptor for the prime minister, surrounded by women at an International Women's Day reception (10 March). It was as if 1975 was an official UN-sanctioned opportunity to mock those uppity women who were getting above their station – or, god forbid, claiming equal status.

It was Christmas for headline writers – every day. They couldn't resist reminding Australians that it was weird to see a woman doing a 'man's job'. When a woman appeared as a police prosecutor in a courtroom: 'Ladies lay down the law in court' (*Daily Telegraph*, 24 October). When an accomplished, middle-aged lawyer was appointed to the Arbitration Commission: 'Career girl judge ...' (*Daily Telegraph*, 9 June). When not trumpeting the exceptionalism of women in men's roles, news writers opted for using a woman's domestic or marital status as descriptor. An aspiring political candidate for the Senate was an 'attractive 32-year-old mother of two – a divorcee' (*The Australian*, 23 September). (Have you ever read 'Handsome divorced father of two runs for the Senate'?) Another who succeeded against all athletic odds and climbed Everest was reminded of her real job: 'Housewife on top of the world' (*Sydney Morning Herald*, 19 May).

The NAC grew increasingly outraged at the coverage of women. Reflecting on the year, its 1976 report to parliament blasted the media: 'This kind of verbal sexism is equally prevalent in radio and the electronic media, and is accompanied by widespread trivialisation, sensationalising and distortion of news relating to women.'[15]

It was also alarmingly prevalent in cartoons. A series on IWY by the infamous cartoonist Larry Pickering in *The National Times* included images of men in what looks like a rugby scrum carrying out a gang rape, with the word bubble: 'We can't keep meeting like this Elsa'. Another showed fearsome women with clubs and a sign – 'Eye for An Eye Rape Squad' – as three women hold a man down on the ground, saying, 'Ok, now we've got 'im, who's going to rape 'im?' (Are you laughing yet?) Others show men's faces cleaved into enormous-breasted women, or sexy nude women with face veils – 'You're a tease Delilah.' (Laughing now?)[16] But it wasn't just the sexist insults the National Advisory Committee worried about. It was the impact such inane commentary and misogyny was having on how women were viewed – and, most importantly, on how they viewed themselves: 'It would be difficult to overestimate the effect that the Australian media's constant and insidious sexism is having on the women, children and men who are exposed to it every day of their lives.'[17]

Out of respect to my media colleagues of yesteryear, I must stress that some individual journalists did make efforts to follow Elizabeth Reid's lead by trying to highlight the inherent sexism in social attitudes. Some brought a new lens to their reporting as they attempted to unpack the truth about women's lives (bless you, Caroline Jones). Some even took a serious interest in IWY, even if their news outlets didn't. But these were individuals up against the might of the men they worked for: media proprietors and male executives driven by hypermasculine news values. Mainstream, commercial media across Australia made a hearty meal of International Women's Year. Attack, ridicule and suggestions of 'catfights' and 'feminist rabble' were good for business. The inevitable disagreements and challenges that occur in any year-long program sent a thrill across media desks: 'Radicals damage feminist cause' (*Courier Mail*, 17 September); 'Despair over women's year' (*The Australian*, 5 September); and then the swift reduction to failure – 'Year a flop for women' (*The Mercury*, 11 December).

Despite the mess of mass media misogyny, a few good, decent men viewed the advance of women in journalism as an important way to bring about change. They could see that young women entering the profession were incredibly diligent and hard working. Nearly all the women journalists I've interviewed who were employed in mainstream publications in 1975 speak about the supportive male mentors they had along the way. Women like political commentator superstar, Niki Savva, who was a tiny, talented young Greek-Cypriot woman when she joined the press gallery in Canberra, working for *The Australian*. Savva was one of six women in a press pack of more than 100 men. She lets out a hooting laugh when I ask her if there was much drinking at work back then. 'Was there much *drinking*?' she repeats, as if it's a fabulously quaint question. The answer: yes, day and night. What about sexual harassment? There are stories of hiding behind locked doors, turning off office lights, trying to appear invisible, and Niki's story of a handsy, drunk MP blocking her exit from his chambers. Her peeling laugh of 'You haven't got a chance, mate!' and her mouthy takedown about his masculine inadequacies did the trick. Humiliation worked. But Savva was lucky. Women don't always duck away from such moments unscathed. (As journalist Jess Hill has theorised, male humiliation can in fact be a precursor to violence against women.[18])

On the other hand, Dany Torsh, who challenged the Journalists' Club in Sydney for banning female membership, speaks fondly of the male journalists who helped her navigate her early career as a reporter at *The Australian*. Emboldened, Torsh went on to set up the Media Women's Action Group (MWAG), a women's collective, to push back against the media sexism sloshing around them, as well as to make demands for basic facilities, such as creches, to help women work the rolling hours required of a journalist. Torsh wanted the MWAG to include women from across all three media monopolies in Australia at the time: Murdoch, Fairfax and Packer. So she invited Elisabeth Wynhausen from *The Bulletin*; Sandy Symons, women's editor at *The Sunday Australian*; and Frances McLean from *The Sydney Morning Herald*. They held their first meeting in the newsroom at Holt Street, where Torsh worked.

Julie Rigg, an inaugural member of the MWAG and co-founder of the groundbreaking *Coming Out Show* on ABC Radio, launched in 1975, also cites various supportive male colleagues who actively encouraged women's training so they could master all aspects of broadcast. The show was produced by the newly formed Australian Women's Broadcasting Cooperative and was a direct product of International Women's Year funding and focus. Incredibly successful in covering issues never previously discussed on air and reaching markets once ostracised by mainstream media, the legendary show became an institution. It launched countless women's careers and remained on air for a whopping 23 years.

So, yes, there were hopeful and even inspiring media moments back then. But, sadly, the overwhelming news response to International Women's Year by commercial media was a shitshow. The industry-wide determination to rubbish everything about International Women's Year was so overtly sexist and demeaning, it's almost funny. Except it's not. Most of the reporting was so misrepresentative of what actually occurred that year, if taken at face value it creates an historical lie.

Gough Whitlam allocated a generous $2 million dollars for the year and a further $1.3 million for the flow-on year. Media men were appalled. '$2 mil. for the sheilas: Surprisingly, it's not a joke', spat *The Age*. It was 'The year of the bird', chirped *The Sunday Telegraph*.[19] Interestingly, both those stories were written by women, who claimed the headline was a direct quote or 'common refrain' from men. The demeaning ridicule of women as 'birds' and 'sheilas' doesn't seem to have registered. *The Australian* pitched the year as some kind of long ladies' luncheon: 'All set for a ladies' affair'.[20] When the second round of money was announced, it was sheer outrage: 'AND THE GIRLS WANT $2m MORE', splashed *The Sun*, referring to the government funds as 'the girls' housekeeping'.[21]

To perhaps try and speak the language of men back to them, at one point government staff hired Paul Hogan to record an endorsement of IWY. 'G'day. The better half has asked me to say a few words about International Women's Year,' he begins. 'So here goes: "Good on yer, loves, good luck and any'ow it's about time."'[22] Although, well-intended, I doubt Hoge's radio intervention did anything constructive towards eliminating stereotypes. Rather, it encouraged them.

Handing over the mic to the sheilas

Interestingly, television media made some concerted efforts to address International Women's Year by offering special coverage 'for the ladies'. Some even devoted a whole program. Unfortunately, it didn't always go well.

A Current Affair celebrated International Women's Year by handing over the show to a female host and reporter for one night only.[23] The opening titles announced the special episode as, 'A Feminist Current Affair, without Mike Minehan'. (I'm not making this up.) The 'stand-in' leaned forward in the host's chair, folded her arms and introduced herself: 'Hi. I'm Claudia Wright and today Pip Porter went to the street to ask the people what they thought of us taking over *A Current Affair*.' The tape rolls and a man in his thirties wearing a tan suit and tie says he thinks putting girls in charge is 'a great idea', as long as it's '… er, not too often'. A young, pimply-faced guy with long hair says, 'I think it's pretty good to listen to what the women have to say. It's their only chance.' A middle-aged woman nods with conditional approval: 'Well, I think if they behave themselves properly, it's a good idea.'

So, did journalist Claudia Wright 'behave' herself? Thankfully, no. Wright, well-known as a 'feminist' on her regular radio gig at 3AW in Melbourne, used her TV spot to throw a few darts. Why not? It was prime-time TV and this singular opportunity wasn't to be wasted.

During the show, Wright took aim at the ACTU for not having any women on its executive and for failing to properly include women at its annual congress. She then coolly introduced the president of the ACTU: 'Well, Bob Hawke has been branded a sexist pig. He joins us now from our Melbourne studio.' (I'm not making that up either.) The camera cuts to Hawke, who launches into a furious tirade. There are no women on the ACTU executive, he declares, because women don't step up. Women are the problem. At one point he thumps the desk with his fist. Women are free to stand for election for an executive position, he says; they just don't try.

When Wright points out that unionist Linda Norton had

tried, that very week, and had lost, Hawke raises his voice again. 'Look, you have the most enormous capacity for interruption!' he scolds. 'You're not too bad yourself,' Wright fires back.

Hawke takes control, and when Wright jumps in again, Hawke cracks it. 'Just a minute, Claudia, it's *equality*, not dominance!' This was an unsubtle way of telling Wright that, as a woman, she had no right to assume a dominant position, even as the host of the show. Dominance, authority – these are male things.

Hawke bangs on, and on. Soon Wright appears withdrawn – head down, chin in hand, staring at the desk.

She wasn't invited back.

I watched this footage in an edit suite at the National Film and Sound Archive in Canberra, where no one could hear me gagging. I spooled backwards and forwards, zooming in to capture what I knew must be there. Somewhere, under that thick sweep of luscious fringe, *surely* Claudia Wright was rolling her eyes. I know, because I've done it myself.

I had a visceral reaction to seeing Wright's shoulders slump because I've been there – at that very desk, as fill-in host on *A Current Affair*, when Ray Martin was on holiday. It was nearly two decades after International Women's Year, and yet it was shocking how little had changed. As a 30-something woman doing my job, I was constantly told by my male guests to stop interrupting. The tougher the interview, the more men buckled down – on me. Yet none of those interviewees would have dared suggest to Ray Martin, or fellow hosts Mike Willesee or Mike Munro, that they were 'interrupting'. Later, when I moved back to the ABC to host *The 7.30 Report* in Adelaide, the then-government tried various ways to intimidate me out of doing my job. The favourite was to refer to me publicly as 'Virginia Interruptus'. Ah, such wags.

Fast-forward to today and you'll quickly notice this is still something men only say to women in media: 'Stop interrupting me!'

Over on ABC TV, the national broadcaster took International Women's Year seriously. Early in the year, *This Day Tonight* had hit the streets to ask women what the year meant to them.[24] The responses are a little alarming (consider that a trigger warning), but it's worth pausing to reflect how much this unadulterated, unfiltered material serves as precious proof of the success of Women's Liberation and the change in social attitudes since this time. Here is some of what they said, beginning with two young women, 20-somethings, both holding babies:

WOMAN 1: I don't take an interest in Women's Lib ... I don't like it.

FEMALE REPORTER: Why don't you like it?

WOMAN 1: I'd rather be the way I am [laughs]. I like to be under my husband's thumb.

WOMAN 2: I reckon the man should wear the pants. He should sort of be the boss of the family. I'd rather him go out to work and earn the money, than me go out and earn the money, and look after the kids. I just don't believe in it.

The reporter roams a shopping mall, to the soundtrack of Helen Reddy's 'I Am Woman'. A bespectacled middle-aged woman declares that IWY means 'nothing' to her and that she doesn't believe in Women's Liberation. An older woman sporting a smart hat and pearls is asked about women's liberation; she says, 'I'm inclined to think that they can overdo all these things. Don't you?' As for issues like equal pay and employment opportunities for women: 'No, I don't go with it really. I think the man is the important one with the jobs and pay and that sort of thing.'

The final vox pop is with a 30-something woman wearing a pink shirt, collar upturned and a dab of shimmering blue eyeshadow: 'I consider a liberated woman is a woman who does what she wants to do, thinks for herself what she wants to think, and is not dominated by a male.' At last: a believer! But then the interviewee, warming to the camera, does a U-turn. 'Actually, I think women are in great danger of being dominated by women, being told to liberate themselves by doing what other women want them to do. Which to me is a great danger ... Women are becoming far too dominant. They're going to end up being women chauvinists.'

What is striking about these comments is the general antipathy from women about women who want to change things: those who demand a better deal, who envisage a better life and perhaps even a feminist future. The ideas of Women's Liberation were not mainstream ideas. They were radical ideas, shared among a small subset of women. Although women's rights and freedoms hardly seem like radical concepts now, the pushback from mainstream women in the '70s is a reminder of how women's progress is fought and won by the radical few – ultimately, for the benefit of the rest. Even when those beneficiaries do their best to disassociate themselves from that radical fringe of changemakers – those women who do the hard work and take the risks that others wouldn't dare.[25]

The ABC of 'Being a Woman'

Unlike the public bullying of Claudia Wright over on *A Current Affair*, there was no chance any bloke would dominate the ABC's International Women's Year feature event. To make sure of that, none were invited to participate in the special hour-long show, titled *On Being a Woman*, hosted by Caroline Jones and broadcast live from Brisbane in front of 200 women.[26] Filmed in late June 1975, during the two-week UN World Conference on Women underway in Mexico, this was a radical departure from the ABC's normal programming. It was a noisy, robust, rollercoaster ride through the big issues for women at the time – many of which are alarmingly similar to the issues we are still discussing today.

Jones was joined by a diverse panel of seven women representing the Women's Electoral Lobby (WEL), the Women's Action Group, an Aboriginal community housing organisation, the Women's Community Aid Association, a Christian women's group, health experts and the Queensland Housewives' Association. As the cameras rolled, Jones opens by explaining that 'this will be unlike any program that you have seen before'. It was a big call. But she was right.

ABC TV had never devoted an entire prime-time program to women talking about women. This would simply not have happened without the impetus of International Women's Year. To ensure both diversity and inclusion, Jones explained that all women's viewpoints were represented in the audience, and she stressed the aim of the show was to unpack confusion about 'that much misunderstood phrase, "the women's movement"'.

One of the opening salvos is from Pam Goring, from WEL, voicing an uncomfortably common complaint during the 1970s – that women are conditioned to compete with each other. When women 'start to achieve things', Goring points out, 'one of the appalling things is that it is not just the men who try to destroy them, it's us. We do it. We pull them down. And I think this is one of the greatest impediments to women taking a greater role in society.'

A murmur of agreement ripples through the audience. Gabby Horan, president of the Queensland Housewives' Association, jumps in: 'I think the greatest enemy we have are women themselves,' she says, 'Women become jealous when they see another woman rising to a position of trust or responsibility.' But just as it seems she is about to call on the sisterhood to unite, Horan flips the agenda to drive the audience towards her central theme – the 'real' role of women. 'Men have had an exclusive club for many years,' says Horan, again to a rumble of agreement. 'Let me clarify that I like men … They have very good points. But God was the creator and he selected women to bear the responsibility of producing the progeny. So that in itself puts us, if not above, then at least equal to them.'

Even Caroline Jones looks bemused at Horan's novel take on equality. But it's her take on women as breeders that triggers argument. 'Most women enjoy their mothering tasks,' argues an audience member, who is quickly backed up by another: 'Mothers at home are being prejudiced against.' The audience groans.

Panellist Barbara Bowers argues that 'the woman who chooses to stay at home and be a mother is psychologically and financially victimised', and Horan digs in: 'I believe the first responsibility of a woman is the contract she entered into with her husband …' The audience begins to scoff loudly. Horan raises her voice. 'Yes,' she states emphatically, 'they entered into a contract with their husbands to provide a home, have his children and bring them up. And that is the first responsibility of a woman.' At this point Horan is howled down. She'd had the devoted mothers and happy homemakers in the audience with her, but seems to have lost them by over-egging claims of a God-given contract.

I can imagine the broad grin on the ABC producer's face at this stage. The show was experimental and minutes in already there's conflict and female outrage: great telly! The cameras zoom in on close-ups of Horan. The issue of a woman's 'real role' was clearly a hot topic this audience was hungry to debate. But Horan was just a grenade pin. If anyone else in the audience believed 'God' made women breeders in the quest for gender equality, they weren't saying so. Of greater interest was that vexed issue of a woman's 'choice': the moral virtue of the homemaker versus the income earner.

After a number of women argue over the inequity of juggling the double load of paid work and housework, a young woman in the audience proffers an articulate summary that sounds achingly familiar:

> We should be redefining the role of women and the role
> of *men*! And [men] must have a lot more to do with the
> care and nurture of children. We have to change our
> work patterns, so that men and women can fulfil their
> potential and men can fulfil their potential. If it means
> shorter working hours so that both men and women
> can care for children, that's what we should do … and it
> seems to me International Women's Year will do nothing
> if these things aren't come to terms with.

When it is suggested men get involved in childbirth, Gabby Horan screws up her face and retorts, 'Eeeew yuck! No. I think [childbirth] is feminine work and [the mother] goes about her business alone.' The audience clearly doesn't agree.

Horan is an easy target in this discussion, but it is a young Indigenous woman, Susie Chilly, whose calm, quietly spoken but razor-sharp moral authority puts Horan in her place. Earlier in the discussion, Chilly, a field officer with Aboriginal Community Housing, had spoken about the housing discrimination experienced by her parents. A doleful-looking Gabby Horan told Chilly – with breathtaking paternalism – that she, Chilly, 'can't help the fact that she's black'. (Yes, she did say that.) Members of the panel and audience verbally pounced on her.

Soon the talk turns to the media and how it misrepresents women and overstates their differences of opinion, an overt feature of IWY media coverage and dominating reports from the global Women's Conference in Mexico. Panellist Barbara Bowers, a journalist herself, accuses the media of a persistent lack of diversity in women's voices. In the clipped accent of a private girls' school, Bowers launches a tirade against only 'elite women's voices' being heard in news media – 'the recognised, privileged vocal minorities, and I would include myself in this,' she says. Jones draws Chilly back into the discussion, and the young woman's slow, carefully chosen words, quieten the auditorium.

'Everyone here is just so far away from what is happening for black people,' she says.

> Everyone is still bypassing [racial] discrimination. Until
> people realise it exists and [stop] saying, 'Yes, sisterhood
> is great' and yet not really understanding each other,
> until black women and white women really understand
> each other … there is no way that International Women's
> Year is going to do anything for the black movement.

They were powerful and prophetic words. The issue of race, and racism within 'white feminism', became a persistent and unresolved issue that percolated through the inaugural World Conference on Women, and continued for decades to come.

In Australia, Elizabeth Reid didn't shy away from this. She ensured some of the major IWY activities set out to specifically challenge and debate issues of racism, and the role and needs of Indigenous women within the women's movement. One of those events, a day-long 'Black Speak Out', was the first time some of the participants had ever met an Indigenous woman, much less heard her speak.

The wild thing about hosting large live panels like the ABC's IWY special is that there is no script. There's an autocue with the host's opening and closing remarks, and a rough plan for questions, but other than that it's a free-for-all. Given this was 1975, when studio technology was basic and the host didn't have the benefit of a bluetooth earpiece connecting her to a producer, Caroline Jones was little more than a traffic director in this fast-flowing conversation. She also happened to have a terrible cold and sounded awful, so mostly stayed silent. But it didn't matter. Women needed no prompting to dive into vigorous debate about the changing status of women in society, and the conflicting social pressures they faced. Reid's IWY agenda was clearly having the intended impact – attitudes were being challenged. Some were even changing. Women were questioning social norms.

On the flip side, most disturbing is the realisation that, 50 years later, so little has changed! We are *still* vexing over the role and rights of women as homemakers, the double juggle of work and family, a lack of sisterhood and fear of female competitiveness. In fact, other than the God lecture from Gabby Horan, there was little in this hour-long broadcast that wouldn't be on the agenda of a similar show today. That strikes me as a miserable admission of failure. Our unresolved cultural mindset around family responsibilities and domesticity still tethers many women like a yoke, just as it did our mothers and grandmothers.

Or worse, when there is nothing yoke-like about it. I am increasingly alarmed by overt indications of young women embracing sex-role stereotypes that I thought we had killed off and buried last century. Not long after viewing *On Being a Woman*, I happened to see an episode of the TV show, *Married at First Sight*. It was early 2025 and I felt like David

Attenborough watching the mating game of a new species. As the happy couple unpack their suitcases, the bride, Lauren, says she needs to do some laundry washing. The groom, Clint, says, 'I actually enjoy washing.' Lauren looks annoyed. 'Yeah? I think it's a girl's job, really.' Clint looks confused: 'What are you saying?' Now Lauren is scornful: 'Just leave the washing to me.' Cut to Lauren telling an interviewer, 'Oh god. I mean … for me gender roles are very important. I want to look after and, like, serve my husband. That makes me happy.'[27]

That doesn't make me sad. It makes me angry.

Funnelling funds for feminist projects

Anger has a rightful place in feminist theory and action. But what I didn't expect to find when I set out on this journey of discovering our feminist past was such a strong spirit of optimism. The collective sense of hope that permeated International Women's Year – despite all the belly-up moments in the sisterhood – was, and remains, profoundly inspiring. Those women who had experienced their own sense of revolution through the advent of Women's Liberation wanted to take others on that journey too. They wanted to change the world – and they believed they could. They knew that in order to change gender-based discriminations and oppressive systems, women – and men – had to discover and understand the nature of these oppressions for themselves. Although it was never said, as such, the main objective of Reid and co's approach to IWY was to effectively create a nation-wide consciousness-raising experience. The distribution of IWY funds was to help citizens find a pathway to their own transformation.

One of the more radical programs funded in 1975 was a series of four suburban 'women's commissions'. Modelled on the Sydney Women's Commission, run by Women's Liberation two years prior, these NSW suburban 'speak outs' were held in Liverpool, Chatswood, Hurstville and Bankstown, attracting over 500 women. They arrived curious, cautious and perhaps anxious. But that didn't stop hundreds of women courageously standing up and taking the microphone. In what turned out to be consciousness raising on a mass scale, women opened up publicly with deeply personal stories about their lives and what it was like to be a woman in Australia.

Some four decades later, in what she rightly calls 'an amazing find', academic Isobelle Barrett Meyering was excited to unearth transcripts of the women's commissions. She says the fact the sessions were recorded was unusual, and it showed how serious organisers were about the value of capturing women's stories. These big public forums were open to whatever subjects women wanted to raise, and the stories that poured out of women were equally fascinating and depressing – a living archive of what has not changed over five long decades.[28]

Almost all the issues raised back in 1975 continue to resonate loudly right now. Women spoke openly about their struggles with motherhood, social isolation, challenges of suburban living, lack of childcare and transport, unemployment and obstacles to promotion at work, health, abortion, drugs and alcohol, and a lack of support services during pregnancy. Importantly, domestic violence and 'psychological abuse' – or what we'd now call coercive control – featured prominently in the discussions. Given the unprecedented nature of these public events, there was plenty of risk involved in asking women to speak freely, with no subject or speaker off limits.

Naturally there were differences of opinion, particularly around abortion rights and access to contraception, and at times tensions spilled over and arguments broke out. But this is perfectly in keeping with the spirit of challenge Elizabeth Reid carefully wove into the IWY program. Her underlying intention was to shake people awake, to make women question, debate and find their way through the maze from personal to political awareness. After an arduous IWY panel discussion in New York, which had got bogged down discussing women only as wives and mothers, Reid's usual patient diplomacy snapped. 'If we're not careful, this whole year will become one *huge* Mother's Day,' she said. Germaine Greer, sitting on the same panel, agreed: 'We in the West still talk about childbirth as women's primary function. It is *one* of women's functions.'[29]

Unsurprisingly, there were battles fought over access to grants, and some sensational – and wildly incorrect – media coverage over who had received what. A $100 000 allocation for a six-part TV series on human reproduction, to be produced by Germaine Greer, was widely trashed as though Greer had pocketed the money for herself. 'There'll be flat-busted, fat-busted, foam-padded females shedding their bras by the bus-load at the feet of the Federal free-givers,' wrote one correspondent to *The West Australian* on 20 June.

Unexpecting grant recipients were thrilled by the generosity of the IWY committee and the unique opportunity to bring their women's projects to life. Lyndall Ryan reportedly chirped a delighted 'Oh goodie!' when she received a $33 000 personal cheque in the mail.[30] The money was for the Leichhardt Women's Health Centre. So chuffed was Ryan that she carried it around in her handbag for days, showing it to everyone.

Others were far from happy. In what developed into an infamous spat with Elizabeth Reid, the Sydney Women's Liberation group did not receive IWY funds for Elsie, the nation's first women's refuge, which had been set up in 1974 by Anne Summers and others in an unused house in Glebe, Sydney. Money for Elsie was desperately needed to help support the hordes of women and children turning up on the refuge's doorstep. But Reid's view was that the International Women's

Year grants were to do what government departments couldn't do, or chose not to do – not to take the place of what they *should* do. Anne Summers took this personally, and Reid and Summers fell out as a result. In truth, this is a major understatement and my way of trying to gloss over the fact that two of my greatest Australian feminist heroes actually had what Summers called 'a catastrophic deterioration' in their relationship.[31] I'll admit, my heart sank when I learned of the stoush between these two exceptional women.

In response to the Sydney women's outrage over their failure to get an IWY grant for Elsie, Reid penned a piece for the feminist journal *Refractory Girl*, in which she bluntly reiterated her position: 'The restructuring of the Australian society in a revolutionary feminist way will not come about through the setting up of women's shelters, or writing articles for women's journals, or creating jobs for the girls,' she wrote. 'These and similar activities are not political acts which undermine the existing society.'[32]

Reid's argument, said Summers, was that 'We should not be propping up a flawed and oppressive patriarchal system by providing stop-gap services such as refuges … Better to let the system disintegrate under its own contradictions so that a revolutionary restructuring could emerge.'

But just when you think the sisterhood has gone belly up, it rights itself – with raw honesty. Summers again: '[Reid's] criticism stung even more because in some ways I agreed with her. From a purely theoretical perspective she was right.'[33]

The clash between the idealism of social revolution and the reality of abused women in desperate need of emergency shelter was painfully uncomfortable. But this wasn't simply a moment of theory versus reality. Reid's view that expenditure on women's services, such as refuges and rape crisis centres, should be integrated into government budgets and not given as one-off handouts or band-aid measures was hard to dispute. The Elsie refuge did receive government funding during International Women's Year, but the money was an allocation from the Department of Health. 'As it should have been,' says Elizabeth Reid.

An animated falling-out between Reid and the Sydney Women's Liberation group ensued. Reid cites the infamous 'lipstick outrage' as a tipping point. Following the devastating cyclone that flattened Darwin on Christmas morning in 1974, the Whitlam government had sent various supplies north, including a consignment of personal items requested by the women of Darwin, which included lipstick. 'A frisson of scorn reverberated around the Sydney women's movement,' wrote Anne Summers.[34]

Writing in her memoir a quarter of a century later, Summers suggested the intervening years had sharpened her insight to what Reid was trying to achieve. Reflecting on the lipstick affair, she noted that in the mid-1990s Parisian women sent lipsticks to women caught up in the Bosnian war. I am reminded here too of when I travelled to Afghanistan in 2009, during the heat of the US-led war against the Taliban. The single thing I was asked for most by impoverished young women and girls was lipstick.

Why did the lipstick issue become such a sticking point among feminists, when there was so much more deserving of women's attention during IWY? I ask Elizabeth Reid, and she smiles: 'Maybe they worried I wanted to turn them into sex objects!' We both laugh at the ridiculous irony here. One of the things Reid was persistently asked by media in the '70s, by women reporters in particular, was why didn't she wear make-up.

Although you would not have gleaned it from media reports back home, the Australian program of events for International Women's Year was considered 'one of the most extensive worldwide' and singled out for international praise by the UN Secretary-General.[35] The diversity of projects spanning political engagement, creative endeavours and social and cultural challenges spread right out across the nation. It was impossible to miss.

When the United Nations' Assistant Secretary-General and head of IWY, Helvi Sipilä, visited Australia in late 1974, she was effusive in her praise for the Australian government's 'exceptional commitment to IWY', particularly in comparison to the US, about which she was much less enthusiastic.[36] Sipilä had met Reid earlier in the year and quickly became impressed by her sharply focused, feminist approach and strong theoretical foundations. A former lawyer, and not one given to hyperbole, Sipilä was openly effusive in citing Australia as 'leading the way towards equality for women'.[37] It was a big call by the UN executive, but well grounded in the political will she witnessed in Canberra, and the evident strength of the women's movement.

It has to be radical when even the PM wants a 'revolution'

In addressing the IWY National Advisory Committee at its inaugural meeting, Prime Minister Gough Whitlam expressed a profound seriousness about what he hoped International Women's Year would do for the women of Australia. But he was also careful to temper expectations: 'Government legislation can only achieve so much and I shall not pretend to you that any government can achieve immediately for Australian women the *revolution required* to allow them to develop fully as individuals.'[38]

The italics are mine. While you can almost hear the deep throttle of Whitlam's voice, what we also hear in these words is a strong echo of Elizabeth Reid. For it was Reid who introduced notions of revolution and the need for 'a revolution in people's heads', most importantly in women's heads. This is a concept she took to Mexico and onto the UN global stage. Whitlam went on to say that 'even if we were to remove all the inequalities of opportunity and of status, it still would not be enough', because 'the inequality of women's position in society is deeply embedded not just in the institutions but also in the *psychology* of the society'. According to Whitlam, 'the first and fundamental step towards freedom is awareness by women themselves of their real inequality, of the extent of this social, political, economic and cultural discrimination and deprivation'.[39]

Again, the italics are mine. Whitlam's focus on the 'psychology' of the society is bold. It acknowledges the overwhelming power of patriarchy to not only control the structures and systems that shape women's lives, but to shape women's *thinking*. His insistence that 'women themselves' need to wake up to what is dominating and diminishing them, was – and remains – an unprecedented prime ministerial admission. It was an admission that a women's revolution was crucial for the future of the nation, for social cohesion and perhaps even for sovereign stability into the future.

Looking back now, from the vantage point of 50 years, Reid says the PM was in fact 'directing the NAC to focus on the problem of sexism within the patriarchy without naming either as such'.[40]

But when it came to standing on centre stage and naming sexism as the problem, in front of a global audience, Elizabeth Reid didn't hold back.

12

MEXICO 1975 AND THE GREATEST CONSCIOUSNESS-RAISING EVENT IN HISTORY

Was Elizabeth Reid nervous? After all, it was only a United Nations world conference and an international stage, an auditorium filled with over 1300 government delegates from across 133 nations, with leading players from the UN and more than 1000 accredited media watching on, and several hundred cameras focused on her.

It was 20 June 1975, in Mexico City, at the World Conference on Women – a wild, chaotic, messy and unexpectedly magnificent conference, supposed to be a one-off, occurring right at a time when women were 'looking at the world from what appeared to be the brink of revolution and trying to imagine their place in a world made anew'.[1] Never before had representatives of the world's women gathered for a conference or forum singularly about women.

As to be expected when any new revolution begins to glow, there were disagreements, open debates, protests and walk-outs. 'This cultivation of disunity ... came about because key players took the risk of inviting chaos and conflict,' wrote historian Jocelyn Olcott.[2] But the critical thing about Mexico was the explosive roar it triggered. Once women were connected and empowered through new networks, there would be no going back. An unstoppable global revolution of women began. It was also a stage on which Australian feminism – shaped by a finely tuned Women's Liberation framework – played a pivotal role.

Who'd be nervous?

Elizabeth Reid laughs when I tell her that the old newsreel footage I've seen shows her standing centre stage, arms stretched out to hold both sides of the lectern, looking perfectly calm, focused and purposeful. *Very* purposeful. 'Oh, my legs completely went to jelly,' she says. Unfortunately, I can't corroborate that claim. At no point do any of the cameras zoom in on her legs.

There was nothing tame about Reid's speech to the conference. It was a long two-week event, but Reid, as head of the Australian delegation, was one of the early speakers. She had written the speech only hours before delivering it, while sitting on the floor of a nearby museum, her notes spread around her and images of Aztec warriors bearing down on her.

The words came quickly. Reid knew precisely what she wanted to say.

Margaret Whitlam hangs out with 'hookers' on the way to Mexico

If I was a headline writer for News Limited back in 1975, me and the boys would have had a few beer-fuelled belly laughs over this one. The PM's wife – hanging out with hookers! Media gold! But women weren't headline writers in those days. And no journalist knew Whitlam and Reid had taken a little detour on their way to Mexico.

According to Reid, the Australian delegation to the conference – ten women, four men – were unified and very well prepared. 'We had drawn up our battle lines,' she says. Some of them had even studied Spanish in the months ahead of their arrival in Mexico City. Reid was leader of the delegation and Margaret Whitlam,

Gough Whitlam's wife, was the co-deputy with Robin Ashwin, Australia's ambassador to Egypt. The group included Susan Ryan, then member of the ACT House of Assembly; Shirley Castley, from the IWY National Advisory Committee; and Sara Dowse, an active member of the women's movement, who had joined the bureaucracy as a new 'femocrat' to set up a women's unit within the Department of the Prime Minister and Cabinet. On their way to Central America, the group stopped off in San Francisco for a rather unusual engagement, one that would have sent the Australian media into a frenzied meltdown if they'd known about it. Which, fortunately, they didn't.

Reid was an exceptional networker and mentor to a diverse range of women. Later in her international career she became known for setting up meetings, outside the UN process, to connect women in various pockets of the world to help build collaborations and strength through feminist collectives. She initiated long-lasting and productive connections among activists in the Pacific, and later in Asia and Africa. Jocelyn Olcott describes them as 'almost like women incubators'. On the way to Mexico in 1975, Reid led the Australian team to one of these informal 'incubators', which cascaded into what sounds like a wild reality TV show – without the script.

As the group passed through Los Angeles, Reid wanted to take the opportunity to meet with COYOTE, a group making waves in the US by advocating for the rights of sex workers. 'They were hookers with a really strong feminist manifesto,' says Reid. 'We wanted to talk to them about our analysis and make sure we were aligned.' When the Australian consul-general in LA heard that Margaret Whitlam would be in town, he organised a cocktail reception party at his home. Reid asked her contact at the consulate to ensure the women from COYOTE were invited, along with their legal counsel, the fabulously flamboyant and outspoken civil rights activist Flo Kennedy.

The women arrived en masse. When the wife of the consul-general heard there were 'hookers in her house', according to Reid, she 'had conniptions'. Police were called, sirens filled the street and the consul-general's children were scurried off to another location. Unperturbed, Margaret Whitlam and the Australian delegates continued their discussions with the sex workers outside the house, on the footpath, despite the commotion. They later met up again in Mexico for extended talks, exchanging ideas around issues of sex workers' rights, protections and ethics. Reid viewed the encounter as a win-win. 'We felt the contact was the most important thing,' she says. 'It was a form of recognition, the very fact that the Australian delegation had asked to meet with them, gave them a certain status, and it gave us an opportunity to sit down with them, talk and get to know their issues.'

As far as the Australian team was concerned, such a meeting was perfectly in sync with the broad remit of International Women's Year. It was about developing a deeper understanding of all women and the intersecting circumstances of their lives and experience.

'We women': Sexism in the global spotlight

Despite the World Conference on Women ostensibly being for and about women, the overwhelming majority of delegates – a quarter of whom were men – were there first and foremost to represent their governments. They all arrived with political agendas.

The conference would expose serious rifts between women from the global south and those from the global north. 'Western, white feminism' – viewed as a product of the north – was being given a shake out by women of the third world, emerging from colonialism and carrying the scars of imperialism. All of this was unfurling at a time when concepts of development, productivity and a 'New International Economic Order' had seized global discussions without any coherent reference to – or understanding of – how this new world order would impact women, nor how they would be included in shaping and building this new future.

Half the delegates, including those from all the Arab, African and Soviet bloc nations, walked out in protest against a speech by Leah Rabin, wife of Israel's prime minister Yitzhak Rabin. Leah Rabin watched coolly as they streamed out, saying, 'I know countries have conflicts and misunderstandings, but not to be willing to sit down and listen to each other is to reject the point and goals of our being together.'[3] Later Rabin told media she would be 'glad' to meet and talk with the wife of the Egyptian president, Jihan el-Sadat, who was also attending the conference. To which el-Sadat curtly replied that she 'couldn't sit down with a lady who is occupying Arab territory'.[4] There was a strong anti-Zionist theme among some delegates, with added encouragement from the host, Mexico. The final Mexico Declaration would call for a global commitment to end Zionism, along with colonialism and apartheid.

I would like to note the irony, but it is more tragedy than irony, that 50 years after this conference we are still grappling with some of the same global conflicts and tensions. Not only was Israel's occupation of Palestine a searing issue at the 1975 conference, but so too was Russia's domination of Ukraine. At the Tribune, a conference for non-government organisations held in parallel with the official conference, Ukraine protesters mounted a hunger strike in protest against Russian detention of political prisoners.[5] Although, in a wacky bit of gossip, it was suggested the Ukrainians may not be Ukrainians at all, but paid by the CIA to stage an anti-Russian protest (now there's a Trumpian somersault to get your head around). Gloria Steinem supposedly was a CIA spy too!

While political differences looked like splitting the conference between those from the global south and representatives of the global north, Reid forged a powerful and strategic path right down the middle of such tensions. 'We accepted that the political issues of the day had their place in a conference for women,' Reid says, 'but only if the links to women were articulated.' The message conveyed in Reid's speech was decidedly not about Australia. In fact, she even used Australia's economic success as an example of why a focus on economic development does not necessarily alleviate women's oppression or discrimination.[6]

None of these issues could be tackled, she believed, without first defining and owning the fundamental problem that afflicted all women, everywhere, regardless of their economic status. So Reid walked onto that stage with a steely determination to force open discussion on the one issue the United Nations did not want on the agenda – 'sexism'.

'If this conference is to be serious in maintaining that there is something wrong with the position of women in society,' Reid said clearly, slowly, 'the clearest analysis ... is that which describes the inferior position of women as arising from sexism ... Sexism is the artificial ascription of roles, behaviours and even personalities to people on the basis of their sex *alone*.'[7]

Sexism had never before been raised at a United Nations intergovernmental forum. The word itself was not part of the UN lexicon. Reid changed all that.

'None of us live in, and it is impossible to imagine living in, a non-sexist society,' she said, eyeballing world leaders:

> We live in societies which are ruled by men – in other words, our societies are patriarchal ... To attempt to work out strategies for changing this situation must therefore be our primary task at this conference. It will be slow and sometimes painful to come to terms

with the realities of our problem, which requires as much a revolution in the heads of people as it does the modification of the structures which reinforce these destructive values.

She had their attention, even though a flurry of flash bulbs had turned to the Philippines' Imelda Marcos, who had taken her seat like a heavily plumed bird sitting in a royal box. (This was years before her infamous fall from grace. Unfortunately, no cameraman thought to shoot her shoes.) Reid pressed on, placing sexism alongside concepts of racism and colonialism. This is where she saw the real fight. Sexism was, she argued, just as harmful to global politics as racism:

> The basis of racism, racial discrimination, colonialism and neocolonialism, alien domination, is similar to the basis of that violence against women which we call sexism. It is based on the need ... for power over other human beings. Patriarchy is yet another form of colonising people. But of course it is such a subtle process ... a colonisation by mute consent.

Fluid and articulate, Reid's fundamental argument around the limitations of focusing on 'equality' – one of the UN's official themes for the conference – challenged the idea that fixing structural and institutional gender inequities would solve women's problems and end gender discrimination. Instead, she argued, the sort of equality that was measured with a ledger risked giving the appearance of a problem 'fixed', when in fact underlying attitudes of sexism and patriarchal dominance had not changed a jot. Reid was also highly attuned to talk of 'development' for poorer, third world nations, being a limp euphemism for 'Westernisation' or colonisation by other means.

These would not deliver improvements to the status of women, she argued. Without substantial changes in attitudes and a global attack on sexism, Reid argued, the rest was just window dressing. Instead, she mounted a solid case for 'culturally appropriate concepts of development' that centred on women.

Well ahead of her time, Reid argued for women's equal participation in conflict and peace negotiations, flagging the very concepts we heard 25 years later, when the UN Security Council passed its first resolution on Women, Peace and Security in 2000. But here again, with an unflinching sense of reality, Reid also spoke about the uselessness of war – including justified revolutions – where women fight alongside men 'to free themselves and their people'. 'Often, the new society benefits women no more than the old,' she pointed out. Ultimately, women always lose: 'The continued oppression of women implies the maintenance of power over women by men through their imposition of sexist values ... Until such time as violence against women is recognised and understood, and ceases, peace will remain unattainable.'

Reid's words on violence were uncompromising. She spelled it out. In a context where cultural relativism played a heavy hand, her boldness was seen for what it was – a radical act:

> Violence includes rape, immolation, forced sterilisation, indecent assault, infibulation, unwanted pregnancy, clitorectomy, unnecessary surgery and wife beating and shackling as well as mental violence ... Violence against women is most often committed by men known to their victims, often fathers and husbands, who are otherwise respectable and acceptable members of society.

Reid's positioning of violence flagged the deeper feminist agenda of linking women's rights with human rights, the link famously immortalised by Hillary Clinton in 1995. But the connection had already been well made by then. Interestingly, Gough Whitlam had alluded to this in 1974, in his inaugural address to the IWY National Advisory Committee.

Back on stage, Reid pushed on. 'Physical assault on women reflects the low status of women in society, the denial to them of the right to respect and dignity,' she said. 'This low status is reflected not only in the perpetration of such acts of violence, but by the frequent sanctioning, condoning, even admiration of such acts.'

Her speech had travelled a precarious path, but Reid had pulled it off. With masterful persuasion and rhetoric that drew on intersecting interests, the speech cleverly navigated the politically charged environment by framing women's rights and issues of oppression as universal concerns that required a universal solution.

As she spoke, the eyes and ears of every member of the Australian delegation were trained on Reid. Sara Dowse lights up when I ask her what it was like sitting in that enormous auditorium back in 1975, watching Australia's representative boldly reframe the collective global challenge facing women and reorient international focus. 'It was thrilling. Truly thrilling. It was a huge moment. I couldn't take my eyes off Elizabeth. You could feel that huge place full of people all listening. We were very, very proud,' Sara recalls. 'Elizabeth's speech was the best thing about the conference. We got the word "sexism" into the language of the UN. And that was really something. Everyone thought Australia was a feminist paradise!'

With an ear for rhythm and the power of good political pentameter, Reid left her best for last. As she drew to a close, she finished with a rolling rally cry:

We women will no longer be excluded from the sphere of decisions …

We women will no longer be relegated, either here or in our own countries, to a secondary place …

We women will no longer be manipulated for political ends …

We women will no longer tolerate paternalism, benign or otherwise, for it deprives us of our self-hood.

This is *our* conference.

Thank you.

The applause was thunderous. In footage, Reid appears to be blushing as cameras follow her off stage, through the audience and back to her seat. Her path is blocked by numerous delegates who jump up to congratulate the slightly overwhelmed Australian. Her serious face softens into a tight smile. It's the smile of someone who knows she's just nailed it. Still moving, she continues to take outstretched hands of congratulations, including at one point from Mother Teresa. The speech was a triumph – a masterclass in intersectionality, well before its time. Elizabeth Reid has just seized the global spotlight and positioned Australia as a feminist thought leader.

The power in the cadence of Reid's punchy conclusion was brilliant. The clarity of her message, pounded out by the force of repetition, was unmissable. 'We women' sounded like a mantra. And if you speak those final lines out loud, you may well hear the echo of another powerful feminist speech made nearly four decades later, the resonant rhythm of 'I will not': 'I will not be lectured about sexism and misogyny … I will not!'

There is something mesmerising about a fiercely intelligent woman firmly lecturing her audience with rhythmic defiance. We watched Julia Gillard in 2012 with the same awe that was directed at Elizabeth Reid in 1975.

Australia wins international acclaim

The world's leading historian on International Women's Year and the Mexico conference, Jocelyn Olcott, does an animated body shake when I ask her about Reid's speech. 'Elizabeth Reid – she was just on fire! I mean she was amazing! And she really changed the dynamics of the conference,' Jocelyn says. 'If you read that address she gave, first of all it gives you the chills. And secondly, it's still true. I mean, it's still a great piece of writing, and there is nothing you would walk back from that. And I don't think you can say that about anyone else at that conference.' Academic Jon Piccini, who has also studied Reid's speech in detail, says it was 'notably out of character' with the rest of the Mexico conference. He describes her politics as 'radical', her attitude 'forceful' and her tone 'provocative'.[8]

None of that was lost on the international media. The speech was widely reported, and Reid, along with members of the Australian delegation, were chased down for interviews. Although aspects of the speech clearly challenged many delegates and conservative media, the issues Reid raised were nevertheless treated with seriousness. Australia was quickly seen as a dominant player in the women's space and Reid a major influence. Olcott says that Reid's impact on the overall conference was so profound, 'It's hard to imagine what it would have been like without her.' Later, in its conference wrap-up, *The New York Times*' reporter Judy Klemesrud showcased Reid and her 'militant feminist viewpoint'.[9] Her statements about women's 'invisibility' in the outside world were discussed, along with her urgent call to change attitudes towards women, 'otherwise there will be no such thing as true equality'.

It perhaps won't surprise you to learn that media interest in the Australian position on women, and Reid's celebrated speech, stopped at the Australian border, blocked by an impenetrable, nation-sized cultural condom. No Australian media reported on Reid's speech – despite the Department of Foreign Affairs releasing the transcript in full. Media outlets who had no journalists on the ground and failed the basic practice of reportage – to seek interviews – ran the occasional wire story, with a few additional flourishes to add a tone of contempt.

The Australian Women's Weekly was the only print media outlet in Australia to send a journalist to cover the Mexico conference. Although reporter Philippa Day Benson arrived days after Reid delivered her speech, she nevertheless felt the afterglow. By the end of the second week, Reid was being courted by international media, who were so impressed with Australia's contribution that Day Benson says her Australian press label became 'a source of pride'.[10] The *Women's Weekly* journalist had also been the lone Australian reporter at the key IWY event in New York months earlier, when Reid and Germaine Greer had appeared on an all-star TV panel to debate 'Women and Men: The Next 25 Years'. Day Benson detailed how impressed UN officials and other international leaders were with Australia's IWY priorities, and with Reid and Greer's 'outstanding insight and ability to see the issues clearly'.[11]

In New York, Reid had done the rounds of talk shows, including an hour-long appearance on the Bill Moyers TV show, where she was joined by Iranian diplomat Zuzu Tabatabai. The two women later become great friends, but Moyers seemed to want to pit them against one another: one a 'Western white woman of privilege', the other a Muslim woman – also of privilege – but from a distinctly different cultural background. The women weren't buying it. Instead of highlighting their differences, they found common ground in the 'basic discriminatory attitudes' faced by all women, regardless of race, religion or social status.

Unable to prise open any disunity or conflict, Moyers eventually slumped into the 'man as victim' role: 'Do you know how hard it is to be a man in this kind of world today?' he asked. Quick as a whip, Reid replied:

> I should imagine that it's a very fearful thing – for two reasons. Firstly, I think that very often men don't even understand their own reactions against women. But secondly, it's a world and time of change and questioning; therefore, its unsettling for everybody. But particularly men.
>
> I mean, women today are beginning to walk differently. Now you may not understand why you react against this. We're not just waddling along; we're not crumbling along and we're not clinging anymore. Some of us are striding along the streets.

I always smile when I hear that line: 'Women today are beginning to walk differently.' I can pick a confident woman a mile away. It's in her walk, the way she holds her shoulders, the way she moves her head, how she listens. Confidence in a woman is the greatest, most enviable beauty, a glorious thing to behold. To picture a whole population of women walking taller, stronger, prouder as a result of the revolution they've experienced within themselves, well, it's an image – and an aspiration – to hold dear.

Ringmaster in a multilingual circus: The World Plan of Action

At all UN global conferences, there is an agreed outcomes document at the conclusion that member states sign on to. Or choose not to. For the first World Conference on Women, producing that document – the World Plan of Action – was a tortuous affair, steered with extraordinary dexterity by Elizabeth Reid. The IWY consultative committee tasked with drafting the

Plan first met in March 1975, in New York. It was headed by Iran's Ashraf Pahlavi, twin sister of the Shah of Iran. Sensing the almighty battle ahead, Pahlavi appointed Reid chair of the working group, which was a little like being made ringmaster of a multilingual circus out of control. What should have been a diplomat's polite picnic turned into a hair-raising rollercoaster ride of bullying, disagreement, threats and exhaustive debate. Twenty-three nations were represented around the table, most with vastly different views on what women needed most. During arguments over economics and equality, Reid continued to push the group towards 'radical revolutionary demands', persisting with the Australian mantra of changing attitudes and cultural restructure. It was a tough sell.

Gun-carrying Mexican delegates – including Mexico's Attorney General (who had managed to get himself elected president of the conference) and the chief of police (who inexplicably appears to have appointed himself to the working group) – fought furiously with the Americans. It was left to Reid to steer a way through what at times looked like becoming an international incident. She recalls chairing those sessions as 'the most difficult meetings' of her life. But she drew heavily on her Women's Liberation framework and theory to shift the dynamic and change the style of engagement to what was later described as resembling a 'feminist political meeting'. She used both candour and diplomacy, as well as a good dose of Australian straight shooting. One of the participants was so impressed with Reid's style that he even commented, 'I think I may be on the verge of taking feminism seriously.'[12]

At one point, Reid pulled the recalcitrant, warring nations (who were all sticking to their national geopolitical agendas) into line with a rousing speech, in which she urged the delegates to challenge their own gender bias around stereotypes such as the typical 'homemaker' and 'breadwinner', and the perceived binary between the two. 'Both men and women must be made aware of our habitual patterns of prejudice,' she lectured them, 'which we often do not see as prejudice but whose existence manifests itself in our behaviour and in our language.' The address energised the room and shifted sentiment. One of the UN attendees passed her a scribbled note: 'You have consciousness raised this whole committee and have changed it from traditional rhetoric to something fundamental and important.'[13] With Reid at the helm, Australia had significant input into the process of arriving at some point of agreement. That kudos further cemented Australia's role as one of the three lead players at the conference, along with Iran, a substantial sponsor, and Mexico, the host.

After argument over every word – and every punctuation point – through a total of 894 amendments, the final World Plan of Action adopted by the Mexico conference was a long way from what Reid and her team had hoped it would be. The document reflected both progress and unresolved tensions around issues of priorities for women, particularly where goals of economic justice and development were seen as competing with equal rights, political participation and education. The perpetually divisive issue of motherhood and traditional roles of women versus recognition of women as independent individuals beyond the family unit touched a raw nerve with most delegates, and discussions were bogged down in conservative politics. The feminist push to broaden the agenda to include individual rights, legal protections and bodily autonomy for women had Elizabeth Reid's influence woven all through it. Therefore, the failure to enshrine some of these critically important progressive steps for women into the Plan of Action severely bruised Reid. She wore her disappointment heavily.

Nevertheless, despite those tensions, this was an historic first attempt at laying out a global agenda for women's rights, and Australia was viewed as the driving force behind the best of it. Elizabeth Reid was credited with corralling the myriad disparate views and competing agendas, and ensuring a final plan was drafted and presented for UN member states to vote on. When the UN proclaimed the 'Decade for Women' would follow International Women's Year, international media referred to the Plan as the quaintly ambitious '10-year action plan for sexual equality'. The document heralded Australia's key goal of changing society's attitudes about women, stating: 'A major obstacle in improving the status of women lies in public attitudes and values regarding women's roles in society.'[14] Australia and circling progressive nations were deeply disappointed that the word 'sexism', much less the concept, was not included in the 49-page plan. But the fact delegates were talking about it and were forced to consider it was thanks to Reid boldly raising it, right there on centre stage, in the first place. No one else did.

Although the Plan of Action failed to meet Reid's hopes and expectations, the secondary document – the Mexico Declaration – gave her heart. Drawn up in a unique collaboration between diplomats and feminists from the global south and non-aligned nations, the Declaration was presented on the final day of the conference.[15] It wasn't well received by the US or Israel, as it specifically called for the elimination of colonialism, Zionism and apartheid, as well as an end to land acquisition by force. But Reid says it was 'the first attempt to try and make the links we had been pushing for, between demands for a more just economic order and the specific needs of women'.

At the parallel Tribune conference for NGOs, many of the delegates argued they should also have input into the World Plan of Action. They didn't get it. But at the completion of the process, the UN's Helvi Sipilä addressed some 2000 delegates to urge them forward. She said what happened next was up to them. It was a reminder that any UN-endorsed action plan is not a legally binding document. Rather, the purpose of the Mexico Plan was to lay out the global consensus around women's rights and gender equality at that point in time. 'The UN cannot change your laws, your education, your economic plans,' she said. 'You are the ones [who can] ... You should be involved in national planning – and you should be heard.'

Later Sipilä told media in her final press conference in Mexico: 'Now I think we may see the beginning of a new world. The women who have been here say they are not the same persons any more.'[16] Liberia's representative to the United Nations went further. Assessing the value of International Women's Year, Angie Brooks told media, 'It was one of the greatest things the United Nations has done in its history. It forced the attention of the world on the injustice that has been practiced.'[17]

The role played by Australia at the UN World Conference on International Women's Year in Mexico cannot be overstated. Yet, back at home, it was severely understated, even ridiculed. In its parliamentary report on International Women's Year, the National Advisory Committee expressed a defiant exasperation over the national media. It noted the Mexico conference not only received surprisingly little coverage, but 'what coverage it did receive was almost universally misinformed, confused, and confusing'.[18] For Elizabeth Reid, the mud of media mockery stuck hard. Despite being internationally hailed at Mexico as a key influencer and authority on gender equity, mastheads such as *The Sydney Morning Herald* had already decided Whitlam's women's adviser gig was a waste of time, and Reid was too. Before the Mexico conference was over it ran an editorial, on 1st July 1975, stating: 'The best thing that can be said of her performance [in the role of women's adviser] is that it has been undistinguished. Indeed, it has been extremely difficult for Australians to discern just what Miss Reid has been doing for the past two years.'[19]

Now, it doesn't take a news junkie to cotton on to what is happening there. The political winds in Australia were changing. Whitlam's enthusiastic championing of International Women's Year, along with his full embrace of the liberation of women, was on the nose. Or, rather, it had got up the media's nose. It was an easy target for media wanting to needle the government. And it was soon to get much worse.

For historian Jocelyn Olcott, the Australian media's poor depiction of both Australia's efforts at Mexico and the impact Elizabeth Reid had on the conference simply doesn't tally with the reality. Reid, says Olcott, was a 'rock star'. 'She was an unapologetic feminist. The only UN meetings that have the word "feminism" in the title are meetings that Elizabeth Reid organised. Which is really telling, right? All these years later, that's still the case.'

Olcott points to Reid's 'moral authority', and her 'empathy to all sides'. 'She never dismissed people. She always listened. And people listened to her.' But she isn't surprised by the media reaction to Reid in Australia.

I think she was probably pretty threatening to those who didn't want to take feminism seriously, because to her feminism just seemed axiomatic: you start from feminism and then figure out the policies from there. But I think it was frustrating for her to realise that not everyone else was starting from the same place.

That photo: False 'facts' and a good feminist fight

Despite the engaged and mostly serious coverage international media outlets gave to the World Conference on Women, the most dominant theme reported – and widely repeated – was hype over 'female fighting'. Gosh, who would have thought? Thousands of women gather to discuss and debate issues of concern, and to prioritise what should be included in the United Nations 10-Year World Plan of Action, and there's *disagreement*? I'd be seriously disappointed if there wasn't. As stated, the intention of the organisers was to invite disruption, embrace disunity and challenge differences. So, women did.

'That photo', snapped and instantly shot around the world, was of an incident that took place not at the official government conference, but at the Tribune conference on the other side of Mexico City. It was attended by 6000 women representing community and non-government organisations from across the globe. When it came to representing feminism in 1975, feuds were a favourite starting place for media, and with some big egos such as Betty Friedan, and celebrity feminists such as Gloria Steinem, Germaine Greer and actor Jane Fonda in attendance at the Tribune, there were always cameras lurking. Waiting.

Ten days into the event, when people were tired, tempers were frayed and impatience with long, verbose speeches was growing, a sudden interruption on stage got photographers rushing to the front with flash bulbs firing. Associated Press secured the shot that within 24 hours swept the world and was reproduced in most major international newspapers. It was a close-up shot of two women fighting over a microphone with gusto. It's not a mere snatch but a moment of fierce altercation. Taken as a wide shot that originally showed a panel of women on stage – one of them laughing – the photo was cropped to zoom in and intensify the physicality of the moment and emphasise the conflict. Given the angle of the shot, it almost looks as if the woman in possession of the microphone, who has her elbowed raised and hand clawed, is about to scratch out the eyes of a woman attacking her from behind. Seemingly evidence of a 'global catfight', that photo, according to Olcott, became 'the most widely circulated image of the 1975 International Women's Year gathering in Mexico City'.[20]

Suddenly, lazy Australian media flexed its muscle. A brawl: joy! Media that had not bothered to report Elizabeth Reid's celebrated speech quickly became animated about the Women's Conference. 'FEMINISTS FIGHT AT MEETING', hollered *The Canberra Times*, which went on to detail how 'feuding feminists grappled for microphones and screamed insults'.[21] *The Sydney Morning Herald* followed suit with the headline 'Feminists scream insults at meeting'.[22] The *Daily Mirror* leapt to declare that 'Women's talks were a failure', quoting a French delegate ('Grotesque, screaming and rather painful …') and again using a single image to represent all that had happened over two weeks in Mexico.[23]

Major media players ran large images of the cropped photo, and *New York Times* correspondent Judy Klemesrud described a 'scene of much shouting, scheming, plotting and general hell-raising'. Her explanation for the fighting on stage was 'a protest by Latin women, who felt their views had been overlooked.'[24]

Time magazine ran an uncropped version of the same photo, which widened out to include a black woman who was apparently also battling the two Latin women for the microphone. *Time* internationalised the brawl by suggesting the three women were from Latin America, Europe and Africa – each representing a different continent's view.[25] That was just plain nonsense. No reporter appears to have spoken to the women on stage. Even worse, no one thought to interview the 'African' woman and ask why she was involved in a vigorous protest by 'Latin women', who were in fact Mexicans. If they had, they would have discovered she wasn't African at all. She was Fijian. Her name was Amelia Rokotuivuna and she was chairing a panel on nuclear disarmament in the Pacific when it was rudely interrupted by the Mexicans, who, for unknown reasons, chose a panel on 'non-violent peace protests' as their moment to disrupt.

As a television journalist, I have an insatiable curiosity about what is happening outside the frame, and immediately before and after an image is frozen. So, I went in search of the footage. Discovering it at Australia's National Film and Sound Archive was like waking up on Christmas morning to find a shiny-new dragster under the tree. I think I squealed with glee. After speaking with many women who were furious about 'the photo' incident and its widespread use by media, I have a very guilty confession: I loved this brawl. If I had been present, as a television reporter, I too would have zoomed in and relished the wild flaying-about of hands, arms and microphone, and the attempts by the ever-smiling Amelia Rokotuivuna to calm the women down. The actual footage is even better than the moment captured in 'that photo'.

The women fight with vigour, and the microphone is yanked from one to the other, like a relay baton snatched from an opposing team. The woman who started it all suddenly gives up on the mic, gulps down a glass of water and then stands up on the table. The crowd goes wild. Her nemesis grabs her from the side. She flings her off. Another woman from the Pacific panel tries to coax her down from the back. She shakes her off too. The panellist grabs the blouse of the woman on the table and tugs, hard. It's stretchy and springs the Mexican woman forward. She steadies herself and waves an arm at the crowd. They're hollering as if at a footy match. Another woman in pink jeans darts forward from the front of stage, grabs her elbow and yanks. The Mexican woman is not giving in. She bucks and kicks. At one point, three women are tugging at her to get down.

I love an action shot, and this footage has it all. And yes, it makes for great TV viewing. Would I have used this footage if I was reporting on the World Conference on Women for the

ABC at the time? Yes. You bet. It was riveting and dramatic, which makes it news – and that is how news media works. But – and here is the critical 'but' – this is just one moment, in fact less than a few minutes, in an historic world conference that lasted two weeks. Without a thorough investigation to put the drama into context, explaining the issues that motivated the angry action and how the incident reflected on the conference in full – without all that, it is not news. It is just titillation. Which, as we know, was the lifeblood of Australian media back in 1975, and, to our shame, remains so today. As for the details? Damn them.

The story that has never been told about the moment of the brawl, and 'that photo', has Australia at the centre. (There we are again.) While arms were thrashing and cameras flashing, there was an Australian on the stage posing as a photographer. With a clear view of the drama, Anne Walker watched it all play out.

Originally from Melbourne, Walker was a student completing her PhD in the US. She was close mates with the Pacific women, having worked with them to set up the Fiji Young Women's Christian Association (YWCA) and develop a program of multiracial kindergartens. When she heard about these 'groundbreaking' women's meetings in Mexico, Walker travelled down south to support her friends. On the day of their Pacific panel, she became 'annoyed that all the journalists and photographers were men'. So, she says, 'I donned a hat and taped "PRESS" on the side so that I could go on stage and take photos.' Although she couldn't understand what the Mexican women were saying, this is what she saw:

Amelia leaned forward and tried to negotiate between the women. She suggested calmly they speak one at a time and she reached out to hold the microphone for them. Then suddenly flashbulbs went off from the floor as dozens or more photographers took their shots. Three women fighting on stage![26]

When Walker later read the media reporting of that moment, particularly the story in *Time* magazine that suggested Amelia was an African protester, she was horrified. In her memoir, Walker writes of how offended they all were on Amelia's behalf, 'who felt it was terribly unfair that she had been used in this way'.

The small crew of Australian and Fijian women had made their way to the Mexico conference to protest against French nuclear testing at Mururoa atoll, in French Polynesia. In the lead-up to the Mexico conference, Elizabeth Reid had met with a broad group of women in the Pacific to encourage them to get involved, to teach them how the UN operates and what they needed to do to participate. One of the women, Ruth Lechte, also from Melbourne, then working as executive officer of the FIJI YWCA, wrote newsy letters home to her parents from the Mexico conference. With a lovely Aussie sense of humour and turn of phrase, she wrote about the opening of the Women's Conference as a dreary endurance. 'We had to suffer all the big ladies,' she said, referring to the Philippines' Imelda Marcos, the prime minister of Sri Lanka and the first ladies from Israel and Egypt, all of whom gave long opening speeches. 'Then, praise God, Australia did the right thing for once,' she wrote:

Margaret Whitlam is here, but Elizabeth Reid is
head of delegation, and she gave the best speech of
the conference – that is one very smart cookie. We
are having an all-Pacific meeting in her apartment
tomorrow night [before the panel] … Margaret
Whitlam is a very natural, pleasant, intelligent and able
woman. Comes up and has a little chat … [she] certainly

does her homework. Eliz Reid is undoubtedly brilliant, and of course stands out in the conference. All the bright people and radicals are over at the Tribune.[27]

Elizabeth Reid had talked the women through their conference strategy, with advice on how to get the most leverage out of their panel opportunity. But no one could have foreseen how their moment in the spotlight would be stolen. It wasn't just the spoiled opportunity that bothered Anne Walker. It was the media's sweeping disregard of the critical substance of the Mexico NGO conference. She says the organisers of the Tribune were stunned that their efforts to bring women together were characterised in this way, and that the photo, 'so unrepresentative and so staged', became the conference's most enduring image. 'It could not have been more wrong in its characterization,' Walker wrote. 'In fact, women came together in a miraculous way, forming alliances, networks, making contacts that have endured to this day. It was the beginning of a new day for women of the world.'[28]

Although you'd be hard-pressed to glean that sense of a 'miraculous' outcome from much of the news coverage and post-IWY media analysis, women themselves were clearly deeply affected by their experiences in Mexico. From the distance of half a century, it's difficult to fathom just how powerful a world gathering must have been for those who had never met women from beyond their own borders before, in an era well before the internet and our 24/7 connectedness. Many of them had never had an opportunity to hear stories of female struggle that mirrored their own. Nigeria's Dr Victoria Mojekwo encapsulated the unrivalled power of this connection when she told *The New York Times*: 'You know, there is something called catharsis, sharing and participation. You have pain for so many years, and now I know that women all over the world have this same pain. If this is all I get out of the Tribune, then that's enough.'[29]

Bringing Aussie order to a global 'spontaneous outpouring'

After Mexico, when everyone returned home and International Women's Year drew to a close, it quickly became obvious that this 'moment' was not over. A global movement was emerging. As Anne Walker later wrote, Mexico created a groundswell: 'The IWY Tribune triggered a chain of events that few could have foreseen.'[30] Women's activism around the globe had been networked for the first time. Unprecedented and precious, no one was going to let that go.

The following year, mid-1976, Anne Walker received a phone call from Mildred Persinger, chair of the NGO International Women's Year Committee at the United Nations in New York, who she had met in Mexico. She was phoning to explain a problem: a room overflowing with correspondence from women who had attended the Tribune. There were literally thousands upon thousands of letters. Could Walker come to New York and set up some kind of communications system to deal with the deluge? Now that the United Nations had declared 1976–1985 the 'Decade for Women', women's actions and enthusiastic expectations were clearly revving up.

When she walked into the New York office, Anne Walker had no idea what to expect. 'I was greeted by thousands of opened letters and packages, heaped and spilling from desks, shelves, chairs and boxes,' she writes. 'I sat crossed-legged on the floor ... and began to read.' Some of the correspondents requested information; others wanted to continue the connection; some proposed new women's projects for their communities and needed support or technical training. Others wrote simply to share what they had been doing back in their home countries since returning from Mexico.

Walker spent weeks reading every word and sorting the material into categories and piles, while she tried to work out what to do with it all. 'We needed a strategy that would allow us to somehow respond to this spontaneous outpouring,' she wrote. And so began a unique and remarkable process of building databases, communication platforms, information packs and eventually training modules for women around the world. The bulk of correspondence was from the third world, where women were keen to know how others had solved various local problems. Soon Walker was developing resource kits, with information adapted to different locations based on information women were sharing. Within months she had established a full resource service: the International Women's Tribune Centre. She landed on the idea of an informative and 'newsy' newsletter, which very soon became an invaluable tool of connection and resource for thousands upon thousands of women, sent out in English, French and Spanish. Amazingly, Walker and her team of three others regularly sent the newsletter to more than 26 000 women and women's organisations. Remember we're talking pre-computer days – no Mailchimp or data apps. It was all done by hand, and the Tribune newsletter continued for an extraordinary 25 years.

Despite disappointment over what was excluded from the final World Plan of Action, the Australian delegation to Mexico returned home in strong spirits. As Ruth Lechte wrote to her parents back in Melbourne, 'Australia got the show on the road!'[31] The Mexico Plan had enshrined a fundamental recognition that all women – regardless of economic status – shared the same painful experience of female oppression, whether they lived in the third world or the global north. This was the first time that women in the development movement had seriously and productively engaged with the feminist movement. That alone was a game changer. Elizabeth Reid refers to those discussions as 'electric': 'Feminists started appreciating that their movement was only one part of a global women's movement, a spontaneous awakening of women from one end of the globe to another.'[32]

With that recognition, women grasped the enormous potential for revolution.

13

THE WOMEN AND POLITICS CONFERENCE

There had never been a gathering like it.

The Australian delegation to Mexico returned home fired with purpose. Back in Canberra, the pile of sensationalist press clippings critical of the global conference didn't merit attention for now. There was too much work to do, too many radical new ideas to explore.

Held in Canberra in early spring, the Women and Politics Conference 1975 was billed as Australia's premier event for International Women's Year. It was an intense week-long program of workshops and lectures that covered every aspect of political participation for women: understanding power, the mechanics of political parties, working the bureaucracy, feminist theory and handling the media. Designed to provoke and challenge, the event was the brainchild of Elizabeth Reid. Tragically, it would also be her undoing.

Anyone who wanted to come to the conference was financially supported to get there. Free childcare and holiday programs for older kids were included. They arrived in groups, on buses, some flying across the country, others came alone: migrant women, rural women, curious housewives, political conservatives, Marxist socialists, Indigenous women. Even a group of nuns turned up, with a string of students in tow.

Barbara Wawn wasn't an official speaker at the conference

but that didn't stop her talking to whoever would listen. A factory worker and shop steward from Melbourne, Barb arrived in the nation's capital carrying a tray of lamingtons for the international speakers. 'I was going to make the lamingtons all last week,' she told a reporter, 'but I was so bloody busy I made them an hour before I left for the plane.' Barb and her Aussie treats hadn't had a smooth trip to the capital. 'I stuck the fork in one of them and I dropped the bastard on the floor. Bloody cake, chocolate and icing everywhere when I'm trying to get on the plane.' She also crocheted three tea cosies in Australian wool as a gift for one of the British keynote speakers, May Hobbs, organiser of the London-based Cleaners Action Group.[1]

Within its radicalism were numerous new and ground-breaking conversations. Participants debated questions around women's identity and fear of power, the meaning of feminism, the difference between equality and liberation, the role of conservative women's voices, women's maligned status in the church, reform versus revolution, the impact of racism within feminism, sexism and the representation of women in media. These were conversations driven by curiosity and the search for a woman's place in a world of changing power dynamics and new opportunity.

The resonance with where we find ourselves now, 50 years later, could not be more profound.

The conversations and debates at the Women and Politics Conference were provocative and life changing because women didn't hold back. They didn't need to; there was little to lose. These sessions were unique and powerful because they were stripped of self-censoring. Women were unconcerned about standing in disagreement with one another. If an audience member thought the speaker was speaking a load of rubbish, she said so. Or she protested by walking out. The aim was to deliberately challenge and provoke. And they did.

The debates and issues women were discussing back then are still with us. They are issues that demand our attention and action right now. This is where we can most clearly see that the work of 1975, International Women's Year, is unfinished business. These are lingering conversations we need to return to.

But first: the opening-night fiasco.

Ladies suit up for a rowdy opening night

Margaret Reynolds was a 25-year-old teacher who had never been to Canberra. A founding member of the Women's Electoral Lobby in Townsville, Margaret made the long trip south with a friend. Proudly wearing their WEL T-shirts, they weaved their way through the buzzing crowd at Parliament House (now quaintly known as Old Parliament House) for the opening-night reception on 31 August, fascinated by the variety of fashions on display. Among the noisy, diverse and colourful crowd of 700 women were young hip women in long skirts and cheesecloth, conservative women in twin-sets and pearls, nuns in habits, women in jeans and all sorts in between. Nearly two dozen women turned up wearing men's suits and ties – a fun jab at the official invitation that idiotically stipulated 'lounge suits'. That sent the media into a frenzy, obsessing about the women's 'disrespect'. *The Daily Telegraph* was so incensed it suggested perhaps the prime minister should have reciprocated by 'bringing a plate'.[2] (Barb's lamingtons wouldn't have gone astray.)

Oblivious to the media furore at the time, Reynolds was enthralled by the exciting vibe: 'The buzz and the atmosphere was just extraordinary,' she says. 'I had never been to an event that was all women. And there were hundreds of us!' Officially, there were also two men registered. Margaret Reynolds would later go on to spend 16 years as a senator, including as Assistant Minister for Women. But on that first trip she had no thoughts of a political career at all – nor, in all the excitement, was she worried about the husband and three kids she'd left behind in Townsville. (That week, budding historian Henry Reynolds became the first man in Townsville seen pushing a pram alone.) King's Hall in Parliament House was hot and stuffy, despite being on the threshold of spring, and the place was pumping. 'Many of us probably drank more than we should have,' says Reynolds. 'It was a very entertaining, exciting and invigorating atmosphere. And yes, there were a few women staggering down the stairs when we left.'

Gough Whitlam began his long opening speech by boldly stating what every woman knew, but no man in power had dared say out loud:

> For most of this country's history women have lived
> without visible political power; they have been excluded
> from almost all levels of government in our society. The
> momentous decisions of war and peace, of finance and
> technology, as well as the everyday decisions which affect
> how all people live, have been made by a minority of
> individuals who happened to be born white and male.

At that time, there was a grand total of three women in Whitlam's government and 92 men – a small improvement on the figures at the 1972 election, when Whitlam had won with not a single woman in his caucus. The PM's speech pushed on with a clarion call to women to step up: 'Women must learn how to make their words effective,' he boomed. 'Women must learn to bring about those changes they want.'[3]

In hindsight, half a century later, Whitlam's emphasis on the burden of change being the responsibility of women could be read as borderline offensive. Once again, women are being told to 'change' or 'fix' themselves, as if the problems of social and political exclusion are of their own making. But that would be a misconstruction of both Whitlam and Elizabeth Reid's intent. The Whitlam government's enormous social reform agenda tackled gender discrimination on myriad fronts. Its $74 million childcare program and the abolition of university fees, which saw a flood of women pour into tertiary education, were complete game changers. Those and other social, economic and cultural policies began the painfully slow process of dismantling the patriarchs' clenched-fisted grip on institutional bias.

But, that said, until women changed their own mindset, and killed off what Whitlam referred to in his speech as 'the deeply ingrained assumption that women are here to serve or assist' – until women smashed that attitude – progress would remain impossible. The clear message was that women must believe in themselves first before they can take up the fight. It's a sentiment echoed in the speech given 45 years later by UN Secretary-General António Guterres, in which he reiterated that 'Power is not usually given. Power must be taken.'[4]

Just as Whitlam warmed to his theme, women protesters began a rowdy chant behind him. A small group unfurled banners criticising Australia's treatment of East Timor. A group of Indigenous women protesters also filled the space, heckling and singing 'We Shall Overcome'. Soon even Whitlam struggled to be heard. Women hung protest placards on the statue of King George V in King's Hall, proclaiming 'Women and Revolution; not Women and Bureaucracy'. There are even rumours of lipstick graffiti – 'Lesbians are Lovely' – scrawled across mirrors in the loos. All in all, it sounds like a fabulous night. For the women lucky enough to be there, it was!

International Women's Year had triggered discussion and expectation among women that was unthinkable only a few years earlier. The world for women was seriously shifting. Now, finally, they had a real shot at power, a chance to influence how the nation is run and what gets prioritised from inside the tent. Among the women crowded into King's Hall that night, it wasn't just a party buzz exciting them. It was a power buzz. Here was a prime minister urging them to learn how political power works – and take it.

For the young mum from Townsville, Margaret Reynolds, women across Australia were primed for real change. 'There was a palpable sense of forward motion among the women. This was their time and they knew it! There was a vibe of "Hey, we can get this done. We can make change happen. We can do this!"' Reynolds says. 'Among some women there was a real impatience for reform. There were also *huge* expectations on Liz Reid.'

Theory and resonance:
Old questions that prod new answers

Thankfully, Elizabeth Reid insisted the seminar and workshop discussions at the 1975 Women and Politics Conference were all recorded. Reading through these fabulous transcripts, I was struck by two things. First was the depth of knowledge and theory shared in these utterly fascinating conversations, and how unafraid women were to question and debate one another. They didn't shy away from taking each other on. Second was how much of what women said back then resonates right now. This is not to say things haven't changed. Of course they have. But what this reveals – or perhaps reminds us – is that many of the fundamental concerns women were battling in the mid-'70s, 50 years ago, still preoccupy us today, as the world around us rolls backwards fast.

Women's lack of access to power was a theme throughout. As was deep anger at the media's representation of women and the focus on women's bodies and appearance. Frustration over sexism wove through much of the talk, in the same way we frequently speak of misogyny today. Additionally, women's frustration over not being treated seriously was a common refrain, overlayed by assumptions that it is women – and not men – who will naturally curb their ambitions to put the needs of family and children first. So, what's changed?

The theoretical approach to understanding women's oppression back in '75 was impressive. Far from a women's whingefest, the Women and Politics Conference was all about unpacking the 'why' and 'how', no matter the theme of the session or workshop. While discussions were well grounded in theory, they were steeped in practicality – and in women's reality.

Although there were exceptions.

Biff Ward tells a funny tale of how she got a little carried away when writing her presentation on 'The politics of feminism'. She says she expected only about '12 sisters to turn up'. To her horror, she walked into a room jam-packed with more than 200 eager-eyed women hungry to learn. Biff says, 'I didn't have the wisdom to scrap the paper, which most of them later said they didn't understand. It was so full of jargon. I was using terms like "the existential faction" and "political entryism".' She laughs about it now, saying even she can't follow it.

Keep in mind that this was not an academic conference and these were not students. This was a public event that attracted women from all walks of life, including young mothers, self-declared homemakers and political novices. Yet the depth of discussion and the seriousness with which women drove questions and shook out answers from speakers – and from one another – was remarkable. Most importantly, there was no agreed groupthink to keep the environment 'safe' and 'nice'.

The issue of Aboriginal women's involvement in the conference was initially a point of tension. A number were invited as official speakers, but plenty more attended and wanted to be heard. So, early in the week, a 'Black Speak Out' was held, in which Indigenous women did the talking and white women were asked to do the listening. Marcia Langton, now a distinguished professor and Indigenous leader, was working as a nutrition coordinator for an Aboriginal health service in Sydney back in '75. Langton told the Speak Out that racism and sexism are an integral part of the imperialist system and that they will not be eradicated until the system is destroyed. Indigenous activist Ruby Hammond told the audience it was 'too early for Aboriginal women to be concerned solely with the feminist cause'.[5]

Unfailingly provocative, American lawyer, civil rights activist and feminist Flo Kennedy led a session on 'Black women in society', in which she used language and imagery that these days would have cancel culture hyperventilating. She was described in parliament as 'that foul-mouthed harridan'. Margaret Whitlam scoffed, telling journalists Kennedy was 'intelligent, charming, wonderful'.[6] Kennedy berated women for thinking they were braver than they really are, and spoke of differences in both the degree and kind of oppression people experienced. She urged women with the least amount of power to stop feeling sorry for themselves and instead figure out a 'hierarchy of enemies'. A forced cleaving of social mores was Kennedy's forte, which of course Elizabeth Reid had known when she invited the famed activist to the conference. Disruption was part of the plan. Kennedy told her audience: 'One of the things that this conference will produce is not unity but a coalition of dissatisfied people who will deal with the enemy.'[7]

The celebrated British feminist theorist Juliet Mitchell led a session at the conference called 'Feminist theory?'. Australian socialist feminists relished the opportunity to quiz her. Did she view 'feminist theory as being quite separate from Marxist theory?' they asked. In her longwinded response she made a passing observation: 'Of course, Marxism to date has very much underestimated the sexual divisions within the classes that it's analysing.'

Reading this half a century after these discussions were thrashed out by women piled around a seminar room in Canberra, sitting on the floor, desks and tables, the comment may slide by us now as unremarkable. However, it was a pivotal contribution to an ongoing debate of the time. Some of the women present expressed a self-consciousness about their status as 'middle class'. 'There is nothing wrong with being a middle-class woman per se,' Mitchell said. 'I mean after all what matters is your politics not your class origin.'

Mitchell went on to do a bit of prodding herself. She wanted women to move past understanding the cause of their oppression to unpacking *why* they were oppressed. Any such investigation, she said, should 'start with the present and work backwards, rather than starting with the past and working forwards'.[8]

This has profound resonance with our New Now and the rapidly escalating backlash women are facing today. If we are to follow Mitchell's model, we return to the fundamental questions and ask not just *what* are women losing now, but *why* they are losing it. Why are global forces actively working to dismantle women's rights and wind back female autonomy at this point in time? We know men have always oppressed women – that much is clear. But why an acceleration of oppression right now? What is the reason for this heightened male fear of women's progress? Why women? And why now? These are the questions our feminist foremothers are girding us to tackle.

But first, back at the Women and Politics Conference, they had a media machine to crush.

Media men explain things to me

It really was a case of 'you had to be there'. By now, it is clear how incredibly transformative this conference was for the women who attended it, and how radical the thinking was that underpinned it. Yet the version of this groundbreaking event that appeared in the Australian media was full-scale mockery. It gave the impression attendees were little more than a big bunch of rabble-rousing feminists, confused about their 'feminine identity', as *The Canberra Times* infamously put it.[9]

Anticipating they would not get fair or serious coverage from mainstream media, the International Women's Year secretariat had set up their own daily newspaper, *New Dawn*, which was distributed each morning of the Women and Politics Conference. Run by Gillian Appleton with a team of journalists, *New Dawn* provided the only detailed media coverage of the conference sessions and debates, along with interviews and feature articles on the issues raised. This small pile of fading newspapers, now half a century old and housed in the National Library of Australia, remains a critical media record of what actually occurred that week. Its front page on day one of the conference drew a line in the sand: 'Watch out media' was the banner headline.

I can only wonder what feminist writer Rebecca Solnit, author of the essay 'Men explain things to me', might make of Australia's media men.[10] In 1975, Elizabeth Reid had more reason than most to despise the Australian media. But a philosopher at heart, she encouraged understanding instead and invited senior journalist Evan Williams, who worked for Prime Minister Whitlam, to lead a session at the Women and Politics Conference on 'Handling the media'.

Williams was super media savvy. Or so he thought. He kicked off by telling the women present what they already knew:

'I think it's fair to say on the whole that the women's movement does have a bad press.'[11] (Well, that nearly knocked the socks off them.) Then, in the spirit of the conference, Williams attempted to dig deep and ask the hard question – the 'why'. Why do women get such lousy press?

Well, that was easy. 'Media still see the cause of women as something of a joke,' he said. The reason was 'moral': media men were, in truth, a bit fuddy-duddy and old-worldly. 'They like to appear trendy and progressive,' he said, 'but their responses are generally old-fashioned and predictable.' They saw anything progressive and 'unconventional' as an attack on the moral fibre of society.

Clearly warming to his theme, Williams pushed on, explaining there was a 'stereotyped picture of the female activist' to which media had a 'reflex reaction': 'She's an intellectual, she's unfeminine … she's probably morally lax, she's shrill, intolerant, slovenly, noisy, and of course she hates men.'

How I wish I could time-travel back to Canberra 1975 and squeeze into the back row of that session to ask out loud, 'And Mr Williams, what do you think made her so shrill and intolerant?' While laying out the problem with women – as perceived by media men – it didn't seem to occur to Williams to unpack why men are free to exercise and publish their prejudices.

Next, Williams turned to the next most important conference question: 'What do we do about it?' Rather than address structural bias, media attitudes and behaviour, or the problem with a monopoly of old, white, anti-progressive men running the show, Williams instead opted for the flaccid solution men have continued to use ever since – just fix the woman! 'I don't have any particular advice to offer on this problem,' he said earnestly, 'but I do believe it's probably best to emphasise the broader, deeper, more humane values of the cause.'

In other words, shut the noisy woman down. And just be nice.

Like Rebecca Solnit, I love it when men explain things to me.

'Angry mob of women' terrify newspaper editor

By the spring of 1975, women had endured months of snide media attacks on the aspirations of International Women's Year. Despite the small presence of talented women in journalism, the institutionalised sexism within the male media monopolies was the problem. Letters of protest weren't cutting through. By now, feminists had media outlets clearly in their sights.

Despite the week-long Women and Politics Conference being held in Canberra, not a single member of the Canberra press gallery attended any sessions. Yet many wrote commentary about it, mostly based on hearsay, according to the report by the National Advisory Committee.[12] Given the Australian media's dreadful coverage of the Mexico World Conference on Women, the advisory committee didn't hold high hopes for the Women and Politics Conference, but it proved much worse than expected: 'the extent of the violent, even hysterical reaction it produced could not have been foreseen'.[13]

Mainstream media coverage focused almost singularly on 'divisiveness' – as if disagreement between women represented some kind of foul moral failing. 'Squabbling Libbers only set back the cause', claimed the *Daily Mirror* (8 September), while others used the 'Black Speak Out' day as evidence of intractable divisions: 'Aboriginal women attack "white elitism"', headlined *The Sydney Morning Herald* (2 September). The opening-night reception was universally reported as if it was a chaotic circus: 'a disgusting display of vandalism', with 'delegates squabbling among themselves', trumpeted *The Daily Telegraph* (4 September). By the week's end, a *Sydney Morning Herald* editorial (6 September) declared the conference 'a waste of money' and 'unproductive', and suggested that 'All Australians are poorer for its failure.'

One fading news item, titled 'Gracious womanhood' and dated 13 September 1975, had pride of place on Senator Margaret Reynolds' office wall in Canberra for years. These days it lives on her kitchen cupboard. Reynolds clipped it from her local paper in Townsville when she arrived home from the Women and Politics Conference all those years ago. In an almost breathless baritone it describes the conference as 'a smog of radicalism and vulgarity constituting an affront to human dignity and decency … a scandalous waste of taxpayers' money'. Reynolds can't stop laughing as she reads it to me.

Australian women were well used to the unflinching sexism of our media, but the sneering tone shocked the international speakers at the '75 conference. Juliet Mitchell described it as 'horrifying', while Flo Kennedy didn't hold back, calling Australian media 'atrocious … sexist, racist and incompetent'.[14]

Frustrated by the relentlessly negative media, the Liberal Party – which ran a number of sessions at the so-called 'socialist feminist conference' – issued a press release, in which the president of the Women's Committee enthusiastically praised the conference. No one reported it.

Then came the shocker editorial that would provoke the women at the conference to take action in an historic anti-media protest. On Tuesday 2 September 1975, in what can only be described as tortured prose, *The Canberra Times* published an editorial titled 'The role of women': a ham-fisted attempt to explain to women their purpose in life (Rebecca Solnit would love this one too) while also berating the Women and Politics Conference for not including men (which it did, but only two came). Seemingly unaware of the patronising and inherent chauvinism, the editorial spoke of 'feminine wisdom', a 'woman's touch' and 'women's role in transmitting, fostering and protecting life'. It berated women who wanted paid jobs as a threat to 'the integrity of the family'.

In a common contortion of the times, the writer suggested women in the women's movement wanted to be men, or viewed themselves as 'a substitute for man', in the belief that the sexes are 'interchangeable'. Then came my favourite line: 'It would be curious if nature had gone to so much trouble to make women and men different merely so the differences could go to waste.' Then the writer heaved a sigh of relief, suggesting that despite all this gender confusion, and women wearing male trousers to the conference, 'hardly any had so far relinquished their feminine identity as to go without a handbag'. Phew.

In response, later that week, an angry swell of 300 women from the conference marched in protest through the city streets to the headquarters of *The Canberra Times*, where they reportedly 'stormed' the office. In truth, they simply walked in. Nevertheless, the protest is what the media focused on.

More than half of the marching women piled into the newsroom. Yes, it was a squeeze. The paper later reported that they were 'standing on desks and chairs and filing cabinets'. A news photographer snapped a now famous shot which shows a hapless John Farquharson, acting editor of *The Canberra Times*, his hands gesticulating and mouth open as he appears to be attempting to placate a throng of women around him. He is the lone male, in a sea of more than 100 women. No one is standing on anything. They are leaning in and listening. But they do not like what they hear.

Farquharson doesn't look terrified. He looks exasperated. And outnumbered. But if you were to believe the rest of the media's account of this moment, you'd imagine him cowering in a corner. 'Angry mob of women marches on newspaper' was a banner headline in the Melbourne *Sun* on 6 September; 'Women take "sexist" paper by storm', bellowed *The Age*.

Those women sound ferocious. Angry? Yes. Pissed off and ready to protest? Absolutely. But 'storming' is a big stretch.

Flo Kennedy was spot-on when she said the Women and Politics Conference would produce 'a coalition of dissatisfied people who will deal with the enemy'. Here they were. Despite their broad diversity of views, there was one thing that unified women at the conference: their fury at the media. *This* was the enemy.

Back at *The Canberra Times*, Farquharson was no doubt cursing his bad luck. If only he was on the weekend shift instead! It wasn't just women's anger over the media in general that fired them up to march in and berate him. Editorials are not necessarily written by the editor, or even the acting editor. Various members of the senior team may write them. But their purpose is to reflect the view of the publication. In this case, although I never knew John Farquharson, I'm willing to take a bold guess and suggest he had a heavy hand in it. At this point, I should disclaim my personal fondness for *The Canberra Times*. I was a columnist for several years at the paper and continue to write occasional commentary for it. However, back in 1975, there were no senior women within cooee of the editor's office. And doesn't it show?

The protesters demanded the paper publish a long and detailed statement in response, written by women attending the conference and the Media Women's Action Group. They also demanded *The Canberra Times* appoint women editorial writers. But that's not all. For nearly an hour they lectured Farquharson on media sexism. He listened. Then they asked him for his definition of feminism. And they listened. Closely.

Mr Farquharson's answer to 'What is feminism?' was concise. 'Feminism is femininity,' he said.

The f-word is always bound to cause trouble, isn't it?

In their statement for publication in *The Canberra Times*, the women included the following:

> This comment demonstrates an inexcusable ignorance of the principles and aims of feminism, and indicates the typical media reluctance to acquire knowledge which contradicts its prejudiced notions. Feminism is not about women becoming men; it is not about femininity and frills. Rather, feminists at the conference were coming together to explore how feminists relate to each other, to institutionalised power and to the Australian political scene.[15]

Under increasing criticism and pressure from within and outside government, Elizabeth Reid staunchly defended the protesters – including those who continued the action that night by marching to *The Canberra Times*' printing plant, in an attempt to stop the press. Biff Ward joined Canberra radical feminist Liz O'Brien at the helm of that march, right up to the doors of the printer's. They kept up a noisy chant for hours. 'It was just a huge outburst of anger and hurt,' says Biff. 'Everyone was just so incensed by the constant belittling by the media.'

Later Reid was interviewed on *A Current Affair* and asked if 'storming' *The Canberra Times* was appropriate. She didn't flinch. It was a 'fine' protest action, she said. Perfectly reasonable. 'But of course protests aren't [necessarily] effective. They don't bring about changes … That night didn't bring about a change in the industry,' she said. 'But it did bring about a change in the women.'

The Canberra Times protest is perhaps one of the few documented occasions when women in Australia have physically, en masse, invaded a news media space to say, 'No more! Stop!

We have had enough. We will not be demeaned by you.' For women on that march who had never joined a protest action before – just like the tens of thousands across Australia who joined the March4Justice in 2021 – they too no doubt felt the transformative impact of collectively pushing back and saying, 'No more!'

It is an empowering experience. One that we never forget.

THE 'BLOODY' FINALE

The dapper Robert Moore, host of the ABC's *Monday Conference*, was in good form at the Canberra Theatre on 1 September 1975. The show was broadcasting a panel discussion about the Women and Politics Conference, in front of a live and feisty audience. One of them wanted to know about feminism going 'hand in hand with other "isms"'. Before Elizabeth Reid could answer, Moore shot in: 'Rheumatism?'

Yes, he got a laugh. But the pointed question was a reference to the ongoing debate at the conference about feminists' embrace of socialism. Such public and continual references didn't play well for Gough Whitlam's government, which was under mounting pressure. All this 'women's stuff' and the media circus around it was seriously driving down Whitlam's approval ratings with the nation's voters. Or so the PM's advisers told him.

By then, the strain was beginning to show on Elizabeth Reid. The lively TV debate quickly turned to one of those deeply unresolved issues that plagued the women's movement in Australia: should feminists work 'inside' or 'outside' the system? This goes to the very heart of the fundamental tug of war within the women's movement in the mid-1970s. Revolution? Or reform? By virtue of being the first woman ever appointed to a senior government advisory role, specifically to advise on women's issues, Elizabeth Reid had the unenviable job of working out how to straddle both – how to be a radical feminist within a political system designed by and for men. Do you smash it? Or do you try to redesign and reform it, brick by bureaucratic brick, in favour of women? This was a vexed issue for Reid.

Rosemary Brown, the first black woman elected to parliament in Canada, was also on the ABC panel that night at the Canberra Theatre. She was another of the international guests Reid had brought to Australia for the Women and Politics Conference. Brown said she had agonised over this issue of 'outside' activism versus 'inside the political system'. Ultimately, she said, she opted to seize the opportunity on behalf of other women and go 'inside', with a fierce commitment to bring generations of women along with her.

'Elizabeth?' said Mr Moore. 'Inside the system or outside … which do you think is more likely to bring fruitful results?'

This is where the cracks begin to show. 'Personally, I think that, for their own personal sakes, women should fight outside wherever possible,' she said. 'I think the system is extraordinarily destructive and extraordinarily harmful. I think the price is too high for many individuals.'[1]

The high price extracted from Elizabeth Reid was already evident to those who had listened carefully. Less than two months earlier, at the Mexico conference, Reid had been interviewed by an ABC documentary crew with two other members of the Australian delegation, Susan Ryan and Sara Dowse. Faced with a camera, some people stiffen and contort. Others melt into a sort of cathartic moment of truth telling and speak with unguarded frankness. This footage has a vibe of the latter.

Susan Ryan, who would later become Senator Ryan – architect of the *Sex Discrimination Act 1984* and the first woman appointed to a Labor cabinet – spoke about how women 'have to take over the bureaucracy and take over the political machine as far as possible'. Sara Dowse nodded in agreement. There was a need, she said, for 'a very strong women's movement outside the system, and a very strong ... united group of women working within the system'.

This is when Elizabeth Reid revealed not only her mounting frustration but a raw sense of being overwhelmed and very alone. Spreading her hands to illustrate her point, as if grasping something illusive and slippery, she spoke of the need to have women in key positions 'on the inside'. Then, frowning furiously, she said, 'but they are under such pressure, such duress, such incredible continual compromise ... Anybody in Australia that has gone "in" has been just isolated.'[2] As the Women and Politics Conference drew to a close in September 1975, Reid's isolation was about to plummet to a new low.

By this late stage in International Women's Year, the media coverage of women's issues had become vicious and vindictive. The 'faceless men'– as Reid calls them – in the prime minister's inner sanctum could no longer take it. On the last day of the conference, Reid was called into the prime minister's office and confronted with a pile of media articles about the conference, spread over Whitlam's desk and spilling onto the floor. This was the moment when the full impact of media misogyny came crashing down on Reid, the world's first woman appointed as women's adviser to a head of government.

Naturally, media salivated over the details of what occurred in that meeting. Under an enormous headline screaming 'LIZ REID QUITS', the Australian Communist Party's *Tribune* newspaper reported that 'This week's events culminated in a flaming row between Whitlam, Reid and [John] Menadue, head of the PM's Department.'[3] Others suggested Reid was 'got at'.[4] There were even obtuse suggestions she had been 'swayed' by radical elements of the women's movement. Which, as anyone close to her knows, is nonsense, given Elizabeth Reid is 'swayed' by nothing other than her own conscience and fiercely clear set of values.

Reid smiles when I ask her about 'the meeting'. It may have been 50 years ago, but it clearly left an indelible mark at an exceptionally painful time in her life. There was no yelling. Reid says she argued her case against an overwhelmingly biased and deeply sexist media coverage, not just of the Women and Politics Conference but of International Women's Year and her role. The coverage had begun from the moment of her appointment. 'I was demeaned, parodied, insulted, belittled, patronised, judged, cartooned, lampooned – and more – by the press,' she said, years later.[5] She tried to impress upon the men in that room that despite all the media muckraking, women themselves were deeply impacted by the conference and the numerous IWY programs. Women were changing. Attitudes were shifting. In her role as women's adviser, Reid had received more letters than anyone else in government other than the PM himself. Women and girls across the nation had reached out – finally there was someone within government representing them.

But the 'faceless men' were determined to distance Whitlam from Reid, whom they described as a 'political liability'. The government was under enormous pressure, for reasons beyond 'the woman problem'. Reid says after she spoke, the men turned to Whitlam and insisted she had to go. He buckled.

She was offered a well-paid role within the bureaucracy that would effectively turn her into a 'femocrat'. It was designed to keep her at considerable distance from the corridors of power: an untenable proposition for someone accustomed to having the ear of the prime minister. But that wasn't why she rejected the job outright. It was a matter of principle. Biff Ward, her close ally, says that 'Elizabeth took the pure Women's Liberation method of operation as her guiding light in that job.' It's not surprising, then, that Reid decided that 'it was impossible to be a bureaucrat and a feminist visionary'.[6]

Reid says she decided to quit on the spot. She left the

meeting and attended the Women and Politics closing dinner that night without telling a soul what had happened, nor what she knew she was about to do.

The prime minister's women's adviser announced her resignation with a press release on 2 October 1975, and flew out of Australia the very next day. Later she said she felt like a political exile, hounded out of the country by the media.

Elizabeth Reid didn't return home for more than a decade.

Too late now. She's gone.

Reid's sudden departure shocked and dismayed women everywhere. Pop-up protests were held by women in city streets carrying banners berating the prime minister for her resignation. Radio talkback was rushed with callers lamenting Australia's loss. According to the final report of the National Advisory Committee, 'The reaction of regret at Elizabeth Reid's resignation was almost universal'.[7] Even the media had a miraculous change of heart. 'An unwanted resignation', was the headline on an Adelaide *Advertiser* editorial (6 October); 'Feminism lives on in Canberra', insisted *The Sun* (4 October). Laurie Oakes, a press gallery heavyweight, wrote admiringly about the considerable power and respect Reid had gained from the prime minister:

> She taught the Prime Minister the ideology of the women's movement. He gave her virtually total freedom – made her the only member of his staff with formal authority to make statements and public appearances in her own right. When Ms. Reid submitted a recommendation to the Government it almost invariably got the Prime Minister's backing.[8]

But none of this reached Elizabeth Reid. By the time the wheels of apology and regret were in motion, she was alone in Canada resting, trying to heal a badly bruised spirit.

Even now, half a century later, as I speak with Elizabeth about her decision to quit and the drama surrounding her departure, a flash of sadness crosses her face. I can see the pain of it in her eyes. It's not a sorrow for herself. Yes, she was exhausted and wrung out. But the sadness is for what was lost. What could have been. The feminist work she left behind in Australia, unfinished.

Once again, I am stuck by the weight of responsibility and the impassioned seriousness with which these dedicated rebels of the Women's Liberation Movement truly lived their revolution – and still do.

For Reid, there was never an end goal – some kind of 'feminist tomorrowland' – in sight. That wasn't the point of the revolution. 'We had to live our revolution ourselves at the same time as fighting for it,' she later wrote. 'The revolution had to be something that we could do, rather than something that we would aim for and hopefully someday arrive at.'[9]

As International Women's Year drew to an end, the world had changed. Women had changed. The government had changed. Gough Whitlam had lost to Malcom Fraser. The chair of the Federal Women's Committee of the Liberal Party, Beryl Beaurepaire, rode Fraser hard about retaining many of the women's policy reforms Whitlam had put in place.

Even the media was showing extraordinary signs of change, almost as if all editors had attended the same consciousness-raising Christmas party and been hit by a collective 'awakening', so dramatic was the change in tone when they assessed the value of International Women's Year at year's end. Most dropped the snide cynicism and ridicule in place of positive and encouraging headlines: 'Women have to keep on fighting' (*Advertiser*,

1 January 1976); 'IWY opens the door to liberation' (*Sydney Morning Herald*, 1 January); 'One year older, one year wiser', (Melbourne *Herald*, 1 January); and 'The world gets a shove' (*Sydney Morning Herald*, 11 December 1975).

In its detailed report to parliament in 1976, the National Advisory Committee was resolute: 'The women's movement in Australia has now entered into the decision-making world, not merely in order to be equal with men, or to learn to play tired old games, but in order to change that world.'[10]

By January 1976, still reeling from the toughest and most turbulent years in her young life, Elizabeth Reid was not dewy-eyed about the outcomes of International Women's Year. An enormous amount had been achieved. Of course. Women were no longer invisible, which itself was a remarkable shift. But there was still so very much more to do, she told a journalist in New York. The work was far from over: 'We women have to keep on fighting. Attitudes to women are so deeply ingrained that we should not delude ourselves that it's going to be easy. It isn't. It's going to be long and it's going to be bloody.'[11]

A CONCLUSION WITH NO END ...

How long, and how bloody? British feminist Juliet Mitchell called it 'the longest revolution' six decades ago. And yet, here we are: in a social revolution with seemingly no end. Those rebels and revolutionaries, even the reformists of the Australian women's movement, know it's not over. Those of us who have followed in their footsteps, tracking their paths and plotting our own, know it too. Now there is an urgency to our knowing.

At the very time we should be celebrating 50 years since International Women's Year, marking women's considerable progress, we are instead anxiously wringing our hands about what we know is ahead: planning what women must do next. Some of us are trawling through old wardrobes, looking for our revolutionary armour, girding ourselves with Australia's strong feminist legacy. There is a rumble out there.

The call to revolt is on. Again.

*

In March 2025, Hillary Clinton sat on stage with an eminent panel of women, including Christiane Amanpour, chief international anchor for CNN. The women were in a fighting mood. The event was to mark the 30th anniversary of the fourth UN World Conference on Women, in Beijing in 1995.

Following the 1975 Mexico conference, in which Elizabeth Reid and the Australian delegation played a pivotal role, the global feminist awakening seemed like it was on an unstoppable roll. Reid went on to have a distinguished international career in women's development and the United Nations. She played a key role as principal officer in the UN Secretariat for the second World Conference on Women, held in Copenhagen in 1980, which marked the UN Decade for Women (1976–1985).

The third UN World Conference on Women was held in Nairobi in 1985, and ten years later the fourth in Beijing. A whopping 47 000 people descended on Beijing for that event, creating a new record for the biggest gathering of women in the world.[1] The Beijing conference produced the most ambitious blueprint for gender equality the world has ever seen: the Beijing Declaration and Platform for Action. Thirty years later, it remains the best roadmap for gender equality we have.

It is the only roadmap we have. There have been no further World Conferences on Women since Beijing in '95.

The global pushback against women's rights is now so overt that the Beijing Platform, a critical document, has never been updated. It remains static and unchanged, almost like a museum piece we mustn't touch in case it crumbles. A total of 189 nations signed on to the Beijing Platform back in 1995, including Australia. But now, if it were opened for review and updating, we know that several far-right, fundamentalist nations, theocracies and dictatorships, along with increasingly conservative and damaged democracies – the United States included – would force a dramatic and devastating wind-back of many of the women's rights enshrined in it, particularly rights around sexual and reproductive freedoms.

By early 2025, instead of celebrating three decades since Beijing and what Hillary Clinton called 'a breathtaking moment of potential', women everywhere were lamenting the global backlash and political pushback against women and girls.

Back on that stage, Christiane Amanpour asked Clinton how she felt in light of President Trump's considerable rollback of rights, including his redefinition of gender – which demonised and effectively 'disappeared' nonbinary and trans people – along with his demolition of USAID and global programs to support and empower women. Clinton didn't mince her words. She urged women to 'take stock, but also to get re-energised'. Then came the rallying cry: 'So, we're back in the fight! We have no choice.'[2]

*

This book began as a private exercise in an attempt to heal. I was angry, burning with a rage I couldn't articulate or tame. Its corrosive effect was leaching into my life – my mood, my view of the world, my relationships. Most of all, it was infecting my work as a journalist.

Each afternoon, in my former role as a TV news presenter, I would drag myself into the ABC News studio in Northbourne Avenue, just down the road from Parliament House in Canberra, lumbering under the weight of a long shadow of gloom. News gloom. On the face of it, this was a seemingly disproportionate emotion, given we were broadcasting from one of the safest, most peaceful and most resource-rich nations in the world. Australia is a place that also likes to boast of great strides in gender equality: 'My boss is a woman', 'The head of Macquarie Bank is a woman', 'The Liberal Party even elected a woman as leader in 2025'. These kinds of comforting facts are meant to reassure us that the revolution is over, that we have won, that women can step back from the fight.

But we know that isn't true. Everywhere there is chaos,

conflict, military strikes, human suffering, political corruption and nepotism, environmental destruction, evidence of systems failing and democracies in collapse, it is men who are in charge. Men dominate. Men are responsible. Yes, I know Italy's prime minister, Giorgia Meloni, is a woman. So too are another nineteen of the 193 heads of government around the world as I write. The rest are men.[3]

It is men we see in news clips sitting around the power tables and on podiums at world leaders' summits. Women, if present at all, are noted by their difference. Their oddity. Their exceptionalism. Or, as we saw in 2020 in Doha, when the United States sat down with the Taliban to sign the most shameful military exit deal written this century, Afghan women were not just absent but banned from the room, their presence not allowed to pollute the eyeline of a Talib. Even the word 'woman' was banned from the discussion.[4] Such is the privilege that comes with the spoils of war – the domestic and sexual enslavement of women. It's a grubby truth that remains unmentioned among those men history calls 'heroic'.

Fifteen years of telling the loyal news viewer that these daily confirmations of male hierarchy and male supremacy are normal and, by implication, acceptable really rots the female soul, feminist or not.

Before I quit TV news, I commissioned a couple of students from the University of Canberra to make a short video of news highlights, showing the big national and international political and business stories of the month. The aim was to focus on the leaders, the key players, the movers and shakers, the people wielding power, and mash it all up to see what happened. When it was finished, the video's title was bleedingly obvious – 'Where are the women?'

After I established the 50/50 by 2030 Foundation in 2017, with a focus on women and leadership, it didn't take me long to realise that the headline data showing women's progress in the public sector was in fact a distraction. The real story was buried in the body of our research: in the data that hinted at growing negative attitudes among men as women rose through the ranks. Men were panicking. The backlash was building. The evidence was soon multiplying and showing up in research everywhere. The global manosphere spread the word faster than a virus. It's a zero-sum game, they said. Women win; you lose. Retaliate. Take back what is rightfully yours. Send them back to the place they should rightfully be: at home.

Alarmist and extremist as this may sound, this is precisely what the US Heritage Foundation blueprint for the new Trump 2.0 administration, Project 2025, advocated. It listed the restoration of the traditional family as its top priority and 'the centerpiece of American life', with men as the breadwinners and women as the homemakers.[5]

If you hear an echo here, you are right. This 'back to yesteryear' gender stereotype mindset is precisely what Elizabeth Reid and the Whitlam government preached *against*, way back in 1975, International Women's Year.

And yet – here we are. Again. After half a century of 'women's progress'.

By the time the Australian 2025 election campaign was underway, the relentless anti-women agenda peddled by the United States was already bleeding into Australian politics. Donald Trump's full-scale attack on diversity, equity and inclusion (DEI) – to specifically stop gender quotas and the promotion of women – rattled Australian organisations with funding connections to the US. Reputable research institutes began panicking about 'the woman thing' and became reluctant to talk about achievements in gender or other forms of equity. Questions that would have been unimaginable as the world became enlightened across the last 50 years were now being raised: do we remove all reference to women's leadership and equity policies from our website? Do we push DEI underground? Do we abandon equity and inclusion efforts altogether?

Before winning back the presidency in late 2024, Trump told the world he would 'protect the women of our country ... whether the women like it or not': an unnerving threat from a president famed for grabbing women by the pussy. The stink of paternalism was foul, but it would soon get worse.[6] *The New York Times* warned MAGA rhetoric was 'growing darker and more menacing', calling one of Trump's biggest rallies a 'carnival of misogyny'.[7] In early 2025, Trump's new tech-bro squeeze, Mark Zuckerberg, famously told Joe Rogan – one of the biggest 'go-bro' podcasters in the world – that there was too much feminine energy in leadership. He argued for more aggression and 'masculine energy', suggesting the corporate world had become too culturally 'neutered'.[8] I suppose I shouldn't have been surprised after that – but I was – when newly elected JD Vance put out his vice president's call to men to be more manly.[9]

It wasn't a message to muscle up. It was a message to double down.

The pumped-up patriarchy's rally cry – we are 'back on top' – reached Australia like a bugle call, blowing combustible streams of misogynistic methane onto the smouldering fires of male discontent. The then leader of the Liberal Party, Peter Dutton, went on Sydney's 2GB radio and told the large, predominantly male audience how happy he was that Trump would 'hit the ground running' in his second presidency.[10]

In no time conservative politicians and candidates in the 2025 federal election were singing from the same 'take back control of women' song sheet. A Liberal Party candidate called for a reversal of laws allowing women to serve in defence combat, explaining they should instead serve 'as the backbone of society'.[11] The word 'homemaker' was no doubt hovering, but the candidate got busy instead blaming pornography for turning men into transgender women. Gunning for a shot as prime minister, Peter Dutton called the guy 'outstanding', while also promising a nation-wide crackdown on 'woke ideology' in schools.[12]

The US reversal of abortion rights had already emboldened Australia's conservatives, with attempts in both South Australia and Queensland to repeal abortion laws back in 2024. The efforts failed. For now. Dutton's awkward attempt at a Trump-lite persona also failed, as his party's lack of policy preparation saw the Liberals thrashed at the 2025 election. But the stench of alt-conservative beliefs lingers.

Clearly, political agendas are changing. The patriarchal pendulum is swinging. Team Backlash has been emboldened.

Not long after President Trump began his pernicious dismantling of women's rights in 2025, leading American gender theorist and philosopher Judith Butler – who uses the pronoun 'they' – was asked by their graduate students what they should do in the face of what they said felt like a new world of anti-gender fascism. Butler's response echoed Hillary Clinton's. 'We reassemble,' they said. It's not a question of what the individual can do, Butler told the students, but rather a question of 'How do I act and what collaboration do I need to be part of?' Butler urged them to connect and find support in the collective. 'When you're acting together with others,' they said, 'you're not just fighting the enemy, you're also regenerating each other. You're giving each other hope and joy.'[13]

Those words have profound resonance here in Australia. As I have highlighted and celebrated in this book, we know the power of collective effort. We have felt the hope and joy. It's in our bones, in our feminist legacy, and in our recent past. It is why we share deep reserves of optimism.

*

In the past, I've managed to write my way out of troubled emotions and brewing anger. Once the words are down, the argument laid bare, the rationale – or lack of – exposed, the catharsis comes. Somewhere in that jumbled method I unknot my pain and find a form of closure. I hoped that might be the case this time, with this book. However, that is not what has happened here. Instead of finding peace within my rage, softening its edge and charting a pathway out of it, I have landed somewhere entirely different and unexpected.

Far from calmed, I am more enraged than ever.

But tempering that rage is a surprising well of optimism ... along with a spirit of hope and even a sense of joy. These emotions surfaced while writing this book, like gifts handed down from generations of women before me.

Australian women have experienced a profound period of change in recent years, change that has empowered us individually and collectively. Across half a century, women's actions have changed laws, work cultures and political behaviours, and forced a public reckoning that has fundamentally reshaped community expectations. Most importantly, women themselves have changed.

We have gathered in numbers too big to ignore, rallied and roared, 'Enough is enough!' The message was heard. We were told it was a 'triumph of democracy' that we weren't shot. But even chief patriarchs can misfire and shoot themselves – in the foot.

We've basked in solidarity when we assembled, our unity validating our anger and reminding each of us that we are not alone. Our combined actions confirm that the grief and frustration we feel is a perfectly valid response to what we see happening around us – and *to* us.

We have witnessed countless women use their voices to say, 'No! I will not.' Imbued with a spirit of solidarity and sisterhood that felt new to many of us, we have collectively celebrated women's courage, and emboldened others to step up. Wearing white outfits, red shoes or black T-shirts, we've fashioned our own revolutionary wardrobe and worn it like armour – a signalling to the sisterhood.

Throughout it all has been the powerful and unmistakable legacy of our feminist lineage, threading connections through much of what we do.

The opening epigraph of this book is a quote from a speech Elizabeth Reid gave back in 2017, when her mood was bellicose and revolutionary. Reflecting on the Australian Women's Liberation Movement, she asked 'Why does such a movement seem so anachronistic today? Have we moved away from the radical feminist discourse of "liberation" and "revolution' … Don't women need liberating anymore?'

Until our world has eradicated all forms of sexism and misogyny, and changed social attitudes and norms to something unrecognisable today, until then, we will need to fight for liberation. Until we have developed a new social narrative that centres women as lead players and primary contributors to our planet's future, the liberation project will not be over. But the courage and collectivism we have seen in Australia over recent years is undeniable evidence that we can do this. We women can rise. We can resist. We can do revolution. The radical and subversive ideas that drove the Australian Women's Liberation Movement remain an undercurrent we can harness to fuel our momentum.

The force of backlash swinging our way is ferocious, but we have what we need for a feminist fightback.

As Elizabeth Reid urged many years ago, we must adopt a true 'revolutionary consciousness', one fit for the times. This means moving past a preoccupation with policy reform and gender equality. Equality lacks ambition. We learned that long ago. New challenges demand a much bigger, bolder, more comprehensive approach: a revolution in our heads and hearts, as well as in our actions.

In a world in which power is not given but taken, revolution is our only option. It starts with courage and is fired by collectivism.

It's time.

NOTES

Epigraph

1   Reid, Elizabeth, 2017, keynote address, *How the Personal Became Political: Re-assessing Australia's Revolutions in Gender and Sexuality in the 1970s*, symposium, Australian National University, Canberra, 6–7 March.

Preface

1   Mitchell, Juliet, 1975, 'Feminist theory?', in *The Women and Politics Conference, 1975*, vol 2, Department of the Prime Minister and Cabinet, Canberra, p 191, <https://archive.org/details/womenpoliticscon0000wome/>, accessed 10 June 2025.

2   Australia's 2022 federal election was smeared by anti-trans hate when Liberal candidate Katherine Deves likened the fight against transgender people to the actions of German people who stood up for Jewish people during the Holocaust. McGowan, Michael, 14 April 2022, 'NSW candidate likens anti-trans activism to opposing the Holocaust', *The Guardian*, <www.theguardian.com/australia-news/2022/apr/14/nsw-liberal-candidate-likens-anti-trans-activism-to-opposing-the-holocaust>, accessed 26 May 2024.

3   Ferber, Alona, 22 September 2020, 'Judith Butler on the culture wars, JK Rowling and living in "anti-intellectual" times', *The New Statesman*, <www.newstatesman.com/long-reads/2020/09/judith-butler-culture-wars-jk-rowling-living-anti-intellectual-times>, accessed 26 May 2024.

4   Casey, Sarah and Watson, Juliet, 2023, *Hashtag Feminisms: Australian Media Feminists, Activism, and Digital Campaigns*, Peter Lang, Oxford, p 18.

Introduction

1   World Economic Forum, 12 June 2025, *Global Gender Gap 2025 Report*, <https://www.weforum.org/publications/global-gender-gap-report-2025/>, accessed June 2025. See also WEF Benchmarking gender gaps, 2025, Performance by region; < https://www.weforum.org/publications/global-gender-gap-report-2025/in-full/benchmarking-gender-gaps-2025/>.

2   Guterres, António, 7 March 2025, 'Spotlighting "mainstreaming of misogyny", Secretary-General urges action to empower women on international day', media release, United Nations, <https://press.un.org/en/2025/sgsm22572.doc.htm>, accessed 10 June 2025.

3   Sky News Australia, 24 February 2025, '"War on men is absolutely over":
      JD Vance delivers inspiring message at CPAC', video, YouTube, <www.
      youtube.com/watch?v=imMcKzmfxrQ>, accessed 26 March 2025.
4   Ipsos and Global Institute for Women's Leadership, 6 March 2025,
      International Women's Day 2025, <www.ipsos.com/en/international-
      womens-day-2025>, accessed 8 May 2025
5   Guterres, António, 6 March 2020, 'Progress towards gender equality ...',
      X post, <https://x.com/antonioguterres/status/1235745110144487424>,
      accessed 8 May 2025; United Nations, 27 February 2020, 'Twenty-first
      century must be century of women's equality, Secretary-General says
      in remarks at The New School', media release, <https://press.un.org/
      en/2020/sgsm19986.doc.htm>, accessed 8 May 2025.
6   Guterres, António, 8 February 2020, 'Secretary-General's remarks at
      high-level meeting on gender equality and women's empowerment',
      <www.un.org/sg/en/content/sg/statement/2020-02-08/secretary-
      generals-remarks-high-level-meeting-gender-equality-and-womens-
      empowerment>, accessed 8 May 2025. See also United Nations,
      27 February 2020, 'Make this the century of women's equality: UN chief',
      video, <https://news.un.org/en/story/2020/02/1058271>, accessed 8 May
      2025; Guterres, António, 27 February 2020, 'Secretary-General António
      Guterres' remarks at the New School: "Women and Power"', <www.
      un.org/sg/en/content/sg/speeches/2020-02-27/remarks-new-school-
      women-and-power>, accessed 8 May 2025.
7   Australian Human Rights Commission, December 2022, 'The positive
      duty in the Sex Discrimination Act', <https://humanrights.gov.au/our-
      work/sex-discrimination/positive-duty-sex-discrimination-act>, accessed
      4 June 2025.

Part 1 Our New Now
1   Columbia SIPA, 12 March 2025, 'Addressing 21st century challenges to
      gender equality: Beijing+30', video, YouTube, <https://igp.sipa.columbia.
      edu/events/addressing-21st-century-challenges-gender-equality-
      beijing30-livestream>, accessed 13 March 2025.
2   Chemaly, Soraya, 2018, *Rage Becomes Her: The Power of Women's Anger*,
      Simon & Schuster, London, p 296.

1   A feminisation of power
1   Solnit, Rebecca, 15 July 2016, '"Hope is an embrace of the unknown":
      Rebecca Solnit on living in dark times', *The Guardian*, <www.theguardian.
      com/books/2016/jul/15/rebecca-solnit-hope-in-the-dark-new-essay-
      embrace-unknown>, accessed 10 October 2024.
2   Haussegger, Virginia, 24 April 2003, 'Feminism's left us in a fix', *Sydney
      Morning Herald*, <www.smh.com.au/national/feminisms-left-us-in-a-
      fix-20030424-gdgned.html>, accessed 10 October 2024. See also Hewett,
      Jennifer, 7 September 2002, 'The mothers' club', *Sydney Morning Herald*,
      <www.smh.com.au/national/the-mothers-club-20020907-gdfm2y.
      html>, accessed 30 January 2025.

3   Milligan, Louise (reporter), 12 August 2024, 'Don't Speak', TV episode, *Four Corners*, ABC TV, <https://iview.abc.net.au/show/four-corners/series/2024/video/NC2403H026S00>, accessed 9 May 2025.

4   Quinn, Tina (host), 15 August 2025, 'Commercial television: The industry that #MeToo forgot', podcast episode, *Fourth Estate*, <https://podcasts.apple.com/au/podcast/fourth-estate/id1006554000>, accessed 9 May 2025.

5   Intersection Pty Ltd, October 2024, *Out in the Open: Changing the culture at Nine Entertainment: An Independent Workplace Review by Intersection Pty Ltd*, Nine Entertainment, <www.nineforbrands.com.au/wp-content/uploads/2024/10/Intersection-Nine-Entertainment-2024-Report-FA.pdf>, accessed 4 June 2025.

6   Intersection Pty Ltd, *Out in the Open*, p 1.

7   Senate Environment and Communications References Committee, 12 March 2021, *Media Diversity in Australia*, <https://parlinfo.aph.gov.au/parlInfo/search/display/display.w3p;query=Id%3A%22committees%2Fcommsen%2F2345169c-f701-48d9-ae97-905c332d6b65%2F0002%22>, accessed 11 June 2025. See also Rudd, Kevin, 'Murdoch's "toxic" and "sexist" culture exposed by former employee at Australian Senate hearing', video, YouTube, <www.youtube.com/watch?v=X68NVLPVzuI>, accessed 11 June 2025.

8   For further discussion of News Corp's appropriation of 'hot' women facing court charges, see Barry, Paul (host), 22 March 2021, 'Sexy snaps', video, *Media Watch*, <www.abc.net.au/mediawatch/episodes/photo/13267836>, accessed 11 June 2025.

9   Hrovat, Bianca, 30 April 2025, '"I'm still in disbelief": Ex-Swillhouse staff take fight global with tears, dancing and packed bars', *Sydney Morning Herald*, <www.smh.com.au/goodfood/eating-out/i-m-still-in-disbelief-ex-swillhouse-staff-take-fight-global-with-tears-dancing-and-packed-bars-20250425-p5lubv.html>, accessed 4 June 2025. Regarding the music industry, see MAPN Consulting, 2022, *Raising Their Voices*, <https://womeninmusicawards.com.au/wp-content/uploads/2022/09/Music-Industry-Review-Report-Raising-Their-Voices-2022-web.pdf>, accessed 11 June 2025.

10   Australian Human Rights Commission, 'The positive duty in the Sex Discrimination Act'.

11   Drummond, Matthew, 2 October 2020, 'The list to be on: 20 years of the AFR Magazine Power Issue', *Australian Financial Review Magazine*, <www.afr.com/work-and-careers/leaders/the-list-to-be-on-20-years-of-the-afr-magazine-power-issue-20200929-p5605w>, accessed 13 September 2024.

12   Mitchell, Susan, 1996, *The Scent of Power: On the Trail of Women and Power in Australian Politics*, Angus & Robertson, Sydney, pp 154–57. Mitchell includes extensive text of Rod Cameron's 1990 speech, which he had faxed to her. 'Feminisation: The Major Emerging Trend Underlying Future Mass Audience Response' was delivered in October 1990 to the Public Relations Institute in Canberra; for more on this, see Neales, Sue,

23 October 1990, 'Leadership trend part of the feminisation factor', *Australian Financial Review*, <www.afr.com/politics/leadership-trend-part-of-the-feminisation-factor-19901023-k442u>, accessed 6 June 2025.

13 For more on 'neurosexism', see Cordelia Fine, 2010, *Delusions of Gender: The Real Science Behind Sex Differences*, Norton, New York.

14 Haussegger, Virginia, December 2006, 'Sex and power', *Vive*, no 87, p 86. Available online at <https://virginiahaussegger.com.au/wp-content/uploads/2023/02/Sex-and-Power.pdf>.

15 Diversity Council Australia, 7 June 2025, 'Capitalising on culture and gender in ASX leadership', <www.dca.org.au/wp-content/uploads/2023/06/capitalising_on_culture_and_gender_infographic_final_0.pdf >, accessed 7 June 2025.

16 Lewis, Helen, 6 May 2020, 'The pandemic has revealed the weakness of strongmen', *The Atlantic*, <www.theatlantic.com/international/archive/2020/05/new-zealand-germany-women-leadership-strongmen-coronavirus/611161/>, accessed 8 June 2025; Taub, Amanda, 15 May 2020, 'Why are women-led nations doing better with Covid-19?', *New York Times*, <www.nytimes.com/2020/05/15/world/coronavirus-women-leaders.html>, accessed 7 June 2025.

17 Friedman, Uri, 19 April 2020, 'New Zealand's prime minister may be the most effective leader on the planet,' *The Atlantic*, <www.theatlantic.com/politics/archive/2020/04/jacinda-ardern-new-zealand-leadership-coronavirus/610237/>, accessed 7 June 2025.

18 Fioramonti, Lorenzo, Coscieme, Lica and Trebeck, Katherine, 1 June 2020, 'Women in power: It's a matter of life and death', *Social Europe*, <www.socialeurope.eu/women-in-power-its-a-matter-of-life-and-death>, accessed 8 June 2025.

19 Haussegger, Virginia (host), 17 December 2020, 'Julia Gillard', podcast episode, *BroadTalk*, <https://shows.acast.com/broadtalk/episodes/juliagillard>, accessed 11 June 2025.

20 Haussegger, Virginia (host), 6 August 2020, 'Dame Annette King', podcast episode, *BroadTalk*, <https://shows.acast.com/broadtalk/episodes/dameannetteking>, accessed 11 June 2025.

21 Cassells, Rebecca and Duncan, Alan, 2020, *Gender Equity Insights 2020: Delivering the Business Outcomes*, BCEC/WGEA Gender Equity Series, no 5, <www.wgea.gov.au/newsroom/more-women-at-the-top-proves-better-for-business>, accessed 11 June 2025.

22 Isabella Vacaflores and Elise Stephenson, 27 May 2025, 'Understanding Female Legislators' Substantive Representation in the Australian Parliament', *Journal of Women, Politics & Policy*, <www.tandfonline.com/doi/epdf/10.1080/1554477X.2025.2507550>, accessed 8 June 2025.

23 Armstrong, Sally, 2019, *Power Shift: The Longest Revolution*, Anansi Press, Toronto, p 1.

24 Armstrong, *Power Shift*, p 4.

25 Heimans, Jeremy and Timms, Henry, 2018, *New Power: How Power Works in Our Hyper-Connected World – and How to Make it Work for You*, Pan Macmillan, p 2; see also Heimans, Jeremy and Timms, Henry,

December 2014, 'Understanding "New Power"', *Harvard Business Review*, <https://hbr.org/2014/12/understanding-new-power>, accessed 14 September 2024.

26   Armstrong, *Power Shift*, p 257.

2   Men manning up

1   *Lehrmann v Network Ten Pty Limited (Trial Judgment)*, 15 April 2024, [2024] FCA 369 (Lee J), <www.judgments.fedcourt.gov.au/judgments/Judgments/fca/single/2024/2024fca0369>, accessed 16 June 2025.

2   Zemek, Steve, 5 March 2025, '"Horror movie": Why Lehrmann says defamation findings should be overturned', *The Australian*, <https://www.theaustralian.com.au/breaking-news/horror-movie-why-lehrmann-says-defamation-findings-should-be-overturned/news-story/8117b62f33cdec98e3f87bd917365c33>, accessed 20 July 2025.

3   UN Women, 25 November 2024, 'Five essential facts to know about femicide', <www.unwomen.org/en/articles/explainer/five-essential-facts-to-know-about-femicide>, accessed 11 June 2025.

4   Morton, Rick, 11–17 May 2024, 'Five-month delays for counselling of violent men', *The Saturday Paper*, <www.thesaturdaypaper.com.au/news/health/2024/05/11/five-month-delays-counselling-violent-men>, accessed 25 September 2024.

5   Badham, Van, 5 May 2024, 'As Australia screams for action against lethal male violence, this is a culture war for survival', *The Guardian*, <www.theguardian.com/commentisfree/article/2024/may/05/as-australia-screams-for-action-against-lethal-male-violence-this-is-a-culture-war-for-survival>, accessed 12 May 2025.

6   Watson, Geoffrey, 24 April 2024, 'Don't let Molly Ticehurst die in vain. I don't care if we restrict civil liberties', *Sydney Morning Herald*, <www.smh.com.au/national/nsw/don-t-let-molly-ticehurst-die-in-vain-i-don-t-care-if-we-restrict-civil-liberties-20240424-p5fm76.html >, accessed 1 September 2024.

7   Turnbull, Malcolm, 24 September 2015, video, in Ireland, Judith, 'Malcolm Turnbull's scathing attack on men who commit domestic violence', *Sydney Morning Herald*, <www.smh.com.au/politics/federal/malcolm-turnbulls-scathing-attack-on-men-who-commit-domestic-violence-20150924-gjtpqt.html>, accessed 16 June 2025.

8   Aly, Waleed, 3 May 2024, 'Holding all men responsible for a violent minority has failed to keep women safe', *The Age*, <www.theage.com.au/politics/federal/holding-all-men-responsible-for-a-violent-minority-has-failed-to-keep-women-safe-20240501-p5fo82.html>, accessed 16 September 2024.

9   Hill, Jess, 6 May 2024, 'Something is changing', *How Do You Smash a Ghost?*, <https://jesshill.substack.com/p/something-is-changing>, accessed 12 May 2025.

10   Hadley, Ray, 30 April 2024, 'We're sick of the soundbites. Bail laws are a joke and must be fixed right now', *Sydney Morning Herald*, <www.smh.com.au/national/nsw/we-re-sick-of-the-soundbites-bail-laws-are-a-

joke-and-must-be-fixed-right-now-20240430-p5fnnm.html>, accessed 12 May 2025.

11   AFL, 1 May 2024, 'AFL to take a stand on violence against women', <www.afl.com.au/news/1119895/afl-to-make-a-stand-against>, accessed 11 June 2025.

12   AFL, 6 May 2024, 'Round eight the third highest round attended of all time', <www.afl.com.au/news/1124750/round-eight-becomes-the-third-highest-attended-round-of-all-time>, accessed 11 June 2025.

13   Turnbull, Tiffanie, 20 April 2024, 'Sydney stabbing: Bondi attack on women devastates Australia', *BBC World News*, <www.bbc.com/news/world-australia-68852486>, accessed 16 September 2024.

14   AP/Channel 9, 15 April 2024, 'Bondi Junction stabbings: Joel Cauchi's father "extremely sorry" for victims – video', video, *The Guardian*, <www.theguardian.com/australia-news/video/2024/apr/15/bondi-junction-stabbings-joel-cauchis-father-extremely-sorry-for-victims-video>, accessed 16 September 2024.

15   9News, 6 May 2024, 'Victim Liya Barko speaks with 9 News reporter Damien Ryan', video, YouTube, <www.youtube.com/watch?v=OptixO8H_LM>, accessed 16 September 2024.

16   Lovett, Ian and Nagourney, Adam, 24 May 2014, 'Video rant, then deadly rampage in California town', *New York Times*, <www.nytimes.com/2014/05/25/us/california-drive-by-shooting.html >, accessed 16 June 2025.

17   AAP, 28 April 2025, 'Women not a target of Bondi Junction shopping centre stabbing attack, inquest hears', *SBS News*, <www.sbs.com.au/news/article/women-not-a-target-of-bondi-junction-shopping-centre-stabbing-attack-inquest-hears/8rzgjycuk>, accessed 11 June 2025.

18   Packer, Clareese, 15 May 2025, 'Psychiatrist withdraws claims "hatred for women" fuelled Joel Cauchi's fatal rampage at Westfield Bondi Junction', news.com.au, <www.news.com.au/national/nsw-act/courts-law/joel-cauchis-psychiatrist-withdraws-claim-a-hatred-for-women-fuelled-his-fatal-rampage-at-westfield-bondi-junction/news-story/aca3bd1ca2cddee8d95dc1508160df86>, accessed 11 June 2025.

19   Dumas, Daisy, 13 May 2025, 'Mass murder at Bondi Junction likely due to Joel Cauchi's "sexual frustration and hatred towards women", inquest told', *The Guardian*, <www.theguardian.com/australia-news/2025/may/13/joel-cauchi-psychiatrist-schizophrenia-medication-westfield-bondi-junction-stabbings-inquest-ntwnfb>, accessed 11 June 2025.

20   Australian Prime Minister's Office, 16 April 2024, 'Press conference – Parliament House, Canberra', <www.pm.gov.au/media/press-conference-parliament-house-canberra-22>, accessed 12 May 2025.

21   Quoted in Australian Prime Minister's Office, 16 April 2024, 'Press conference – Parliament House Canberra'.

22   Eltahawy, Mona, 17 April 2024, 'Essay: Femicide – The approved terrorism', Feminist Giant, <www.feministgiant.com/p/essay-femicide-the-approved-terrorism?utm_source=publication-search>, accessed 18 September 2024.

23 Speers, David, 18 April 2024, 'The Bondi Junction and Wakeley stabbings involved extreme violence and caused fear, so why was only one labelled terrorism?', *ABC News*, <www.abc.net.au/news/2024-04-18/two-knife-attacks-bondi-junction-wakeley-terrorism-target-women-/103736578>, accessed 19 September 2024.

24 Barton, Greg, 16 April 2024, 'Why is the Sydney church stabbing an act of terrorism, but the Bondi tragedy isn't?', *The Conversation*, <https://theconversation.com/why-is-the-sydney-church-stabbing-an-act-of-terrorism-but-the-bondi-tragedy-isnt-227997>, accessed 12 May 2025.

25 'How many more women have to die before we get serious about this epidemic?', 26 April 2024, editorial, *Sydney Morning Herald*, <www.smh.com.au/politics/nsw/how-many-more-women-have-to-die-before-we-get-serious-about-this-epidemic-20240425-p5fmhw.html >, accessed 16 June 2025.

26 White, Daniella and Duffin, Perry, 22 April 2023, 'Man on bail charged with "brutal" alleged murder of former partner', *Sydney Morning Herald*, <www.smh.com.au/national/nsw/man-on-bail-charged-with-brutal-alleged-murder-of-former-partner-20240422-p5flrr.html>, accessed 19 September 2024. The comments were made by Detective Inspector Jason Darcy, Central West Police District crime manager.

27 Salter, Michael, 30 April 2024, 'In a society where male violence seems inevitable we need much more than education and awareness', *The Guardian,* <www.theguardian.com/commentisfree/2024/apr/30/in-a-society-where-male-violence-seems-inevitable-we-need-much-more-than-education-and-awareness>, accessed 20 September 2024.

28 Gilmore, Jane, 2019, *Fixed It: Violence and the Representation of Women in the Media*, Penguin, Melbourne.

29 Ferguson, Hannah, 28 April 2024, in Boyd, Abigail, 'Hannah Ferguson at Sydney's rally …', video, TikTok, <www.tiktok.com/@abigailboydgreens/video/7362799448260431120>, accessed 20 June 2025.

30 Crabb, Annabel, 30 April 2024, 'Albanese was so desperate to prove he cares about gendered violence, he forgot one thing: if you're a proper leader, it's not about you', *ABC News*, <www.abc.net.au/news/2024-05-01/albanese-gendered-violence-rally/103785858>, accessed 20 September 2024.

31 Shields, Bevan, 26 April 2024, 'Note from the Editor: Australia cannot afford to wait to act on violence against women', *Sydney Morning Herald*, <www.smh.com.au/politics/nsw/australia-cannot-afford-to-wait-to-act-on-violence-against-women-20240426-p5fmqo.html>, accessed 12 May 2025. In this impassioned editorial, Shields writes that if a national Royal Commission into family and sexual violence cost $100 million, it would equate to 0.00015 per cent of Commonwealth spending, an amount that is 'nothing, given the scale of the problem it would seek to address'.

32 Baker, Jordan and Schultz, Amber, 28 April 2024, 'Misogyny driving violence', *Sydney Morning Herald*, p 1.

3 Misogyny, parliament, witches, liars and leers

1   At the time, the interview with Gillard worried me. It was for my first
     book, *Wonder Woman: The Myth of 'Having It All'*, with its central theme
     of childlessness. No matter how hard I tried to provoke Gillard into
     discussing her choice to be childless, she just wouldn't take the bait. She
     said she made the decision when she was a kid, about 12 years old, and that
     was that. Nothing to see here. Eventually I dropped the interview from
     my book. Yet, ever gracious and generous, Gillard nevertheless agreed to
     launch it for me, in a live ABC broadcast at the National Press Club in
     2005.

2   Donaghue, Ngaire, 2015, 'Who gets played by "The Gender Card"?',
     Australian Feminist Studies, vol 30, no 84, p 164. Donaghue makes the
     point that Gillard could be called the 'model post-feminist woman'. It is
     well documented that Gillard rarely acknowledged sexism and certainly
     never discussed the disadvantages experienced by women until the
     Misogyny Speech. See also Goldsworthy, Anna, 'Unfinished business:
     Sex, freedom and misogyny', *Quarterly Essay*, no 50, 2013.

3   Delahunty, Mary, 2013, 'Liars, witches and trolls: On the political
     battlefield', *Griffith Review*, no 40, p 27.

4   National Film and Sound Archive of Australia, 2012, 'The Misogyny
     Speech by Julia Gillard', video, <www.nfsa.gov.au/collection/curated/
     asset/100595-misogyny-speech-julia-gillard>, accessed 13 May 2025.

5   See Looby, Tosca (director), 2021, *Strong Female Lead*, documentary,
     SBS, <www.sbs.com.au/ondemand/tv-program/strong-female-
     lead/1936064579922>, accessed 13 May 2025.

6   Summers, Anne, 17 September 2021, 'I see no sign that "ugly Australia"
     has learnt from its treatment of Gillard', *Sydney Morning Herald*,
     <www.smh.com.au/politics/federal/i-see-no-sign-that-ugly-australia-
     has-learnt-from-its-treatment-of-gillard-20210916-p58s4s.html>,
     accessed 13 May 2025.

7   Jabour, Bridie, 12 June 2013, 'Julia Gillard's "small breasts" served up
     on Liberal party dinner menu', *The Guardian*, <www.theguardian.com/
     world/2013/jun/12/gillard-menu-sexist-liberal-dinner>, accessed 13 May
     2025.

8   Summers, Anne, 31 August 2012, 'Her rights at work: The political
     persecution of Australia's first female prime minister'. An essay version of
     the public speech is available online at <https://griffithlawjournal.org/
     index.php/gjlhd/article/view/589/550>.

9   Mao, Francis, 16 May 2019, '2019 election: Why politics is toxic for
     Australia's women', *BBC World News*, <www.bbc.com/news/world-
     australia-48197145>, accessed 5 October 2024.

10   Ellis, Kate, 2021, *Sex, Lies and Question Time*, Hardie Grant Books,
     Melbourne, p 123.

11   Mao, '2019 election'.

12   Manne, Kate, June 2024, 'The future of misogyny', *The Monthly*,
     <www.themonthly.com.au/issue/2024/june/kate-manne-future-
     misogyny>, accessed 10 October 2024.

13 Beard, Mary, 2022, 'The history and culture of misogyny, from the ancient world to today', in Gillard, Julia (ed.), *Not Now, Not Ever: Ten Years On From the Misogyny Speech*, Vintage Books, Melbourne, p 66.

14 Beard, 'The history and culture of misogyny', p 66.

15 Hanson-Young, Sarah, 2018, *En Garde*, Melbourne University Press, Melbourne, p 23.

16 Hanson-Young, *En Garde*, p 24.

17 Tolentino, Jia, 2019, *Trick Mirror: Reflections on Self-Delusion*, 4th Estate, London, p 235.

18 Hanson-Young, *En Garde*, pp 37–38.

19 Karp, Paul, 3 March 2021, 'David Leyonhjelm to pay Sarah Hanson-Young $120,000 after losing defamation appeal bid', *The Guardian*, <www.theguardian.com/australia-news/2021/mar/03/david-leyonhjelm-to-pay-sarah-hanson-young-120000-after-losing-defamation-appeal-bid>, accessed 4 October 2024.

20 Duffy, Conor, 10 May 2016, 'Election 2016: Betrayal claim against "sex appeal" MP splits Liberal campaign in crucial seat of Lindsay', *ABC News*, <www.abc.net.au/news/2016-05-09/sex-appeal-mp-accused-of-stabbing-abbott-in-back/7395544>, accessed 13 May 2025.

21 Grattan, Michelle, 10 August 2018, 'Inquiry finds Husar behaved badly to staff but dismisses allegations of lewd conduct', *The Conversation*, <https://theconversation.com/inquiry-finds-husar-behaved-badly-to-staff-but-dismisses-allegations-of-lewd-conduct-101385>, accessed 13 May 2025.

22 Grattan, Michelle, 29 August 2018, 'Liberal MP Julia Banks to quit at election, calling out bullying', *The Conversation*, <https://theconversation.com/liberal-mp-julia-banks-to-quit-at-election-calling-out-bullying-102340>, accessed 13 May 2025.

23 Banks, Julia, 2021, *Power Play: Breaking Through Bias, Barriers and Boys' Clubs*, Hardie Grant Books, Melbourne, p 82

24 Australian Institute of Company Directors, 25 October 2024, 'Number of women directors climbing, but not women chairs', media release, <www.aicd.com.au/news-media/media-releases/2024/number-of-women-directors-climbing-but-not-women-chairs.html>, accessed 12 June 2025.

25 Chief Executive Women, 2024, *CEW Senior Executive Census 2024: Keeping Score of a Losing Game*, <https://cew.org.au/research-resources/research>, accessed 13 June 2025.

26 Guardian News, 13 April 2021, 'Christine Holgate fronts inquiry over Australia Post departure: "I have done nothing wrong"', video, YouTube, <www.youtube.com/watch?v=PNzHlew0VUo>, accessed 13 May 2025.

27 McClymont, Kate and Maley, Jacqueline, 22 June 2020, 'High Court inquiry finds former justice Dyson Heydon sexually harassed associates', *Sydney Morning Herald*, <www.smh.com.au/national/high-court-inquiry-finds-former-justice-dyson-heydon-sexually-harassed-associates-20200622-p5550w.html>, accessed 13 June 2025.

28 Gleeson, Hayley, 27 June 2020, 'Dyson Heydon sexual harassment allegations: Is this the start of the law's "Me Too" moment?',

<www.abc.net.au/news/2020-06-27/dyson-heydon-sexual-harassment-legal-profession-open-secrets/12395386>, accessed 14 May 2025.

29 McClymont, Kate and Maley, Jacqueline, 'High Court inquiry finds former justice Dyson Heydon sexually harassed associates'.

30 BBC, 23 June 2020, 'Dyson Heydon: Inquiry finds top Australian ex-judge harassed women', *BBC News*, <https://www.bbc.com/news/world-australia-53140910>, accessed 20 July 2025.

31 Milligan, Louise (reporter), 9 November 2020, 'Inside the Canberra Bubble', TV episode, *Four Corners*, ABC TV, <www.abc.net.au/news/2020-11-09/inside-the-canberra-bubble/12864676>, accessed 5 October 2024.

32 Milligan, 'Inside the Canberra Bubble'.

33 Hitch, Georgia, Borys, Stephanie, 2 December 2021, 'Education Minister Alan Tudge stands aside amid abuse allegations, PM tells parliament', *ABC News*, <https://www.abc.net.au/news/2021-12-02/alan-tudge-stands-aside-amid-abuse-allegations/100669592 >, accessed 20 July 2025.

34 Niki Savva, vote of thanks, at 'In conversation with Julia Banks', ANU Meet the Author, Australian National University, Canberra, 8 July 2021, <https://soundcloud.com/experience_anu/in-conversation-with-julia-banks>, accessed 16 June 2025.

35 Baker, Richard, 16 August 2020, '"Sexually harassed" AMP executive says the company is still covering up', *Sydney Morning Herald*, <www.smh.com.au/business/companies/sexually-harassed-amp-executive-says-the-company-is-still-covering-up-20200816-p55m7n.html>, accessed 20 April 2024.

36 McClymont and Maley, 'High Court inquiry finds former justice Dyson Heydon sexually harassed associates'.

Part 2 The awakening

1 Kovac, Tanja, 10 March 2021, 'Women unite in anger to march on Parliament and across the nation', *Sydney Morning Herald*, <www.smh.com.au/national/women-unite-in-anger-to-march-on-parliament-and-across-the-nation-20210310-p579bk.html>, accessed 26 June 2025. At the time of writing, Tanja Kovac was CEO of Gender Equity Victoria.

2 Dowse, Sara, 6 June 2013, 'The femocrat factor', *Inside Story*, <https://insidestory.org.au/the-femocrat-factor/>, accessed 26 June 2025.

4   The mood that triggered a movement

1 Mostyn, Sam, 3 March 2021, '"This howl of pain is the soundtrack to millions of women's lives"', *Sydney Morning Herald*, <www.smh.com.au/national/this-howl-of-pain-is-the-soundtrack-to-millions-of-women-s-lives-20210303-p577k6.html>, accessed 3 August 2024.

2 Karp, Paul, 8 March 2019, 'Scott Morrison wants women to rise but not solely at the expense of others', *The Guardian*, <www.theguardian.com/world/2019/mar/08/scott-morrison-wants-women-to-rise-but-not-solely-at-expense-of-others>, accessed 20 April 2024.

3   Crabb, Annabel, 28 March 2021, 'A new power has risen in Australian politics – and it's not coming quietly', *ABC News*, <www.abc.net.au/news/2021-03-28/new-power-emerges-in-australian-politics-not-coming-quietly/100030876>, accessed 20 September 2024.

4   Lewis, Helen, 2021, *Difficult Women: A History of Feminism in 11 Fights*, Vintage, London, p 8.

5   ABC News, 26 January 2021, '"Hear me now": Australian of the Year Grace Tame's speech in full', *ABC News*, <www.abc.net.au/news/2021-01-26/grace-tame-australian-of-the-year-speech-in-full/13091710>, accessed 14 May 2025.

6   ABC News, 3 March 2021, 'Australian of the Year Grace Tame's full National Press Club address', video, YouTube, <www.youtube.com/watch?v=LJmwOTfjn9U>, accessed 22 April 2024.

7   Contos, Chanel, 15 March 2021, '"Do they even know they did this to us?": Why I launched the school sexual assault petition', *The Guardian*, <www.theguardian.com/commentisfree/2021/mar/15/do-they-even-know-they-did-this-to-us-why-i-launched-the-school-sexual-assault-petition>, accessed 4 July 2024.

8   Contos, '"Do they even know they did this to us?"'

9   Teach Us Consent website (original). These testimonies were included on the original website in 2021, representing examples of the several thousand testimonies sent to Chanel early in her campaign. An updated website with fewer examples is available at Teach Us Consent, <www.teachusconsent.com>, accessed 26 June 2025. Also hear author's interview with Chanel Contos: Haussegger, Virginia (host), 24 June 2022, 'Chanel Contos: Changemaker', podcast episode, *BroadTalk*, <https://shows.acast.com/broadtalk/episodes/chanel-contos-changemaker>, accessed 14 May 2025.

10   Haussegger, Virginia (host), 12 March 2021, 'Isobel Marshall and Eloise Hall', podcast episode, *BroadTalk*, <https://shows.acast.com/broadtalk/episodes/isobelmarshallandeloisehall>, accessed 14 May 2025.

11   Haussegger, 'Chanel Contos: Changemaker'.

12   Ackland, Richard, 21 July 2017, '"This doesn't get to be over for me": The rape case that put consent on trial', *The Guardian*, <www.theguardian.com/society/2017/jul/21/this-doesnt-get-to-be-over-for-me-the-case-that-put-consent-on-trial>, accessed 13 July 2024.

13   Oldfield, Jessica C and McDonald, Dave, 2022, 'I Am That Girl: Media reportage, anonymous victims and symbolic annihilation in the aftermath of sexual assault', *Crime Media Culture*, vol 18, no 2, pp 223–41.

14   AAP and SBS, 23 November 2021, 'NSW passes "common sense" affirmative consent bill after advocacy work of Saxon Mullins', *SBS News*, <www.sbs.com.au/news/article/nsw-passes-common-sense-affirmative-consent-bill-after-advocacy-work-of-saxon-mullins/2z3ucw45j>, accessed 3 July 2024.

15   Nicholls, Sean (reporter), 22 March 2021, 'Don't Ask, Don't Tell', TV episode, *Four Corners*, ABC TV, <https://iview.abc.net.au/video/NC2103H008S00>, accessed 14 July 2024. In an interview with Sean Nicholls, Parliament House security guard Nikola Anderson details

what she saw on the night Higgins and Lehrmann arrived at Parliament House on Saturday 23 March at 2 am.

16   Nicholls, 'Don't Ask, Don't Tell'.

17   ABC News, 15 February 2021, 'Staffer Brittany Higgins allegedly raped in minister's Parliament House office', video, YouTube, <www.youtube.com/watch?v=qUdNCFt93Zg>, accessed 14 July 2024.

18   Wright, Shane, 20 April 2024, '"It is now time to heal": Higgins breaks silence on Lehrmann case', *Sydney Morning Herald*, <www.smh.com.au/politics/federal/it-now-it-s-time-to-heal-higgins-breaks-silence-on-lehrmann-case-20240420-p5flcr.html>, accessed 20 April 2024. Also see Federal Court of Australia transcript of *Lehrmann v Network Ten Pty Limited (Trial Judgment)*, <www.judgments.fedcourt.gov.au/judgments/Judgments/fca/single/2024/2024fca0369>.

19   Wright, '"It is now time to heal"'.

20   Haussegger, Virginia, 2019, 'The gender agenda: Boom, bust and bullyboys', in Mark Evans, Michelle Grattan and Brendan McCaffrie (eds), *From Turnbull to Morrison: The Trust Divide*, Melbourne University Press, Melbourne, pp 187–99.

21   Basford Canales, Sarah, 22 August 2024, 'Brittany Higgins said "no one goes for Morrison and gets away with it", according to husband's messages,' *The Guardian*, <www.theguardian.com/australia-news/article/2024/aug/22/brittany-higgins-linda-reynolds-defamation-trial-scott-morrison-david-sharaz-samantha-maiden-text-messages-ntwnfb>, accessed 23 August 2024.

22   Stayner, Tom, 3 March 2021, 'Grace Tame tells Scott Morrison "having children doesn't guarantee a conscience"', *SBS News*, <www.sbs.com.au/news/article/grace-tame-tells-scott-morrison-having-children-doesnt-guarantee-a-conscience/ukeum5vdq>, accessed 15 May 2025.

23   Chemaly, *Rage Becomes Her*, p xix.

24   Haussegger, Virginia, 17 February 2021, 'Why Brittany Higgins' story has stoked women's rage', *Canberra Times*, <www.canberratimes.com.au/story/7131517/why-brittany-higgins-sordid-story-has-stoked-womens-rage/>, accessed 16 June 2025.

25   Whitbourn, Michaela, 4 April 2024, 'Lehrmann invoiced Seven for "bender" with cocaine and sex workers, court told', *Sydney Morning Herald*, <www.smh.com.au/national/judge-to-hear-from-ex-seven-producer-in-lehrmann-defamation-fight-20240403-p5fh3s.html>, accessed 10 August 2024.

26   Edna Ryan Awards, 2021, 'Brittany Higgins | Grand Stirrer & For Making a Feminist Difference in Community Activism', accessed 15 May 2025.

27   The Project, 21 November 2021, 'Brittany Higgins powerful speech after winning incredible award', video, YouTube, <www.youtube.com/watch?v=3dUYGgWJGQk>, accessed 16 July 2024.

28   Hitch, Georgia, 12 March 2021, 'Defence minister Linda Reynolds retracts "lying cow" comment towards Brittany Higgins', *ABC News*, <www.abc.net.au/news/2021-03-12/linda-reynolds-retracts-lying-cow-comment-brittany-higgins/13242902>, accessed 20 June 2025.

5   It began with a tweet

1   Mostyn, Sam, 3 March 2021, '"This howl of pain is the soundtrack to millions of women's lives"', *Sydney Morning Herald*, <www.smh.com.au/national/this-howl-of-pain-is-the-soundtrack-to-millions-of-women-s-lives-20210303-p577k6.html>, accessed 3 August 2024.

2   Haussegger, Virginia (host), 1 April 2021, 'Janine Hendry', podcast episode, *BroadTalk*, <https://shows.acast.com/broadtalk/episodes/janinehendry>, accessed 30 May 2024.

3   March4Justice, n.d., 'Janine', <www.march4justice.org.au/about/janinehendry/>, accessed 16 May 2025.

4   Haussegger, Virginia, 14 March 2021, 'March4Justice taps into the power of recent acts of courage as well as a deep and ancient anger', *Canberra Times*, <www.canberratimes.com.au/story/7165564/the-intensity-and-rage-of-this-moment-is-powering-a-new-movement/>, accessed 22 April 2024.

5   Murphy, Katharine, 7 March 2021, 'Sex discrimination commissioner says Australia at "turning point" on sexual harassment and assault', *The Guardian*, <www.theguardian.com/australia-news/2021/mar/07/sex-discrimination-commissioner-says-australia-at-turning-point-on-sexual-harassment-and-assault>, accessed 25 April 2024.

6   Gunia, Amy, 12 March 2021, '"We've had enough." Furious Australian women force a reckoning on sexism after a rape allegation in the government', *Time*, <https://time.com/5945614/australia-protests-rape-allegations/>, accessed 22 July 2024.

7   Dawson, Emma, D'Rosario, Michael and Jackson, Shirley, May 2022, *The Way In: Representation in the 46th Australian Parliament*, Per Capita, Melbourne, p 8, table 1, <https://percapita.org.au/wp-content/uploads/2022/05/The-Way-In-46th-Parliament-May-2022-UPDATED.pdf >, accessed 26 June 2025. See also World Economic Forum [WEF], *Global Gender Gap Report 2021*, WEF, Geneva, p 103, <www.weforum.org/publications/global-gender-gap-report-2021/in-full/>, accessed 27 June 2025.

8   ABC News, 'Australian of the Year Grace Tame's full National Press Club address'.

9   Gunia, '"We've had enough"'.

10   openDemocracy, 3 July 2020, 'What can a world in crisis learn from grassroots movements?', video, YouTube, <https://youtu.be/TpOg5FnphDI?si=Xto1MB5O8HaMpe2a&t=885>, accessed 16 May 2025. Eltahawy's definition of patriarchy begins at 14:45.

11   50/50 by 2030 Foundation, May 2017, 'Towards inclusive leadership: Bridging the intersectionality deficit through co-design', Office for Women project proposal, University of Canberra. This grant proposal aimed to fill the gap in evidence-based data 'on women experiencing complex identities or intersectionality (gender/CALD, gender/class, gender/disability, gender/ethnicity and gender/indigeneity)'. We argued that at the time there was no comprehensive research that provided 'an understanding of the intersectionality landscape for the APS (Australian Public Sector)

or examines specific issues around the intersectionality of identities for women'.

6   The March4Justice hits the streets

1   Gunia, '"We've had enough"'.
2   Ferrier, Tracey, 10 March 2021, 'The March4Justice women who are raring to rally: "A time of reckoning for Australia"', *The Guardian*, <www.theguardian.com/australia-news/2021/mar/10/the-march4justice-women-who-are-raring-to-rally-a-time-of-reckoning-for-australia>, accessed 7 June 2024.
3   Overington, Caroline, 15 March 2021, 'Why all fathers should join the March4Justice', *The Australian*, <www.theaustralian.com.au/commentary/why-all-fathers-should-join-the-march4justice/news-story/c5d5808b539e961fcc76646c054a22a6>, accessed 7 June 2024.
4   Lake, Marilyn, 1999, *Getting Equal: The History of Australian Feminism*, Allen & Unwin, Sydney, p 282.
5   ABC News, 15 March 2021, 'Read what Brittany Higgins had to say when she spoke at the women's march', *ABC News*, <www.abc.net.au/news/2021-03-15/brittany-higgins-speech-womens-march-parliament-house-canberra/13248908>, accessed 19 May 2025.
6   Goodall, Jane, 16 March 2021, 'A place of greater safety', *Inside Story*, <https://insidestory.org.au/a-place-of-greater-safety/>, accessed 3 April 2021.
7   Haussegger, Virginia (host), 25 March 2021, 'Aminata Conteh-Biger', podcast episode, *BroadTalk*, <https://shows.acast.com/broadtalk/episodes/aminataconteh-biger>, accessed 19 May 2025.
8   Topsfield, Jewel, 15 March 2021, '"A tidal wave" of tears and rage sweeps the nation as tens of thousands rally', *The Age*, <www.theage.com.au/national/a-tidal-wave-of-rage-protests-field-anger-at-women-s-long-fight-20210315-p57ayo.html>, accessed 10 August 2024.
9   Lowrey, Tom and Snape, Jack, 16 March 2021, 'Scott Morrison's "bullets" for protesters comment stuns Australian UN representative', *ABC News*, <www.abc.net.au/news/2021-03-16/bullets-women-march-4-justice-scott-morrison/13251804>, accessed 27 July 2023.
10   Summers, Anne, 19 March 2021, 'Nothing will change for women while Morrison is PM', *Australian Financial Review*, <www.afr.com/politics/federal/nothing-will-change-for-women-while-morrison-is-pm-20210318-p57c0d>, accessed 22 July 2024.
11   Solnit, Rebecca, 16 September 2013, 'Rebecca Solnit: Joy arises, rules fall apart: Thoughts for the second anniversary of Occupy Wall Street', *Guernica*, <www.guernicamag.com/rebecca-solnit-joy-arises-rules-fall-apart/>, accessed 19 May 2025.

7   A national appetite for change

1   Sex Discrimination and Fair Work (Respect at Work) Amendment Bill 2021, <www.aph.gov.au/Parliamentary_Business/Committees/Senate/Education_and_Employment/RespectatWork>, accessed 11 August

2024. See also Vrajlal, Alicia, 21 August 2021, '18 months on, women call on government to take the Respect@Work report seriously', *Refinery29*, <www.refinery29.com/en-au/what-is-the-respectwork-report-and-why-does-it-matter>, accessed 20 May 2025.

2   Importantly, the following year – when Labor won government – the new prime minister, Anthony Albanese, immediately committed to implementing each of the 55 recommendations in the Jenkins report.

3   Jenkins, Kate, November 2021, 'Commissioner's foreword,' in Australian Human Rights Commission, *Set the Standard: Report on the Independent Review into Commonwealth Parliamentary Workplaces*, p 8, <https://humanrights.gov.au/sites/default/files/document/publication/ahrc_set_the_standard_2021.pdf>, accessed 20 May 2025.

4   See, for example, Steggall, Zali, 22 August 2024, 'The introduction of the Independent Parliamentary Standards Commission ...', Instagram post, <www.instagram.com/zalisteggall/reel/C-85bBAMUUI/>, accessed 23 August 2024.

5   Such comments were numerous, but the specific quotes referenced were included in the following: Gillespie, Eden, 8 April 2021, 'Female journalists painted as "subjective" and "emotional", experts say', *SBS News: The Feed*, <www.sbs.com.au/news/the-feed/article/female-journalists-painted-as-subjective-and-emotional-experts-say/kndr8qyox>, accessed 20 May 2025; Muller, Denis, 1 April 2021, 'Yes, politicians need to change the way they treat women. But so, too, do some in the media', *The Conversation*, <https://theconversation.com/yes-politicians-need-to-change-the-way-they-treat-women-but-so-too-do-some-in-the-media-158123>, accessed 20 May 2025; Meade, Amanda, 2 April 2021, 'AFR hit job on Samantha Maiden backfires spectacularly', *The Guardian*, <www.theguardian.com/media/2021/apr/02/afr-hit-job-on-samantha-maiden-backfires-spectacularly>, accessed 20 May 2025; Murphy, Katharine, 6 March 2021, 'Canberra's pale, stale and male tribe is missing the moment – as it did with Julia Gillard's misogyny speech', *The Guardian*, <www.theguardian.com/australia-news/2021/mar/06/canberras-pale-stale-and-male-tribe-is-missing-the-moment-as-it-did-with-julia-gillards-misogyny-speech>, accessed 20 May 2025.

6   Patrick, Aaron, 31 March 2021, 'PM caught in crusade of women journos', *Australian Financial Review*, <www.afr.com/companies/media-and-marketing/pm-caught-in-crusade-of-women-journos-20210326-p57eee>, accessed 20 May 2025.

7   Meade, 'AFR hit job on Samantha Maiden backfires spectacularly'.

8   Gillespie, 'Female journalists painted as "subjective" and "emotional", experts say'.

9   Milligan, Louise (@milliganreports), 31 March 2021, 'No-one commissions snarky profiles ...', X (Twitter) post, <https://x.com/Milliganreports/status/1377035111716118528>, accessed 15 November 2024; Middleton, Karen (@KarenMMiddleton), 31 March 2021, 'Pathetic, irrelevant & sexist hatchet job ...', X (Twitter) post, <https://x.com/KarenMMiddleton/status/1377085319829364737>, accessed 15 November 2024; Murphy,

Katharine (@Murpharoo), 31 March 2021, 'Haven't really wanted to engage substantively ...', X (Twitter) post, <https://x.com/murpharoo/status/1377175311117209605>, accessed 15 November 2024.

10 Murphy, 'Canberra's pale, stale and male tribe is missing the moment'.

11 Muller, Denis, 1 April 2021, 'Yes, politicians need to change the way they treat women'.

12 Safety. Respect. Equity, 6 March 2022, 'Safety. Respect. Equity', video, YouTube, <www.youtube.com/watch?v=CSGEbuhMQl4>, accessed 20 May 2025.

13 Karvelas, Patricia (@PatsKarvelas), 21 May 2022, 'One overwhelming story ...', X (Twitter) post, <https://x.com/PatsKarvelas/status/1527985381710254080>, accessed 23 May 2025.

14 Nelson, Camilla, 22 May 2022, 'Women stormed the 2022 election in numbers too big to ignore: What has Labor pledged on gender?', *The Conversation*, <https://theconversation.com/women-stormed-the-2022-election-in-numbers-too-big-to-ignore-what-has-labor-pledged-on-gender-183369>, accessed 20 May 2025.

15 Kelly, Paul, 3 April 2021, 'Able is Albo, but will poll be Morrison's Waterloo?', *The Australian*, <www.theaustralian.com.au/inquirer/able-is-albo-but-will-poll-be-morrisons-waterloo/news-story/7567bbf0726ca699084d92ac6dcef4ca>, accessed 17 June 2025.

16 Muller, Denis, 9 May 2022, 'As News Corp goes "rogue" on election coverage, what price will Australian democracy pay?', *The Conversation*, <https://theconversation.com/as-news-corp-goes-rogue-on-election-coverage-what-price-will-australian-democracy-pay-181599>, accessed 5 November 2024.

17 Kenny, Mark, 16 May 2022, 'Teal is telling. What Independents reveal about government and media failure', *Canberra Times*, <www.canberratimes.com.au/story/7719077/teal-is-telling-what-independents-reveal-about-government-and-media-failure/>, accessed 5 November 2024.

18 Stephenson, Elise and Williams, Blair, 26 May 2025, 'Labour women make history by overtaking men in cabinet. So is the job done?', *The Conversation*, <https://theconversation.com/labor-women-make-history-by-overtaking-men-in-cabinet-so-is-the-job-done-256603 >, accessed 17 June 2025.

19 Ipsos and Global Institute for Women's Leadership, *International Women's Day 2025*.

20 University of Melbourne, 18 July 2024, 'Radical anti-feminism a prevalent form of violent extremism', <www.unimelb.edu.au/newsroom/news/2024/july/radical-anti-feminism-the-most-prevalent-form-of-violent-extremism-in-australia,-report-finds>, accessed 26 May 2025; Meger, Sarah, Johnston, Melissa and Riveros-Morales, Yolanda, 2024, *Misogyny, Racism and Violent Extremism in Australia*, University of Melbourne, <https://rest.mars-prod.its.unimelb.edu.au/server/api/core/bitstreams/d6245487-7e2d-4241-84b0-1b6f78621e80/content>, accessed 26 May 2025.

21 Guterres, António, 7 March 2025, 'UN Secretary-General's remarks at the International Women's Day event 2025', <www.unwomen.org/en/

news-stories/speech/2025/03/un-secretary-generals-remarks-at-the-international-womens-day-event-2025>, accessed 26 May 2025.

Part 3 Feminist foundations
1 Summers, Anne, 2000, *Ducks on the Pond: An Autobiography 1945–1976* (1999), Penguin, Melbourne, p 259.
2 Reid, Elizabeth, 2023, 'When Sally met Harry: Whitlam and the Women's Liberation Movement', unpublished paper provided to the author.

8 The great 'spontaneous awakening'
1 Whitlam, Gough, 8 March 1975, 'Speech by the Prime Minister The Hon. E.G. Whitlam, M.P., at an International Women's Day Reception: Melbourne, 8 March, 1975', Department of the Prime Minister and Cabinet, Canberra, <https://pmtranscripts.pmc.gov.au/sites/default/files/original/00003643.pdf >, accessed 22 June 2025.
2 Olcott, Jocelyn, 2017, *International Women's Year: The Greatest Consciousness-Raising Event in History*, Oxford University Press, New York, p 235.
3 Olcott, *International Women's Year*, p 5.
4 Ryan, Julia, 2024, *Julia @ Women's Liberation: Inside the Movement*, Fox Place, Canberra, p 3.
5 After Ryan's death in 2023, a group of her closest friends, led by her lifelong 'bestie' Biff Ward, published *Julia @ Women's Liberation*, an edited collection of her diary notes, meeting logs and musings on the Canberra Women's Liberation group. This fabulously raw and sharply observed account is testament to the messy magnificence of the movement and the exceptionally strong bonds it fostered. It's also a golden record of what was discussed at these weekly meetings.
6 Ward, Biff, 2025, 'Letter to Julia', private letter to Julia Ryan's family, provided to the author by Biff Ward.
7 Smith, Evan, 2018, 'When the personal became too political: ASIO and the monitoring of the Women's Liberation Movement in Australia', *Australian Feminist Studies*, vol 33, no 95, pp 45–60.
8 Smith, 'When the personal became too political'.
9 The panel was 'Feared and revered: Rebels, radicals and reformers', Canberra Writers Festival, 10 July 2023, following the launch of Arrow, Michelle (ed.), 2023, *Whitlam and Women: Revisiting the Revolution*, NewSouth, Sydney. I asked Michelle Arrow and five of the contributors to join me for this feature event: Elizabeth Reid, Biff Ward, Gail Radford, Gillian Appleton and Cathy Eatock (daughter of Indigenous trailblazer Pat Eatock).
10 Gail Radford, a veterinarian, was a member of the Canberra group and a founding member of WEL. Her appointment as the inaugural Director of the Equal Employment Opportunity Section within the Public Service Board, late 1975, made her the first EEO Officer in Australia. She had previously sat on the National Committee on Discrimination in Employment and Opportunity. The appointment was roundly criticised

by the media as a political appointment and 'nepotism', given Gail was married to Dr Peter Wilenski, the former principal secretary to Whitlam and later head of the Department of Labour and Immigration. A furious Whitlam hit back at the press, suggesting undertones of racism in the press criticism as Wilenski was a Polish Jew.

11   Mitchell, Juliet, 1971, 'Women: The longest revolution', in *Woman's Estate*, Penguin, London, pp 75–122, <www.marxists.org/subject/women/ authors/mitchell-juliet/longest-revolution.htm>, accessed 23 June 2025. The first version of this essay was published in *New Left Review* in 1966; Mitchell revised and exapnded it for her 1971 book *Woman's Estate*.

12   Mitchell, 'Women: The longest revolution'.

13   For further discussion on this, see Mitchell, 'Women: The longest revolution'.

14   Summers, *Ducks on the Pond*, p 352.

15   The terms 'suffragette' and 'suffragist' are often used interchangeably as if they are one and the same. But they are not. They were two distinctly different groups who employed significantly different means and strategies to achieve the same outcome – the vote for women. The suffragists were peaceful protestors who avoided violence or social disruption as they petitioned for the vote, while the suffragettes were spectacularly radical, using any means they felt necessary to draw attention to their cause and the profound gender inequity in voting rights and political participation. Suffragettes who were jailed for violent actions attempted to go on hunger strikes. In addition to beatings, they were force-fed by prison guards, who shoved tubes down their throats as a hideous form of gendered torture. The 2015 film *Suffragette*, directed by Sarah Gavron, was the first mainstream feature film to highlight these practices.

16   Lake, *Getting Equal*, p 222.

17   Smith, 'When the personal became too political', p 55.

18   Arrow, Michelle, 2002, *Upstaged: Australian Women Dramatists in the Limelight At Last*, Currency Press, Sydney, p 185, quoted in Smith, 'When the personal became too political', p 47.

19   Smith, 'When the personal became too political', p 53.

20   Smith, 'When the personal became too political'.

21   Lake, *Getting Equal*, p 219.

22   Taylor, Jean, 2009, *Brazen Hussies: A Herstory of Radical Activism in the Women's Liberation Movement in Victoria 1970–1979*, Dyke Books Inc, Melbourne, p 62.

23   ACTU Institute, 13 October 2021, 'Zelda D'Aprano's equal pay protest', blog post, *Union History Blog*, <https://atui.org.au/2021/10/13/zelda- dapranos-equal-pay-protest/>, accessed 21 June 2025.

24   Greer, Germaine, 1997, 'Foreword', in Liz McQuiston, *Suffragettes to She-Devils: Women's Liberation and Beyond*, Phaidon, London, p 6.

25   Jennings, Kate, 2010, *Trouble: Evolution of a Radical. Selected Writings 1970–2010*, Black Inc, Melbourne, pp 3–9.

9   Building the Women's Movement

1   Summers, *Ducks on the Pond*, p 259.
2   Ryan, *Julia @ Women's Liberation*, pp 24, 277.
3   Summers, *Ducks on the Pond*, p 260.
4   Summers, *Ducks on the Pond*, p 260.
5   Ward, 'Letter to Julia'.
6   It must be noted that reference to women 'having the vote' in Australia, which was granted in 1901, fails to account for the fact that Aboriginal women did not receive this same right until 1962. So while we proudly boast that Australia was the first country in the world to grant women both the right to vote and to stand for national parliament, the claim needs to be qualified against the reality of the racially discriminating Australian Constitution of 1901.
7   Ryan, *Julia @Women's Liberation*, p 4.
8   Reid, Elizabeth, 2017, 'How the personal became political: The feminist movement of the 1970s', *Australian Feminist Studies*, vol 33, no 95, p 11.
9   See Ann Curthoys writing about this in the first issue of *MeJane*, March 1971.
10 Fitzgerald, Alan, 5 November 1970, 'Show of strength by "weaker sex"', *Canberra Times*, p 3.
11 Ryan, *Julia @ Women's Liberation*, p 9.
12 Henderson, Beryl, 12 November 1970, 'Women's liberation', letter to the editor, *Canberra Times*, p 2.
13 Summers, Anne, 1994, *Damned Whores and God's Police*, updated edition, Penguin, Melbourne, p 23.
14 Lumby, Catharine, 1998, 'Media', in Caine, Barbara (ed.), *Australian Feminism: A Companion*, Oxford University Press, Melbourne, p 216.
15 Greer, 'Foreword', in McQuiston, *Suffragettes to She-Devils*, pp 6–7.
16 Greer, 'Foreword', in McQuiston, *Suffragettes to She-Devils*, pp 6–7.
17 Edgar, Patricia and McPhee Hilary, 1974, *Media She*, William Heinemann, Melbourne, p 1.
18 Edgar and McPhee, *Media She*, p 2.
19 Mitchell, Juliet, 1971, 'The Women's Liberation Movement', in *Woman's Estate*, p 42.
20 Quoted in Lumby, 'Media', in Caine (ed.), *Australian Feminism*, p 216.
21 Moore, Robert (host), 20 October 1975, *Monday Conference*, ABC TV, National Library of Australia, Nq 330.994 MON, no 163.
22 'Liberation "leads to suicide"', 3 June 1972, *Canberra Times*, p 11. See also 'Women's Lib "will lift crime"', 18 July 1973, *Canberra Times*, p 7.
23 Paine, Justin, 8 September 1975, 'Women threaten after-work drink', *Daily Telegraph*, p 7.
24 'Women's Lib "frightens" the men', 26 January 1972, *Canberra Times*, p 17.
25 Morgan, Robin, 1978, *Going Too Far: The Personal Chronicle of a Feminist* (1968), Vintage Books, New York, p 65.
26 'Bras burnt: Thousands of women march for equality', 28 August 1970, *Canberra Times*, p 6.

27 'Demonstration', 16 December 1970, *Canberra Times*, p 8.

28 Greer, 'Foreword', in McQuiston, *Suffragettes to She-Devils*, pp 6–7.

29 D'Alpuget, Blanche, 2 September1975, 'Plenary Session 1: Let's do a super marketing job', *New Dawn*, Vol 1, No 2. Note: Mitchell went on to point out, 'In countries in which there has been equal pay for women for 20 years, women still get only 72 percent of male pay.' A sobering thought back then, but even more sobering now when we consider that five long decades of 'women's progress' later, women's total pay in Australia is just 78 cents to the male dollar. Despite equal pay legislation and countless efforts and pay gap awareness campaigns, the fact Australia is still grappling with a total remuneration gender pay gap of 21.8 percent, according to January 2025 data from WEGA, is damning proof that as a nation we still fail to treat gender equality seriously.

30 Reid, Elizabeth, 1975, 'Statement by the Leader of the Australian Delegation, Ms Elizabeth Reid, at Mexico City on Friday, 20 June 1975', United Nations World Conference of the International Women's Year, Mexico City, p 5, <https://pmtranscripts.pmc.gov.au/sites/default/files/original/00003796_0.pdf>, accessed 29 May 2025.

31 For greater detail on the post-feminist, neoliberal push towards a theory of feminist 'solvedness', see Donaghue, Ngaire, 2015, 'Who gets played by "the gender card"? A critical discourse analysis of coverage of prime minister Julia Gillard's sexism and misogyny speech in the Australian print media', *Australian Feminist Studies*, vol 30, no 84, pp 161–78.

32 'The Mothers' Club', 7 September 2002, *Sydney Morning Herald*, <www.smh.com.au/national/the-mothers-club-20020907-gdfm2y.html>, accessed 30 January 2025.

33 Reid, Elizabeth, 1995, 'Development as a moral concept: Women's practices as development practice', in Noeleen Heyzer (ed.), *A Commitment to the World's Women: Perspectives on Development for Beijing and Beyond*, UNIFEM, New York, 1995, p 3.

34 Reid, Elizabeth, 2023, *Revolution and Reform: The Women's Liberation Movement and the Whitlam Years*, Whitlam Institute, Sydney, p 9, <www.whitlam.org/publications/elizabeth-reid-legacy-paper>, accessed 29 May 2025.

35 See 50/50 by 2030 Foundation, 2018, *From Girls to Men: Social Attitudes to Gender Equality in Australia*, University of Canberra, <www.broadagenda.com.au/wp-content/uploads/attachments/From-Girls-to-Men.pdf>, accessed 29 May 2025.

36 Greer, Germaine, 1972, *The Female Eunuch* (1970), Bantam Books, New York, p 352.

37 Adelaide Writers' Week, 2008, unnamed news clipping.

38 Reid, *Revolution and Reform*, p 7.

39 Reid, *Revolution and Reform*, p 13.

10 Sisterhood and strategy

1 Summers, *Ducks on the Pond*, p 270.

2 Ward, Elizabeth [Biff], 'On being late', in Jocelynne A Scutt (ed.),

Different Lives: Reflections on the Women's Movement and Visions of its Future, Penguin, Melbourne, 1987, p 78. For further discussion on this, see Reid, Elizabeth, 2025, 'International Women's Year 1975: A view from Australia', unpublished manuscript, p 4.

3   Reid, 'How the personal became political', p 17.

4   Reid, keynote address, *How the Personal Became Political* symposium.

5   Summers, *Ducks on the Pond*, p 271.

6   Summers, *Ducks on the Pond*, p 272.

7   Sarachild, Kathie, 1973, 'Consciousness raising: A radical weapon', in Redstockings of the Women's Liberation Movement and Kathie Sarachild (eds), *Feminist Revolution: An Abridged Edition with Additional Writings* (1975), Random House, New York, p 144, <https://redstockings. org/images/stories/CatalogPDFs/FR/26-Feminist-Revolution-Consciousness-Raising--A-Radical-Weapon-Kathie-Sarachild.pdf>, accessed 30 May 2025.

8   Reid, Elizabeth, 'International Women's Year 1975: A view from Australia', p 2.

9   Summers, *Ducks on the Pond*, p 272.

10 Summers, *Ducks on the Pond*, p 272.

11 Evans, Alice (host), 2020, 'Consciousness raising: Elisabeth Jay Friedman', podcast episode, *Rocking Our Priors*, <https://soundcloud.com/user-845572280/consciousness-raising-professor-elizabeth-jay-friedman>, accessed 13 February 2025.

12 Contos, in Haussegger, 'Chanel Contos: Changemaker'.

13 Contos, Chanel, 2023, *Consent Laid Bare*, Macmillan, Sydney, p 7.

14 Morgan, Robin, 1970, 'Introduction', in Robin Morgan (ed.), *Sisterhood is Powerful: An Anthology of Writings from the Women's Liberation Movement*, Vintage Books, New York, p xv.

15 Morgan, 'Introduction', in *Sisterhood is Powerful*, p xv.

16 Steinem, Gloria, December 1971, 'Sisterhood', *New York Magazine*, pp 47–49.

17 Summers, *Ducks on the Pond*, pp 270–71.

18 Quoted in Magarey, Susan, 2014, *Dangerous Ideas: Women's Liberation – Women's Studies – Around the World*, University of Adelaide Press, Adelaide, p 33, <https://library.oapen.org/handle/20.500.12657/33184>, accessed 30 May 2025.

19 Quoted in Magarey, *Dangerous Ideas*, p 32.

20 Huggins, Jackie, 1987, 'Black women and Women's Liberation', *Hecate*, vol 13, no 1, p 77.

21 'Feared and revered: Rebels, radicals and reformers', Canberra Writers Festival, 10 July 2023.

22 Spender, Dale, 1983, *'There's Always Been a Women's Movement This Century'*, Pandora Press, pp 4–6.

23 Crozier De-Rosa, Sharon, 8 February 2024, 'Radical books: Dale Spender, *There's Always Been a Women's Movement This Century* (1983)', *History Workshop*, <www.historyworkshop.org.uk/feminism/radical-books-dale-

spender-theres-always-been-a-womens-movement-this-century-1983/>, accessed 26 June 2025.

24 Crozier De-Rosa, 'Radical books: Dale Spender'.

25 Kinder, Sylvia, 1980, *Herstory of Adelaide Women's Liberation 1969–1974*, Salisbury Education Centre Adelaide, Adelaide, p 31, quoted in Magarey, *Dangerous Ideas*, p 32.

26 Daniels, Kay, 1972, 'Womens [*sic*] liberation national conference June 10–12, a personal report', *Liberaction*, no 3, 1972, pp 4–5, quoted in Magarey, *Dangerous Ideas*, pp 34–35.

27 Freeman, Jo, 1973, 'The tyranny of structurelessness', Jo Freeman, <www.jofreeman.com/joreen/tyranny.htm>, accessed 2 June 2025.

28 Summers, *Ducks on the Pond*, p 278.

29 Summers, Anne, March 1973, 'Where's the women's movement moving to?', *MeJane*, no 10, p 7.

30 In 2013, Nova Peris became the first Indigenous woman elected to federal parliament, winning a Senate seat for the Northern Territory. See Richards, Lisa, 15 June 2021, 'Indigenous Australian parliamentarians in federal and state/territory parliaments: A quick guide', Parliament of Australia, Quick Guide 2020–21, <www.aph.gov.au/About_Parliament/Parliamentary_departments/Parliamentary_Library/Research/Quick_Guides/2020-21/IndigenousParliamentarians2021>, accessed 25 June 2025.

31 Ward, Biff, 2023, 'Sisterhood', in Arrow (ed.), *Women and Whitlam: Revisiting the Revolution*, p 43.

32 Reid, 2025, 'International Women's Year 1975: A view from Australia'.

33 For more on Whitlam's embrace of International Women's Year and his efforts to get Australia to sign onto the UN Convention on the Political Rights of Women, see Reid, Elizabeth, 2025, 'Australia's international role in International Women's Year, 1975', unpublished manuscript, pp 17–19.

34 Summers, *Ducks on the Pond*, p 341.

35 Rees, Jacqueline, 26 March 1973, '"Supergirls" want inquiry on status of women', *Canberra Times*, p 1.

36 Olcott, *International Women's Year*, p 29.

37 Hamilton, John, 21 August 1973, 'But what do I tell my girl? Asks the PM's Miz', *The Herald*, p 2.

38 Ryan, *Julia @ Women's Liberation*, pp 21–22.

39 Steinem, Gloria and Reid, Elizabeth, 10 January 1976, 'Gloria Steinem and Elizabeth Reid talk about revolution', *The Bulletin*, p 39.

40 Olcott, *International Women's Year*, p 235.

Part 4 International Women's Year, 1975

1 Australian National Advisory Committee on International Women's Year [NAC], 1976, *International Women's Year: Report of the Australian National Advisory Committee*, Parliamentary Paper no 210/1976, AGPS, Canberra, p 27, <https://nla.gov.au/nla.obj-1474154417>, accessed 4 June 2025.

2 Olcott, *International Women's Year*, p 16.

11   Eyes on '75 as the sheilas shift the focus

1   Santamaria, Bob, 1975, in *Point of View*, GTV 9, National Film and Sound Archive of Australia, P.V. 449, NFSA ID 18969, <www.collection.nfsa.gov.au/title/18969>.

2   Klemesrud, Judy, 24 June 1975, 'Americans ease stand at women's conference', *New York Times*, p 7.

3   For more detailed discussion about this aspect of the Population Conference debacle, see Reid, 'Australia's international role in International Women's Year 1975'.

4   Reid, 'Australia's international role in International Women's Year 1975', pp 5–7.

5   Olcott, *International Women's Year*, p 31.

6   Olcott, *International Women's Year*, p 31. The *New York Times* article was published 3 March 1974. The letter from the UN staffer was from Susan Jane Kedgley.

7   United Nations, 'Stories from the UN Archive: Hillary Clinton's bold stand in Beijing', UN News, 13 March 2024, <https://news.un.org/en/story/2024/03/1147572>, accessed 2 June 2025.

8   Columbia SIPA, 13 March 2025, 'Addressing 21st century challenges to gender equality: Beijing+30', video, YouTube, <https://igp.sipa.columbia.edu/events/addressing-21st-century-challenges-gender-equality-beijing30-livestream>, accessed 13 March 2025.

9   Whitlam, Gough, 11 September 1974, 'Speech by the Prime Minister: International Women's Year: Inaugural meeting of the National Advisory Committee', Department of the Prime Minister and Cabinet, Canberra, p 3, <https://pmtranscripts.pmc.gov.au/sites/default/files/original/00003385.pdf>, accessed 25 June 2025.

10   Whitlam, Gough, 4 December 1974, 'International Women's Year: Priorities and considerations: Statement prepared for the information of the Parliament and tabled by the Prime Minister, the Hon. E.G. Whitlam, 4 December 1974', Department of the Prime Minister and Cabinet, Canberra, p 7, <https://pmtranscripts.pmc.gov.au/sites/default/files/original/00003519_0.pdf>, accessed 4 June 2025.

11   Reid, Elizabeth, 1974, document provided to the author.

12   NAC, *International Women's Year: Report of the Australian National Advisory Committee*, p 7.

13   United Nations, 10 January 1974, *Influence of Mass Communication Media on the Formation of a New Attitude Towards the Role of Women in Present Day Society*, report of the Secretary-General, UN Social and Economic Council, Commission on the Status of Women, 10 January 1974.

14   NAC, *International Women's Year: Report of the Australian National Advisory Committee*, p 38.

15   NAC, *International Women's Year: Report of the Australian National Advisory Committee*, p 40.

16   Pickering, Larry, 23 June 1975, 'On women's year', *National Times*, p 14.

17   NAC, *International Women's Year: Report of the Australian National Advisory Committee*, pp 40–41.

18 See Hill, Jess, 2019, *See What You Made Me Do: Power, Control and Domestic Abuse*, Black Inc, Melbourne, 2019.

19 Dexter, Nancy, 1 January 1975, '$2 mil. for the sheilas: Surprisingly, its not a joke', *The Age*, p 13; Lee, Katrina, 9 March 1975, 'The year of the bird', *Sunday Telegraph*.

20 NAC, *International Women's Year: Report of the Australian National Advisory Committee*, p 42.

21 '... And the girls want $2m more', 14 August 1975, *The Sun*, p 2.

22 Murray, Paul, 8 March 1975, 'Any'ow, it's about time', *West Australian*, p 33.

23 Wright, Claudia (host), 19 September 1975, *A Current Affair*, GTV 9, National Film and Sound Archive of Australia, 1975.09.19, NFSA ID 280123, <www.collection.nfsa.gov.au/title/280123>.

24 ABC TV, 14 April 1975, 'What does International Women's Year mean to you?', *This Day Tonight*. See online at <www.youtube.com/watch?v=_0RGftlqei8>, accessed 23 June 2025.

25 For more discussion on this theme, see Crispin, Jessa, 2017, *Why I Am Not a Feminist: A Feminist Manifesto*, Black Inc, Melbourne.

26 Jones, Caroline (host), July 1975, 'On Being a Woman, Part One', ABC TV, National Film and Sound Archive of Australia, NFSA ID 593935, <www.collection.nfsa.gov.au/title/593935>; 'On Being a Woman, Part Two', NFSA ID 593950, <www.collection.nfsa.gov.au/title/593950>.

27 *Married at First Sight*, 25 February 2025, Channel 9, series 13, episode 18 (Lauren and Clint).

28 Barrett Meyering, Isobelle, 2018, 'Feminism in Sydney's suburbs: "Speaking out", listening and "sisterhood" at the 1975 Women's Commissions', *Australian Feminist Studies*, vol 33, no 95, pp 61–80.

29 Day Benson, Philippa, 16 April 1975, 'Australia wins world praise', *Australian Women's Weekly*, p 4.

30 Author interview with Biff Ward, 2024.

31 Summers, *Ducks on the Pond*, pp 351–52.

32 Reid, Elizabeth, June 1974, 'The women we ignore', *Refractory Girl*, no 6, pp 9–12.

33 Summers, *Ducks on the Pond*, pp 359–62.

34 Summers, *Ducks on the Pond*, p 361.

35 Barrett Meyering, 'Feminism in Sydney's suburbs'; see also Sawer, Marian, 1990, *Sisters in Suits: Women and Public Policy in Australia*, Allen & Unwin, Sydney, pp 1–33.

36 *The Australian*, 9 October 1974, quoted in Olcott, *International Women's Year*, p 33.

37 Olcott, *International Women's Year*, p 35.

38 Whitlam, 'International Women's Year: Priorities and considerations', p 10.

39 Whitlam, 'International Women's Year: Priorities and considerations', pp 10, 15–16.

40 Reid, 'International Women's Year 1975: A view from Australia', p 22.

12 Mexico 1975 and the greatest consciousness-raising event in history

1   Olcott, *International Women's Year*, pp 15–16.
2   Olcott, *International Women's Year*, p 5.
3   'The sexes: Letting their hair down', 7 July 1975, *Time*, <https://time.com/archive/6846996/the-se×ed es-letting-their-hair-down>, accessed 6 March 2025.
4   'Many exit as Mrs. Rabin speaks at conference', 26 June 1975, *New York Times*, p 2.
5   Olcott, *International Women's Year*, p 3.
6   For more on this theme, see Piccini, Jon, 2018, '"Women are a colonised sex": Elizabeth Reid, human rights and International Women's Year 1975', *Australian Historical Studies*, vol 49, no 3, pp 307–23.
7   Reid, Elizabeth, 20 June 1975, 'Statement by the leader of the Australian delegation, Ms Elizabeth Reid, at Mexico City on Friday, 20 June 1975', Department of Foreign Affairs, Canberra, <https://pmtranscripts.pmc.gov.au/sites/default/files/original/00003796_0.pdf>, accessed 25 June 2025.
8   Piccini, '"Women are a colonised sex"'.
9   Klemesrud, Judy, 2 July 1975, 'As the conference ends, what now for women?', *New York Times*, p 40.
10 Nichol, Leah, 2022, 'The Royal Commission on Human Relationships and the *Australian Women's Weekly*, 1977–1980: The personal, the political, the popular', *Australian Feminist Studies*, vol 37, no 111, pp 71–85.
11 Day Benson, 'Australia wins world praise', p 4.
12 Olcott, *International Women's Year*, pp 79–81.
13 Olcott, *International Women's Year*, p 80. The note was passed by Susan Jane Kedgley, who had become friends with Reid through the IWY process.
14 United Nations, 28 June 1975, 'World Plan of Action: Introduction and Chapter I of the Draft World Plan of Action', <https://digitallibrary.un.org/record/3800549?ln=en&v=pdf>, accessed 23 June 2025.
15 United Nations, 2 July 1975, 'Declaration of Mexico on the Equality of Women and Their Contribution to Development and Peace', in *Report of the World Conference of the International Year of Women: Mexico City*, 19 June – 2 July 1975, pp 2–7, <https://digitallibrary.un.org/record/586225?ln=en&v=pdf>, accessed 23 June 2025.
16 Day Benson, Philippa, 30 July 1975, 'Looking to Australia for a lead in women's politics', *Australian Women's Weekly*, pp 4–5.
17 Klemesrud, Judy, 2 January 1976, 'For women, gains and losses in '75', *New York Times*, p 46.
18 NAC, *International Women's Year: Report of the Australian National Advisory Committee*, p 50.
19 'Women's deliberation', editorial, *Sydney Morning Herald*, 1 July 1975, p 6.
20 Olcott, *International Women's Year*, p 1.
21 NAC, *International Women's Year: Report of the Australian National Advisory Committee*, pp 50–53; 'Feminists fight at meeting', 30 June 1975, *Canberra Times*.
22 'Feminists scream insults at meeting', 30 June 1975, *Sydney Morning Herald*, p 5.

23 Kertesz, Lilla, 4 July 1975, 'Women's talks were a failure', *Daily Mirror*, p 18.

24 Klemesrud, Judy, 29 June 1975, 'Scrappy, unofficial women's parley sets pace', *New York Times*, p 2.

25 'The sexes', 7 July 1975, *Time*.

26 Walker, Anne S, 2018, *A World of Change: My Life in the Global Women's Rights Movement*, Arcadia, Melbourne, pp 14–15.

27 Lechte, Ruth, 17 June 1975, private letter to her parents, supplied to author by Diane Goodwillie.

28 Walker, *A World of Change*, p 16.

29 Klemesrud, 'Scrappy, unofficial women's parley sets pace', p 2.

30 Walker, *A World of Change*, p 6.

31 Lechte, Ruth, 4 July 1975, private letter, supplied to author by Diane Goodwillie.

32 Reid, Elizabeth, 1984, 'Since Mexico '75: A decade of progress?', *Development: Seeds of Change, Village Through Global Order*, no 4.

13 The Women and Politics Conference

1 Wynhausen, Elisabeth, 5 September 1975, 'The great lamington hijack', *New Dawn*, vol 1, no 5, p 8. *New Dawn* was the daily newspaper produced for the Women and Politics Conference.

2 'Libbers well suited', 1 September 1975, *Daily Telegraph*, p 4.

3 Whitlam, Gough, 31 August 1975, 'Speech by the Prime Minister, the Hon. E.G. Whitlam M.P., at the opening of the Women and Politics Conference: Canberra, 31 August 1975', Department of the Prime Minister and Cabinet, Canberra, <https://pmtranscripts.pmc.gov.au/release/transcript-3874>, accessed 6 June 2025.

4 United Nations, 'Make this the century of women's equality: UN chief'.

5 See Wynhausen, Elisabeth, 4 September 1975, 'Blacks' Day: "Too soon to be solely feminist"', *New Dawn*, vol 1, no 4, p 2; Langton, Marcia, Hammond, ruby and Scott, Evelyn, 1975, 'Bureaucracy and Aboriginals', in *The Women and Politics Conference 1975*, vol 2, pp 55–62.

6 'Activist called "foul-mouthed"', 12 September 1975, *Courier Mail*, p 2.

7 Kennedy, Flo, 1975, 'Black women in society', in *The Women and Politics Conference 1975*, vol 2, p 200.

8 Mitchell, Juliet, 1975, 'Feminist theory?', in *The Women and Politics Conference 1975*, vol 2, pp 191–97.

9 'The role of women', editorial, 6 September 1975, *Canberra Times*, p 2.

10 Solnit, Rebecca, 20 August 2012, 'Men explain things to me' (2008), *Guernica*, <www.guernicamag.com/rebecca-solnit-men-explain-things-to-me/>, accessed 16 June 2025.

11 Williams, Evan, 1975, 'Handling the media', in *The Women and Politics Conference*, vol 2, p 224.

12 See NAC, *International Women's Year: Report of the Australian National Advisory Committee*, pp 61–66.

13 NAC, *International Women's Year: Report of the Australian National Advisory Committee*, p 61.

14   Appleton, Gillian, 17 August 2023, *'Feared and Revered: Radicals, Rebels and Reformers'*, CWF 2023, speech notes shared with author.

15   The full statement is transcribed in the official conference papers; a substantially edited version appeared in *The Canberra Times*, 6 September 1975.

14   The 'bloody' finale

1   Moore, Robert (host), 1 September 1975, *Monday Conference*, ABC TV, National Library of Australia, Nq 330.994 MON.

2   NFSA Online, 28 February 2014, 'Australian delegation at the 1975 World Conference of the International Women's Year', video, YouTube, <www.youtube.com/watch?v=UinNIfzUglQ>, accessed 25 June 2025.

3   Stevens, Joyce, 8 October 1975, 'Liz Reid quits ... while the government responds to right-wing pressures', *Tribune*, p 5.

4   'Ms Reid quits govt in row on advisor's role: Blocked by disgruntled bureaucrats', 3 October 1975, *The Australian*, p 1.

5   Forbes, Sandy (host), 18 October 2013, 'Landmark women: Elizabeth Reid', interview transcript, National Museum of Australia, <www.nma.gov.au/audio/landmark-women/transcripts/landmark-women-elizabeth-reid-181013.mp3-transcript>, accessed 9 June 2025.

6   Reid, 'How the personal became political', p 26.

7   NAC, *International Women's Year: Report of the Australian National Advisory Committee*, p 32.

8   Quoted in Forbes, 'Landmark women: Elizabeth Reid'.

9   Reid, *Revolution and Reform*, p 13.

10   NAC, *International Women's Year: Report of the Australian National Advisory Committee*, p 35.

11   Kedgley, Susan, 1 January 1976, 'Women have to keep on fighting', *The Advertiser*, p 4.

A conclusion with no end ...

1   UN Women, 6 March 2025, 'Women's rights then and now: "Beijing 1995 changed our lives"', <www.unwomen.org/en/news-stories/interview/2025/03/womens-rights-then-and-now-beijing-1995-changed-our-lives>, accessed 2 July 2025.

2   Columbia SIPA, 'Addressing 21st century challenges to gender equality: Beijing+30' (see from 1:43).

3   UN Women, 12 June 2025, 'Facts and figures: Women's leadership and political participation', <https://www.unwomen.org/en/articles/facts-and-figures/facts-and-figures-womens-leadership-and-political-participation#_ednref3>, accessed 26 June 2025.

4   AKIpress, 22 June 2023, 'Doha Agreement excludes Afghan women from political engagement – Human Rights Watch', <https://akipress.com/news:716353:Doha_Agreement_excludes_Afghan_women_from_political_engagement_-_Human_Rights_Watch/>, accessed 26 June 2025. See also Allen, John R and Felbab-Brown, Vanda, September 2020, 'The fate of women's rights in Afghanistan', Brookings Institute,

<www.brookings.edu/articles/the-fate-of-womens-rights-in-afghanistan/>, accessed 26 June 2025.

5 The Heritage Foundation, 2023, *Mandate for Leadership: The Conservative Promise. Project 2025*, The Heritage Foundation, Washington, DC, <https://static.heritage.org/project2025/2025_MandateForLeadership_FULL.pdf>, accessed 9 June 2025.

6 Lebowitz, Megan, 31 October 2024, 'Trump says he would "protect" women "whether the women like it or not"', NBC News, <www.nbcnews.com/politics/2024-election/trump-protect-like-it-or-not-rcna178147>, accessed 26 June 2025.

7 Goldmacher, Shane, Haberman, Maggie and Gold, Michael, 6 November 2024, 'Trump at the Garden: A closing carnival of grievances, misogyny and racism', *New York Times*, <www.nytimes.com/2024/10/27/us/trump-msg-rally.html>, accessed 8 April 2025.

8 New York Post, 12 January 2025, 'Mark Zuckerberg talks benefits of masculinity on Joe Rogan podcast', video, Facebook, <www.facebook.com/watch/?v=1267884854496327>, accessed 1 July 2025.

9 Fox 4 Dallas-Fort Worth, 21 February 2025, 'JD Vance to young men: You're not a bad person because you're a man', video, YouTube, <www.youtube.com/watch?v=gRW1huhDPpg>, accessed 1 July 2025.

10 Fordham, Ben (host), 23 January 2025, 'Thursday Show – 23rd January', radio broadcast, 2GB, <www.2gb.com/podcast/thurday-show-23rd-january/>, accessed 2 July 2025.

11 Basford Canales, Sarah, 4 April 2025, 'Liberal candidate says women should not serve in ADF combat rules amid a range of controversial views', *The Guardian*, <www.theguardian.com/australia-news/2025/apr/04/liberal-candidate-says-women-should-not-serve-in-adf-combat-roles-amid-range-of-controversial-views>, accessed 6 April 2025.

12 Katanasho, Gabrielle, 3 April 2025, 'What does "woke" mean? Peter Dutton's warning to schools is deliberately vague', *SBS News*, <www.sbs.com.au/news/article/what-does-woke-mean/lxh4u1859>, accessed 6 April 2025.

13 Essig, Laurie (host), 16 January 2025, 'We talk to really smart people: Judith Butler', podcast episode, *Feminism, Fascism, and the Future*, <https://podcasts.apple.com/gb/podcast/we-talk-to-really-smart-people-judith-butler/id1712028499?i=1000684096223>, accessed 9 June 2025.

ACKNOWLEDGEMENTS

Not just a village, but a tribe. Many wonderful people have helped birth this book. My thanks to NewSouth, Elspeth Menzies and Kathy Bail for bringing writers' words to the world and investing in the national conversation. A special, grand thank you to publisher Harriet McInerney, who believed in this project and urged me on with endearing and calm encouragement throughout every chaotic iteration. What a gift to work with one of the most skilled editors on earth, Emma Driver. If only I could bottle her orderly brain and meticulous judgment. This book owes an enormous debt to Emma's methodical and wise decision making. My thanks also to the delightful Paul O'Beirne and all the NewSouth team.

Chrys Stevenson, you are invaluable and a writer's treasure – thank you for everything you do. My thanks also to the many people interviewed and those whose work opened pathways of exploration and informed my thinking, including the brilliant Jocelyn Olcott, Elisabeth Jay Friedman, Frank Bongiorno, Meredith Edwards, Sharon Crozier-De Rosa, Michelle Arrow, Marilyn Lake, Marian Sawer, Isobelle Barrett Meyering, Helen Dalley-Fisher and Stephen Brady.

To the women from the March4Justice, your generosity, warmth and fighting spirit was pivotal to shaping this story: thank you Janine Hendry, Fiona Scott, Peta Swarbrick, Bethany Williams, Kuljeeta Singh, Kate Walton, Kathryn Allan,

Renee Jones, Blair Williams, Michelle Dunne Breen, Aunty Violet Sheridan and Tjanara Goreng Goreng, and the woman who pulled me in, Kerry Burton. To all the women who joined the march, you have helped change the world – your every step and chant adding to an ocean swell.

My thanks also to the young feminists who spent time yarning with me as we mused over the way of the world, including Amaani Siddeek, Zoe Mitchell, Maddie Chia and Avan Daruwalla. To the women whose stories of bold courage I have shared – Saxon Mullins, Chanel Contos, Grace Tame and Brittany Higgins – your role in our revolution goes down in history.

I also wish to acknowledge and thank those tireless media colleagues who continue to shift the 'centre of gravity'. Louise Milligan, your work has been critical to pushing the cultural dial. Journalists such as Jess Hill, whose dedication to unpacking the complexity around women and violence, and Jane Gilmore, who unpacks how we talk about it, have helped shift the national conversation. Anna Rogers, I salute you. Kate Jenkins, thank you for your generosity and culture-shifting impact. To those wise women of media Niki Savva, Anita Jacoby and Helen McCabe, thank you for chewing the fat. My thanks also to Bevan Shields for unflinching honesty. And to John-Paul Moloney from *The Canberra Times* – may those rowdy women stay away from your printing press!

While the themes in this book, and the ebb and flow of emotion that drove it, are an indelible part of me, there would not have been a book without the women on whose shoulders I stand. I don't know how to begin to thank Elizabeth Reid. If I could fashion bronze into a statue for generations of women and girls to gaze upon, I would. Thankfully, Elizabeth, you are such a prodigious writer and meticulous memory keeper that there is a treasure trove of material now safely housed in the

National Library of Australia. Your work has been invaluable to my research and helped shape this book's journey. Most importantly, your unflinching commitment to women's true liberation and full empowerment across the globe, along with your sharply defined feminism, has helped sharpen my own. I am deeply grateful for the gift of your friendship, your unfailing encouragement and your revolutionary spirit that kept urging me forward.

Anne Summers, your outstanding body of work and exceptional journalism over more than half a century has not only been a driving inspiration but a rich well of information. Thank goodness you have never stopped writing. The patchwork quilt of our feminist legacy is largely stitched together thanks to you. On that score, a big shout out also to Wendy McCarthy.

Biff Ward, perhaps I will never stop asking 'just one more question'! Thank you for being such a patient teacher. You didn't explain sisterhood. You didn't need to; you live it. Thank you for the baton you passed all those years ago. Overwhelmed, I buried it like a bone until I was finally ready to dig it up and take a bite. Your encouragement and support helped give me lift-off. As did our writing group, the Rammies, my first, gentle readers in sisterhood: Dianne Lucas, Karen Viggers, Robyn Cadwallader, Jenni Savigny and Andra Putnis. Thank you too Beejay Silcox, Qin Qin and the magnificent team at the National Library of Australia – what treasures you are. My gratitude also to those caring keepers of Australian culture at the National Sound and Film Archive.

I also wish to thank those radicals and reformers whose energies keep the story alive: Gillian Appleton, Gail Radford, Sara Dowse, Daniela Torsh, Julie Rigg, Margaret Reynolds and Cathy Eatock in memory of her mother, Pat. A special thank you also to Diane Goodwillie for sharing the letters of Ruth Lechte, and to Claire Slatter and the writings of Anne Walker.

I have agonised over the issues in this book and the process of writing it with many thoughtful and dear friends and my beloved family. I apologise for driving you all mad, but you did it – you helped get me over the line. Your enthusiasm for the importance of this discussion and its timeliness, along with your belief in it, kept me afloat. My deep thanks to Tritia Evans, who keeps me balanced with her special gift for nurture, her global-sized heart and beautiful friendship; Helen Sykes, for unrelenting optimism and forward motion; Margaret Evans, for never, ever giving up; and Suzanne Olb for lifelong encouragement. My heartfelt thanks to Quentin Bryce, for fabulous gasbagging, storytelling and making me laugh through the pain, 'now just get on with it!' you'd say. Your wise counsel is woven through these pages. Thank you also to the ever-inspiring Daryl Karp for the rich conversations, tireless encouragement and the invitation to participate in MOAD's bold Changemakers exhibition.

To my fam – my siblings Fiona, Jane, Louise, Tony and Andrew – none of it would be any fun without your wise, crazy, nutty, bullish and brilliant suggestions. I thought our hearts would explode when Petrus said goodbye. I am so grateful we hold one another so carefully. I am deeply proud of our spirit and your creativity. To Fynn, Taoh, Lily, Charlie, James, Mia, Zara, Lauren, Angie, Paris, Zac and Indiana, you inherit this revolution. Fight it well!

Mark, I leave you to last, because this is the hardest. I am out of adjectives, and I know how you hate superlatives. There aren't the words to express my gratitude for the space, time and love you so freely gift me, asking nothing in return. Your gentle care is breathtaking. Our endless conversation, sorting the world, reshaping ideas and testing our resolve is the richest form of nurture. Thank you – for all of it.

INDEX

Scott, Fiona 77, 125, 132–33, 136, 137, 156, 157
Sex Discrimination Act 1984 14, 34, 332
sex education 102, 234
sexism 15–16, 181, 211, 213, 219–21, 242, 256, 264, 286, 290–96, 302, 319–21, 346
   in Australian culture 63, 96, 100, 104
   in the media 12–14, 28–34, 65, 204–209, 215, 267–70, 315, 325–30
   in politics 64–91, 96
   protest against 41, 151–75, 193–95, 196, 223, 228, 238
   see also misogyny; patriarchy
sexual abuse *see* sexual assault; sexual harassment; sexual violence
sexual assault 2, 6, 31, 33–34, 42–43, 45, 95, 97–98, 99–102, 102–105, 106–107, 108–15, 116, 117, 127–28, 144, 234, 294–95
   bail laws 49
   gag laws 101
   victims 45–47
   see also rape; sexual violence
sexual harassment 23, 29–31, 33–34, 41, 43, 74, 76, 79, 84–85, 87, 97–98, 100, 113, 117, 123, 126, 158–61, 162, 181, 243, 268
   in the workplace 18, 23, 30–31, 33, 34, 76–77, 79, 87, 110, 126, 144, 155, 158–61, 161–62, 221
   see also #MeToo
sexual revolution of the 1960s 7, 182, 193
sexual violence 16, 59, 61, 100–101, 138, 147, 232; *see also* femicide; rape; sexual assault
shame 46, 75, 86, 88, 109, 119, 144, 222
   body shame 204
   male 49
   see also slut-shaming
Sharaz, David 111
Shepherd, Helen 238

Shields, Bevan 58–62, 65
Siddeek, Amaani 67
Singh, Kuljeeta 125, 126
Sipilä, Helvi 260, 285, 302–303
sisterhood 7, 8, 82, 88, 126, 140–45, 147, 148, 156, 184, 222, 231, 235–39, 239–43, 244–46, 246–48, 250, 278–79, 283, 345–46
   clenched fist symbol of 121, 148, 149, 251–52
   Sisterhood is Powerful book 235–36
   see also feminists, second-wave; women; Women's Liberation Movement
Sky News 48, 138, 170
slut-shaming 4, 75–76, 95; *see also* shame
social media 32, 69, 102–103, 121, 122, 135, 163, 167, 173, 215, 226, 232, 243, 244
Solnit, Rebecca 27, 149, 323, 325, 326
Solomon, Thelma 192
Speakman, Mark 107
Speers, David 54
Spender, Dale 241–43, 246
Steinem, Gloria 14, 217, 237, 255, 291, 305
Stott Despoja, Natasha 16, 59
Stutchbury, Michael 163
suffragettes 11, 82, 189, 242, 365 n. 15
Summers, Anne 14, 69–71, 149, 177, 188–90, 196, 197–98, 203, 225, 228–31, 237–38, 247–48, 249, 251–52, 282–84
Swarbrick, Peta 125, 126–29, 151–52, 153
Swillhouse 34
Sydney Morning Herald, The 34, 48–49, 55, 58, 303, 306, 325, 337
   Violence Against Women campaign 59–62
Symons, Sandy 269
systems failure 340–41

Tabart, Chelsea 84, 90
Tabatabai, Zuzu 298

www.ingramcontent.com/pod-product-compliance
Lightning Source LLC
Chambersburg PA
CBHW030856270326
41929CB00008B/449